COLLECTION OF MARVELLOUS THINGS

GAIUS JULIUS SOLINUS

Collection Of Marvellous Things

(*also known as* The Polyhistor)

Translated by Arwen Apps

eglantyne books

Published by Eglantyne Books Ltd,

The Club Room, Conway Hall, 25 Red Lion Square, London WC1R 4RL.

www.eglantynebooks.com

©2023 Eglantyne Books

ISBN 978-1-913378-06-6

Printed in the UK by Imprint Academic Ltd;

Seychelles Farm, Upton Pyne, Exeter, Devon EX5 5HY, ImprintDigital.com

A CIP record for this title is available from the British Library.

Book layout and design by Eric Wright

Production team: Robert and Olivia Temple, Michael Lee, and Eric Wright

Introduction: Solinus and his Work

The curious story of Gaius Iulius Solinus' *Polyhistor* ("Multi-history"), also known as the *Collectanea Rerum Memorabilium* ("Collection of Marvellous Things") or, later, as *De Mirabilibus Mundi* ("The Wonders of the World") or *De Situ Orbis* ("Description of the World"), began somewhere in the Roman Empire during the third or fourth century A.D. A geographical compilation with a firm emphasis on *res memorabiles*, or "marvels", the book is a brief sketch of the world as known to later Greco-Roman antiquity, diversified by digressions on a jumble of other topics.

The *Polyhistor* is no more nor less than its title advertises. While the work is brief, it is jam-packed with an erratic hotchpotch of information. According to Solinus' first prefatory letter, he aimed "to recall, in order, the famous sites on land, and the famous features of the seas, preserving the differences in the world. I have put in a good many other things", he goes on, "so, if nothing else, the ennui of readers might be assuaged by the very variety."[1] Within the chapters of his book, geographical sketches, comprising lists of towns, distances and topographical features, sit cheek-by-jowl with snippets of folklore, etymologies, and mythological references. Accounts of volcanic and meteorological occurrences, such as the geothermal activity of the Aeolian Islands, and the flooding of the Nile, are included. Plants and stones with interesting properties are afforded space. Animals abound, both real and fabulous, from the humble dog to the crocodile and the Indian mantichore, a nightmarish man-eater with the body of a lion and a scorpion's sting. Birds also feature, from the quail and the partridge to the maleficent gryphon, a gold and emerald-hoarding monster inhabiting the Scythian steppes. Ethnologies of far-flung races are attempted. Fantastic tribes, such as the serpent-resistant African Psylli, compete for space with a one-legged people of India and four-eyed Aethiopian hunters. Juxtaposed with all this are fables, historical notices, chronologies and occasional digressions attempting technical explanations of natural phenomena such as tidal fluctuation.[2]

I. The Reception of Solinus, Ancient and Modern

If we may trust the account contained in the author's second prefatory letter,[3] the *Polyhistor* was seized upon by an eager public soon after its dissemination. Catching the imaginations of Solinus' contemporaries and successors alike, the work was destined to have a profound effect upon the history of geography, and to trace a bizarre trajectory through Western consciousness. Quoted and used by a variety of authors from Ammianus Marcellinus and Augustine downwards,[4] the work was to enjoy sustained popularity for over a thousand years. To quote M. E. Milham, Solinus "remained the chief Latin geographer to a millennium.[5]" The sheer volume of Solinean material produced and its wide distribution stands as concrete testimony to this. We possess some 250 manuscripts, from the ninth to the fifteenth centuries, and more than 80 printed editions produced before 1600, including at least twelve incunables. A verse epitome of the work was written in the 11th century by one Theoderic of Trond, and in the 12th, another abstract was composed by Petrus Diaconus. It is possible he was used as a school text.[6] Solinus' narratives are reflected on the world maps of the schoolmen of the late Middle Ages, and his menagerie of fantastic creatures re-appear in an array of mediaeval bestiaries. During the Middle Ages, Solinus was particularly popular as a source of geographical knowledge,[7] and some of his more picturesque fables were transcribed almost in their entirety onto the thirteenth-century Hereford and Ebstorf maps.[8] The *Polyhistor* may even have had some influence on European exploration in the 14th and 15th centuries.[9]

Curiously enough, even when first-hand knowledge of the more far-flung areas he wrote about had been acquired, the European enthusiasm for Solinus continued unabated. The *Polyhistor* remained in vogue during the Renaissance and was extensively commented upon by a wide range of scholars. By 1600, the *Polyhistor* had been translated into French, Italian, Spanish, English and German. Several commentaries also appeared. It is interesting to note that the persistent appeal of the *Polyhistor* stood in awkward juxtaposition with the rising tide of empiricism at this time, as well as the general broadening of geographical knowledge.[10] That is to say, the book ought (at least, from our modern perspective) to have been consigned to obsolescence, but remained paradoxically popular. Paul Dover demonstrates that Renaissance readers accordingly reacted to Solinus in different ways, "reflecting an intellectual atmosphere of ambivalence".[11] Some continued to regard Solinus as an authority, while others saw his work as a window into the ancient world and a platform for rhetorical and philological study.[12] This odd intellectual trend certainly extended the *Polyhistor's* already surprising lifespan, but the die was cast. Eventually, the accumulation of data from voyages of discovery and other kinds of practical investigation led to wholesale changes in geographical thinking, increasing scepticism and a general reduction of interest in the book. With the turning of the tide, fascination for Solinus began to die out by the beginning of the 17th century.

However, in the years that followed, Solinus was not to be permitted a dignified retirement. The *Polyhistor* was to experience a reversal of fortunes almost as spectacular as its meteoric rise: in more modern times, the book was subject to such severe criticism that it was to emerge as one of the most unappreciated and even despised Latin works of Antiquity. Today, the book is virtually unknown, even to many specialists.

How could this fate have befallen an author who was "the chief Latin geographer to a millennium"?

The answer to this question has two parts. One of these concerns Solinus' apparent lack of originality, which from the first formed a pillar of the modern criticism of the *Polyhistor*. As early as the Renaissance, when the encyclopaedic *Natural History*, written in the first century A.D. by the Roman naturalist Pliny the Elder, and the *Geography* of Pomponius Mela (also written in the first century A.D.) gained wider circulation, it had been noticed that Solinus' material, his arrangement of it, and even his words themselves were frequently to be found in these works, particularly that of Pliny. The long-lived nickname "Pliny's Ape" was coined, marking the inception of a protracted and tortuous debate on the relationship between the two authors.[13] This relationship was studied in detail by the 17th century French scholar Claudius Salmasius (Claude Saumaise), Solinus' first really trenchant critic. In 1629, Salmasius produced his *magnum opus*, a detailed commentary on the *Polyhistor*, which runs to almost a thousand closely-printed folio pages. Paradoxically, Salmasius did not esteem Solinus' work, believing it obvious the book contained nothing which was not derived from Pliny.[14] He also found the style affected, and penned many remarks critical of Solinus' general perspicacity. The process of marginalisation was all but complete in the nineteenth century, when Theodor Mommsen, the great German classicist, produced his critical edition of Solinus' work. First published in 1864,[15] this publication (again paradoxically) sounded a virtual death-knell for the *Polyhistor*. In the tradition of Salmasius' *Exercitationes*, Mommsen made no attempt to hide his disdain, and despised what he perceived as being the weakness of Solinus' mind. In his view, Solinus was an altogether undistinguished author, a "ridiculous little teacher" (*ridiculus magistellus*),[16] and his production, most of which, so he thought, derived ultimately from Pliny, essentially worthless. That Mommsen nevertheless undertook the task of editing the work can be explained by the intellectual challenge posed by the complex manuscript tradition, though he described the labour as "great rather than fruitful" (*maiorem…quam fructum*).[17] Further enquiry, he felt, was futile: "we leave the criticism of this author and the triumph over such an enemy to those who hunt flies, and whom no victory does not shame".[18] Mommsen's assessment had far-reaching repercussions for Solinus, and is still felt today. His sentiments are reflected in the writings of a string of subsequent scholars (the *detractores Solini*, as one commentator has it).[19] In his *Geschichte der Römischen Litteratur*, Wilhelm

Teuffel, in a similar vein, characterised Solinus' book as pretentious, worthless, and devoid of taste; C. Weymann nastily described its author as a "schwachköpfigen Kompilator" ("dim-witted compiler"). In the early twentieth century, E. H. Bunbury described it as "rude". According to W. H. Stahl, the work was "wretched", "trivial" and "careless".[20] Richard Coniff even goes so far as to express concern lest he portray what he calls "a very bad book" in too positive a light.[21]

As well as its scope and content, the other feature of the *Polyhistor* which seemed to inspire intense dislike was its style. Undeniably, Solinus' book contains many obscurities and much unfamiliar vocabulary;[22] this, and other features of his style, characteristic of later antiquity rather than of the classical authors, led to the *Polyhistor* being consistently and viciously lambasted for its Latin in the 19th and 20th centuries. Mommsen found Solinus' style nauseating (he termed it "prolix, perplexing and insipid" — *tumide et perplexe et insipide*). To E. H. Bunbury, it was "repulsive to a scholar of the present day… barbarous and obscure", peppered with distortions and "attempts at rhetorical grandiloquence". Raymond Beazley, while in general inclined to take a more sympathetic view, still found the book "pompous and inflated".[23] Many other scholars penned similar indictments. This rejection, along with that of many other authors of later antiquity, came about as a direct result of the Humanist preoccupation with the "quality" of Latin and the overweening emphasis on classical forms. The obsession with Ciceronian elegance left no place for authors such as Pliny,[24] let alone Solinus. In Solinus' defence, Zweder von Martels (who, in contrast, describes Solinus' style as "felicitously mannered") makes the fair comment that there is no indication Solinus was criticised for his style in antiquity, or indeed at any time before the rise of Classicism.[25] While Albertus Magnus questioned the veracity of several of Solinus' claims,[26] he had nothing to say against his Latin. Augustine, Martianus Capella and Isidore of Seville all turned to Solinus, as did the Latin grammarian Priscian, who quotes him several times as an exemplar.[27] As von Martels comments, the thousands who read Solinus in the millennium after his appearance "were trained in a much larger variety of authors" than those of more modern times, who had more limited tastes.[28] The simple truth is that Solinus' style went resoundingly… well, out of style. Michael Roberts, in his plea for late antique poetry to be viewed on its own terms, makes much the same observation in relation to criticism of the works of Claudian and Augustine.[29]

Perhaps more pertinent is the accusation also frequently levelled at Solinus of being careless and ignorant. Mommsen contemptuously highlighted IV§67 and V§13, when Solinus, somehow misled, founds the new towns of Abdelos and Addirim from the words which appear in Pliny as *ab Delos* and *ad Dirim*. There are several other like instances in the *Polyhistor* which certainly might be interpreted as carelessness (e.g., identifying Arcesilaus' hometown as Pitane in Laconia rather than Pitane in Aeolis at VII §8) or ignorance (confusing the number of humps possessed by Bactrian camels and dromedaries at LXIX §9). Again in Solinus' defence, von Martels reasonably counters that, like Pliny, he had to deal with enormous amounts of contradictory and unverifiable information.[30] It is certainly unsurprising that he made errors of this sort, easy to condemn from the days of libraries well-stocked with reference works and with well-established scientific methods for distinguishing fact from fiction.

Mommsen and others seemed only too glad to detail what it was that they found objectionable in the *Polyhistor*. What, then, was the key to its erstwhile popularity? What did it have that recommended it to those who could read, as well as the many more who were read to? Its relative brevity? Its reasonably systematic progression? Certainly, Solinus' method (to quote Raymond Beazley, of "extracting the dross and leaving the gold")[31] might have been designed to appeal to the masses. He reduced the interminable lists of his sources and produced a work much more accessible to readers, an easy-to-consult compendium, in contemporary parlance, of "highlights". Additionally, as the *Polyhistor* did not overtly conflict with Christian theology, the Latin Fathers did not trouble to injure his reputation, and it is likely that references to his work by such important Christian writers as Augustine and Isidore of Seville contributed to his enduring popularity. The relative shortness of the work must also have made it much more manageable for copyists. But the emphasis on the miraculous must supply most of the answer. The *Polyhistor* was an unqualified success because it was perfectly suited to the tenor of later Antiquity and the mediaeval era, climates of increasing "superstition and awe", as Lloyd A. Brown has it.[32] Ignorance and apathy supplied the superstition; Solinus supplied the awe. As an account of the world's natural heterogeneity, the work was bound to win popularity. The idea of Solinus' tales filling an intellectual void was taken up by J. N. Wilford, who wrote that, in the absence of further scientific enquiry, "someone like Gaius Julius Solinus was bound to come along and find an enduring, uncritical audience".[33] Anthony Grafton appropriately compares the fascination of generations of mediaeval and Renaissance readers to Desdemona, seriously inclining to hear Othello's wondrous tales.[34]

Surely few works of literature can claim so chequered a history as the *Polyhistor*. The story of Solinus is a stark illustration of the results of interplay between worldviews and shifting intellectual climates. It is also an interesting cautionary tale. Due to his long period of popularity, Solinus' work had profound impact on European thought, and over the centuries, the *Polyhistor* became inextricably intertwined with the cultural fabric of Western civilisation. As well as shaping geographical thought and perceptions of the natural world, giving us the terms "Mediterranean" and "the Orient",[35] Solinus' tales have influenced many a folkloric tradition. They have also inspired artists, supplying details for plays, poems, and even operas.[36] Notwithstanding this, the *Polyhistor* has been relegated to the little-trodden byways of classical scholarship. The verdicts of Salmasius, Mommsen, and their intellectual heirs, refusing to allow the historical significance of the *Polyhistor*, were not based on the circumstances in which Solinus lived and worked, and resulted in the devaluing of this small master work[37] and the denial of its true significance. Surely the aim now, as pleaded by von Martels, is to foster a fairer picture of the book by re-evaluating it in a less anachronistic context.[38] The ancient world is revealed by far too few surviving literary sources for any such document to be lightly cast aside, and the *Polyhistor* today certainly represents an under-utilised resource. Rather than as nothing more than a zealous plagiarist, Solinus may be seen as valuably illustrating a third/fourth century Roman world perspective. There is much of interest to be mined from the *Polyhistor's* pages, and the unique information given therein may provide insights to historians and anthropologists alike. Solinus, it should be understood, offers a window into a significant discourse, and one with a major impact on medieval and Renaissance conceptions of the world.[39]

II. The Author

Nothing is known of the personal history of our author. We cannot even be sure of his full name. One group of manuscripts[40] allows him the three names "Gaius Iulius Solinus", but another group[41] has only "Iulius Solinus", while Priscian and Isidore of Seville specify the cognomen alone. The dedicatory letters are also prefixed with only the one name. The cognomen "Solinus" has been found on various inscriptions scattered throughout the western empire, but the distribution of these does not give up any clue worth the name of a possible area of origin or influence for a family group.[42] "Solinus" is unlikely to have been an eastern ethnic, as the easternmost epigraphical instance of the name is at Solona, in Dalmatia;[43] it has been suggested that the name was theophoric, from "Sol",[44] or even from the Celtic "Sul".[45]

According to Mommsen, the cognomen "Solinus" was non-existent amongst the *personae honestiores*, and indeed, was also exceedingly rare amongst the plebeian class. The epithet "Grammaticus", appended to

Solinus' name in some of the manuscripts,[46] may be an indication of the profession he followed. Perhaps, as is suggested by his almost excessive admiration for men of learning,[47] Solinus devoted his entire life to study. The *Polyhistor* is his only known work, though it is of course possible, in the words of the introduction to Arthur Golding's 1587 translation, that "he left other monuments also of hys wytte, which eyther by force of time are perished, or els perchaunce lie hid in some blind corner among Mothes".

Clearly, Solinus was a Roman citizen—in the tradition of Roman writers,[48] he speaks of Romans as his countrymen, and of Roman religious ceremonies as "ours"—but there is no concrete evidence concerning his country of origin. We might suppose that he lived and worked in Rome itself,[49] as the description of that city contains more details than any other, and he is accustomed to add, when treating ancient buildings there, what currently occupied the site.[50] While certain peculiarities of Solinus' style have given rise to the conjecture that Latin was not his native tongue,[51] he does call Latin "our" language.[52] However, in view of the fact he also claims ownership of Greek,[53] this is hardly helpful.

Enquiry into the times in which Solinus lived is barely more fruitful. Dating the *Polyhistor* with any degree of accuracy is impossible, as the scarce contemporary references courtesy of the work itself are almost invariably dubious,[54] and external evidence is totally lacking.

This in no way deterred Mommsen from authoritatively placing Solinus in the first half of the third century, in the times of Valerian and Gallienus.[55] While conceding his arguments were individually weak, he considered them to have collective force, and believed that overall the indications were "neither dubious nor few".[56] The chief of these indications he detailed as the absence of any allusion in the work to Christianity (unlikely, he argued, if the book was composed following the conversion to Christianity of the Emperor Constantine), a seeming lack of awareness on Solinus' part of Diocletian's division of the provinces, and the fact that Solinus refers to Byzantium rather than to Constantinople. He adds that Solinus' supposed *praenomen*, Gaius, was becoming rare by the fourth century, and reiterates an ingenious argument originally devised by Salmasius, concerning Solinus' reference to silk garments. At L§3, Solinus tells us silk was first worn by women, but "now it is even worn by men" (*nunc etiam viris*). Elagabalus (A.D. 218–222), according to the *Historia Augusta*,[57] was the first to popularize the fashion (under Tiberius, men were forbidden to wear silk, though Caligula reportedly appeared in public thus clad)[58] and the same source reports that Aurelian had no all-silk (*holoserica*) garment, evidently by that time an unusual deficiency. However, Aurelian's successor Tacitus purportedly banned it (again).[59] Following these parameters gives a confidence interval of some 60 years, that is, between A.D. 220–280.

Subsequent scholars have disagreed with this conclusion primarily on the strength of Solinus' style and language, more characteristic of the fourth century than of the third. Raymond Beazley expressed the opinion that the composition of the *Collectanea* should therefore be dated to the latest period consistent with other limitations.[60] More recently, Peter Schmidt, followed by von Martels, has decided for the second half of the fourth century.[61] Schmidt again adduces Solinus' vocabulary and style, but he supports his case with the novel argument that, in several manuscripts for the second version of Solinus' work, the addressee of the first dedicatory letter is written as "Constantius" or "Herennius", not "Adventus".[62] Schmidt proposes the visit of Constantius II to Rome in 357 as a credible date for the work's dissemination. To this is added Schmidt's and von Martels's detection of the Christian influences Mommsen refused to allow.[63] As an example, Schmidt points to Solinus' revulsion for human sacrifices in Gaul.[64] In an article devoted to the subject, Von Martels perceives further Christian influence in Solinus' condemnation of various cannibalistic Scythians, comment not present in the comparable passages of Mela and Pliny. Von Martels's other examples include Solinus' castigation of the lack of chastity among the Garamantic Aethiopians, and his remarks on Judaea, especially his praise for the Essenes.[65] We might add to this (along with Beazley) that Solinus' book is clearly antiquarian in nature, and its judgments often derivative. Why then should it reflect the circumstances, habits or views of the author's own time? Mention (or lack thereof) of the activities of Diocletian, or of Christianity, is therefore potentially meaningless as a line of reasoning. Hermann Walter[66] notes that Martianus Capella's work exhibits no trace of Christianity or Diocletian's provincial division, and that he also calls Constantinople by its old name. In his effort to discredit Mommsen, Von Martels[67] points to Eutropius, whose history of Rome, composed during the reign of Valens (A.D. 364–78), discusses Constantine and the succeeding emperors, yet mentions Christianity only once, in connection with Julian the Apostate. One might extend this kind of reasoning to the silk remark at L§3, by way of pointing out that the reference may well have appeared in an earlier source used by Solinus. In any case, silk garments for both men and women were prevalent enough by the early fifth century for laws to be enshrined forbidding their use and manufacture by private persons.[68]

On the other hand, none of these arguments, barring the linguistic one, compellingly strengthen the case for the later date, which otherwise relies on a suspect name in a late manuscript and the detection of subliminal Christian influences which are by no means explicit.[69] In the end, it must be accepted that the only real certainty is that the *Polyhistor* cannot have been composed *later* than the 4th century. Ammianus Marcellinus, who wrote during the closing years of this century, frequently consulted the work.[70] It had already been copied by the reign of Theodosius II (408– 50; some of the manuscripts include the transcription *studio et diligentia d. n. Theodosii invictissimi principis*).[71] Augustine's *City of God*, composed in the 420s, also makes use of Solinus. Approximately thirty years later, the first author to mention Solinus by name was the author of the *Liber Genealogus*, followed by the grammarian Priscian.[72] (A point in favour of Schmidt's hypothesis is Mommsen's necessary 150+ year hiatus between the book's dissemination and it being used by other authors. A 50 – 60 year gap, as suggested by Schmidt, is certainly more plausible).

To this we may add that it is likely the *Collectanea* was written *no earlier* than the third century. Several other isolated instances in the text do suggest a late third-century date. There is a possible allusion to the province of Syria Phoenice, which was not in existence until A.D. 194, at XXIII §16, and a more concrete reference to "Tripolis" in Africa (i.e., Regio Tripolitana) at XXVII §8. The area, formerly Regio Syrtica, took this name from the fact that there were three principal cities in the region between the Syrtes (i.e., Oea, Sabratha, and Leptis Magna). The new name came into being around the beginning of the 3rd century A.D., and the area was made into a separate province, perhaps by Septimius Severus, who was a native of Leptis. At another juncture, at XLV §5, Solinus opines that horses bred in Cappadocia excelled all others. While Cappadocian horses had always been highly prized, their reputation rose to new heights in Roman racing circles in the 3rd century A.D., probably due to the Imperial acquisition of some large studs there. The third century writers Oppian, Nemesias and Vegetius, seemingly influenced by contemporary circumstances, all mention the Cappadocian breed as superior, while Pliny (et al.) does (do) not.

Hermann Walter advances Solinus' rider regarding the African Blemmyae (XXXI §5),[73] which, he argues, must have been inspired by events which occurred after A.D. 250 (though we may note the Blemmyae must have been a force to be reckoned with considerably prior to this date; in 194 Pescennius Niger attempted to enlist their aid against Septimius Severus). In view of the paucity of more solid evidence, the best we can do is date Solinus' work to an interval of some 130 years, that is, between the 220s and the 350s.

III. The Work

Solinus opens the *Polyhistor* with a treatment of the two subjects he deemed the most important: Rome itself, and the human species:

> Those who imitate the shapes of bodies, setting the rest aside, figure the head before determining the lines of the other limbs. You might say they make their beginning at the very citadel of form. So I also will make my beginning with the "head" of the world, that is, the city of Rome...[74]

What follows forms the first, and by far the lengthiest, chapter of the book. Solinus concludes his description of Rome with a lengthy excursus on the history of the Roman calendar. From here he is able to segue to his dissertation *de Homine*, which opens with a treatment of elements of human reproduction. He goes on to enumerate some very tall tales on an assortment of topics related principally to human *lusus naturarum*.

The second chapter continues his literary peregrination, going on to deal with the remainder of the Italian peninsula. He complains at some length that on this theme there was "nothing now to be found which the old authors' diligence did not anticipate", although, in order to escape accusations of having ignored Italy entirely, he brings himself to treat several topics "which have been more sparingly investigated",[75] dilating on such subjects as the Sibyls, the Hirpi (a tribe of Italian fire-walkers), dumbfounding wolves, and the curious Birds of Diomedes.[76] From here, Solinus proceeds to treat the rest of Europe. He passes through Corsica, Sardinia, Sicily and the Aeolian Islands (chapters III–VI), Greece (VII), Thessaly, Magnesia and Macedonia (VII–IX). Thrace follows (X), and Crete and the Cyclades (XI). Next, Solinus travels eastwards to the Hellespont, the Propontis and the Bosporus (XII). Then come Pontus and Scythia (XIII–XV) where there are cannibals and one-eyed hunters, and Pterophoros, the land of perpetual snow.[77] Beyond, at the back of the North Wind, he finds the territory of the Hyperboreans (XVI). After visiting the Caspian Sea, he doubles back westwards, and treats Germany, Gaul, Britain, Ireland and Spain (XX–XXIII). Chapters XXIV–XXXII describe Africa, from the Gardens of the Hesperides to the Pyramids, and from the Atlas Mountains to the monstrous tribes of darkest Aethiopia. In chapter XXXIII, Solinus arrives in Arabia, replete with flying serpents and exotic perfumes.[78] Passing through Syria and Judaea in chapterS XXXIV–VI, the marvels of Mesopotamia (XXXVII) are detailed before an abrupt turn westwards to Asia Minor (XXXVIII–XLV). From here Solinus travels through Media to the Caspian Gates, crosses the Oxus and the Jaxartes, and arrives in the elusive Land of Silk. India, seemingly envisaged by Solinus as the end of the Continent, and the isle of Taprobane, are finally reached in chapters LII and LIII. The *Polyhistor* concludes with brief descriptions of the Outer Sea, where it first assumes the name "Atlantic"[79] (chapters LIV–LVI), and of the Fortunate Isles.

The *Polyhistor* is known as a geography, but of course, it is not really recognisable as such in any modern sense. Solinus was not, in the vein of Claudius Ptolemy, concerned with mathematical or geographical theory, devoting no space whatsoever to description or discussion of scientific geography. Nor was he interested in composing a guide-book, in the style of Pausanias. At first glance, the *Polyhistor* appears to adhere to the tradition of presenting geography as a *periplus*, or coastal voyage, as do Pliny, Pomponius Mela and others, but closer scrutiny reveals that his modes of description were not quite in keeping with this tradition. Kai Brodersen has shown that, instead of following a linear route along coasts and rivers, as was customary, he innovatively described large *areas* of space, adding neighbours and directions, and making noticeable use of the concept of terrestrial regions (*plagae*). Brodersen further suggests that this change was due to Solinus (or his sources), unlike his forebears, having access to a map of sorts. Solinus' descriptions certainly allow a map, with relative positions, to be envisaged.[80]

In his first dedicatory letter, Solinus thus expresses his *modus operandi*: "to collect interesting stories of far-flung, monstrous savages, strange creatures, and wonders of the lands and seas".[81] His overall mission might be described as a literary quest for the curious—as reflected in the title the work was initially given, *Collectanea Rerum Memorabilium* ("A Collection of Marvellous Things")— within the framework of a description of the known world. This quest shaped both his methods of composition and his selection of material; the mundane is routinely passed over in favour of bizarre details or quirky near-*non sequiturs*. We hear next to nothing, for example, of the physical geography of Germany, but are treated to extensive descriptions of the weird creatures which inhabit the Hercynian Forest— birds which glow in the dark and oversized bovines with curious grazing habits.[82] At another juncture, Solinus dismisses years of Macedonian dynastic struggle in half a sentence, and chooses instead to focus on omens predicting the mishap of a famous king.[83] He interrupts his Scythian chapter in order to tell a series of stories about the marvellous exploits of dogs.[84] This is a recurrent pattern; the prevailing tone of the *Polyhistor* is one of mystery and romance, spiced with sensationalism. The emphasis is firmly on the unknown, the unusual, the unbelievable. Beazley might well be excused for thinking that the book was "perhaps the most completely miraculous view of the world ever put forth in Europe".[85] Yet in reality, Solinus was not concerned with the "miraculous", at least as we today understand the word. Contrary to the belief of many,[86] he did not purposefully spin untruths. He is at pains to point out in his first dedicatory letter that he had followed the opinions of "the most accepted writers" (*scriptoribus...receptissimis*). Instead, he was merely credulously interested, fascinated by the infinite variety of Nature and the bounds of the possible.[87] He adorned his *locorum commemoratio* ("observation of places")[88] accordingly, touching on oddities which aroused his interest, and which, he deemed, were less well-known and likely to prove novel to his audience. What Solinus wanted, therefore, was to entertain and amuse, by way of appealing to the same instincts in his readers as had inspired him in composing the book in the first place. Concerned lest the attentions of readers wander, he designed his work with a view to brevity. Judging by his long-lasting popularity, he succeeded indeed.

Solinus had one other obvious intention, an educational one. For this reason, the accuracy of his information was also of paramount importance. He was concerned to give the true account, and (ironically) not to mislead posterity, criticizing writers he deemed careless. In the first prefatory letter, he speaks of the "yeast of knowledge" (*fermentum cognitionis*) the addressee will discover if he earnestly considers what follows (*si animum proprius intenderis*).[89] At several points he refers to the reader learning something from studying the information given.[90] The subjects he chose to dilate upon, as well as entertaining his readers, were also to function as complements to the general knowledge of educated Romans.

Perhaps as a corollary of this, Solinus liked to think he favoured substance over style. According to his own avowal, his book was leavened with knowledge rather than gilded with superficial eloquence. He believed he had avoided *damnosa concinnitas*, an injurious beauty of style.[91] In other words, he professed not to be interested in windy rhetoric, but in solid facts, about "the famous sites on land and the famous features of the seas".[92] He considered his method as being primarily functional; *eloquentia* was not to be allowed to dominate to the detriment of his subject matter.

This aim is achieved to an extent. The *Polyhistor*, though brief, manages to cover an extraordinary amount of ground, partly due to the concentrated style of many of its sections. In such sections we are gifted with avalanches of towns, peoples, topographical details, and terse references to points of interest.[93] But the *Polyhistor* is very far from structurally homogenous. Some subjects are treated in greater detail (many seemingly at random; it is not hard to imagine Solinus becoming carried away by their sheer interest value) and with contrasting use of language. There are large numbers of long digressions, usually only tenuously connected to their contexts. There are also occasional periods of reflective commentary, which, with their opaque ellipses, present sharp stylistic contrasts. This disunity, almost certainly in part due to Solinus' compositional methods, does not sit well with most modern readers. To some, the *Polyhistor* may come across as something of a rag-bag, loosely organized, with a distracting unevenness.

Solinus' work has a complicated transmission history, having come down to us in two different versions. This fact is lent a certain interest by the two letters included with the text, which purport to have been penned by the author, and which appear to reflect the editorial process. The first letter, clearly dedicatory in character, is addressed to one Adventus, about whom, as with Solinus himself, nothing can be told for certain. It has been suggested he was the M. Oclatinius Adventus who was consul in A.D. 218, though this is unlikely for a number of reasons. For one thing, the date is rather early: according to Dio, Oclatinius was a very old man by the time of his consulship, and Solinus does not in any way imply his Adventus had been involved in public affairs. In any case, Dio tells us that Oclatinius, who had pursued a chequered career, was unable to read through lack of education.[94] Needless to say, there would be very little point in dedicating a book to someone who was illiterate! Solinus very deferentially writes that his Adventus excelled everyone (*praestare te ceteris*) in the study of the best arts (*optimarum artium studiis*).

The first letter presents the work as being entitled the *Collectanea Rerum Memorabilium*. The second letter, addressed to a person unknown (clearly not the same person as to whom the first letter is addressed),[95] explains that the book, previously circulated in a rough and unfinished state (*rudis et inperfecta*), has now been refined, and will henceforth go under the name *Polyhistor*. The two versions are both traceable via different manuscripts. The second version is only superficially different to the first, containing a number of textual changes and additions. In constructing his edition, Mommsen investigated some 175 manuscripts,[96] and identified three different manuscript classes amongst the earliest exemplars. Class I, which descended from a pre-6th century archetype, appeared to be free of noteworthy interpolation, and represented Solinus' first version, with which the first letter belonged. Mommsen's Class I is further distinguishable into two "families", a northern and a southern one. The earliest witnesses to the northern family are a number of excerpts from Solinus in the Irish monk Dicuil's *De mensura orbis terrae*, written in 825. The oldest witness to the southern family is a 10th-century manuscript now at the Vatican, possibly written at Montecassino. Then there is Class II, an offshoot of Class I, with its own variations. The oldest surviving manuscript of this class is at Leiden. Class III, which contained significant additions to the text, along with the second dedication letter, is represented by readings found in "contaminated" copies of Class I and II manuscripts. Class III also represents Solinus' second version of his work.[97] Mommsen chose Class I as the basis of his edition, rejecting the additions of Class III as the work a 6th- or 7th-century interpolator (possibly, he thought, an itinerant Scottish monk, resident at Lake Constance).[98] As a corollary, Mommsen refused to accept the title *Polyhistor*. To him the text of the second letter seemed objectionable, and he denounced it as some nonentity's exercise in style. Breaking with tradition, he subsequently took up the title used in the first letter.[99] Mommsen's opinion on this textual issue, as with his general opinion regarding Solinus, has prevailed. But in the 1960s, Hermann Walter took up arms against Mommen's thesis.[100] In addition to an array of technical textual arguments, Walter suggests that the styles of Classes I and II and the "interpolations" of III are too similar to allow multiple authors. There is also the point that Priscian, in the early 6th century, had quoted the title of the edited version (this was suspected by Mommsen as an interpolation in itself, or even as an inspiration for the new title).

Another intriguing issue is the relation of the two introductory letters to each other as well as to the two different "editions". At first glance, it is difficult to make sense of the content of the second letter, which explains that the work has now taken its final form, with all "rough unshapeliness" (*scabrae informitatis*) expunged. The fact that the second version hardly keeps this promise, having only several additions, and very limited revision of the existing material, provided an obvious basis for the doubt of Mommsen and his followers.

Arguing for the second letter's authenticity, Walter imagined the evolutionary process of Solinus' work as follows:

(1) The first version, as good as finished, was transferred into a fair copy and circulated by well-meaning friends against Solinus' wishes.

(2) The planned dedicatory letter (letter one) had to be held over until it could be revised.

(3) Corrected and enlarged on the basis of the fair copy, the work, prefaced with the dedicatory letter (letter one) was sent by the author with a private accompanying letter (letter two) to a friend. Acting on private initiative, this friend undertook the publication of the second version, and both letters were included.

Schmidt dismisses Walter's reconstruction of events as contrary both to probability and ancient practices, though he himself offers a hypothesis which is (at least on the grounds of the available evidence) hardly more likely. Schmidt posits that the first version was published along with letter one, and (as mentioned above) that it was addressed to no less a person than the Emperor Constantius II,[101] upon the occasion of his visit to Rome in 357. Solinus, argues Schmidt, then revised his work, and Constantius no longer being present, he found a second influential person to stand in his place. Due to the exalted status of Constantius, there was thus no fear that this second addressee (possibly the mysterious Adventus) would feel affronted by being offered a second edition.

Walter's conclusion that the second version was Solinus' own is accepted without question by Peter Schmidt[102] and von Martels. Primarily in view of Walter's textual arguments, and to a lesser degree the pure improbability of Mommsen's theory,[103] I also have chosen to accept the authenticity of the second version of the text, and of its traditional title, the *Polyhistor*. I have accordingly re-introduced the "interpolations", as—despite Mommsen's *auctoritas*—no convincing case can be made for omitting them.

IV. The Sources and Solinus' place in the Roman Chorographic Tradition

Whence had Solinus his information? The problem of the *Polyhistor's* textual antecedents has to date inspired more comment than any other Solinian issue, spawning a number of genealogies of varying degrees of probability. Certainly, in keeping with the contemporary practice in late antiquity of producing new works assembled from condensed versions of older texts, Solinus was far from original. He is the first to admit this: in the first dedicatory letter he mournfully asks: "For what can we claim as our own, since nothing has been passed over by the diligence of old? What remains untouched up to our own era?"[104] Having followed the "traces of the old stamps" (*vestigia monetae veteris*), he writes, he prefers to follow the "universal opinions" (*opiniones universas*) rather than to innovate. Previous to this, Solinus assures his addressee that the authors he has consulted are "most accepted" (*receptissimis*). Having openly presented himself as a dependent writer, he accordingly names sixty-eight different authorities in the *Polyhistor*, some of which—for example, the "Praenestian books"[105] —are otherwise unknown. The rest are almost exclusively classical.[106] The chapters treating Rome (I), Italy (II) and Crete and the Cyclades (XI), are by far the most heavily referenced (one is tempted to conclude Solinus grew tired of foot-noting as his work progressed). Varro is Solinus' most popular authority, cited 12 times in total,[107] followed by King Juba, cited seven times.[108] Occasionally, multiple sources are cited on contested points,[109] but more often, names seem to have been included, as per Solinus' introductory assertions, purely to lend weight to his pronouncements. Many of the citations are certainly at second-hand, in view of the textual parallels with Pliny (see below), but beyond these points, it is difficult to determine much of a pattern.

At the heart of the controversy of Solinus' sources lies the question of the *Polyhistor's* precise relationship with the work of Pliny the Elder. While Solinus never once mentions Pliny or the *Natural History* by name,[110] the existence of a connection between the two works is outstandingly clear, inasmuch as within the *Polyhistor*, we very frequently find re-treatments of Pliny's subject-matter, reflections of his order of topics, vocabulary and even the re-appearance of whole phrases. It has thus been widely accepted that Solinus drew almost exclusively on the *Natural History* for his information, relying on second- or third-hand citations of other authors. As intimated above, this conception of Solinus as nothing more than a plagiarist has had much to do with the latter-day contempt of his work. Ever since he was dubbed "Pliny's Ape", Solinus has lived in the shadow of his industrious predecessor, with most references to him in modern works on the history of geographical writings similarly describing him as a Plinian "imitator" or "copyist". Teuffel even goes so far as to write that Solinus did not himself compose what he calls "this epitome", but merely abridged.[111] Certainly, the bulk of Solinus' text (just over half)[112] possesses an undeniable relationship with the *Natural History* (of varying degrees of closeness). There are multiple parallels with the *Natural History's* Books III–VI (the geographical books), as well as with the books on humankind (Book VII), animals (Books VIII–XI), plants (Books XII–XIII) and stones (Book XXXVII). Material analogous with passages of Book 2 (on astronomy and meteorology), Book XVI (on trees), Books XIX, XXI, XXII, XXV (on other plants), Books XXVIII, XXX and XXXI (on the medicinal uses of human, animal and marine productions), Book XXXII (on the medicinal uses of marine animals), Book 33 (on metals) and Book XXXV (on the uses of earth) appears less frequently. But the idea that Solinus merely copied out whole passages of Pliny, or epitomised him, will not stand up to even cursory scrutiny. A great many of the Solinian passages which Mommsen designates as Plinian provide fuller information than does Pliny. Sometimes more details are given, and sometimes different items relating to the same "Plinian" topic are present. On occasion, Solinus gives Latin *praenomina* where Pliny doesn't (or different ones).[113] Often, Solinus' details differ from Pliny's. On a few occasions, Solinus appears to expressly contradict Pliny's material; at XI §4, for example, he labels those who report the island of Crete as having 100 *urbes* (as does Pliny, at *NH* IV.58) as "prodigally (*prodige*) giving tongue", saying instead that there were many significant *oppida* ("cities") there. At XV §30, Solinus jibes at the idea that rock-crystal was formed by the compression of ice, a theory endorsed by Pliny at *NH*

XXXVII.23. At XXXIII §11, Solinus accepts the existence of the Phoenix in the face of disbelievers (amongst them Pliny; see *NH* X.3, 5).[114]

But what of Solinus' "unPlinian" sections? A portion of the remaining text may be correlated with passages of Pomponius Mela, though the relationship is often less close The remainder of the text cannot be aligned with any extant work. Some scholars have argued for the existence of an intermediary between Pliny and Solinus, which Solinus must necessarily have used as the basis for his own work. Mommsen was the pioneer of this idea and argued that Solinus did not in fact know Pliny directly, but through another work which was itself heavily dependent on the *Natural History*. This work, he hypothesised, was geographical in nature (drawing primarily on books I –XIII of the *Natural History*) and was augmented with chronological details courtesy of a chronological work of the time of Augustus (*optimae aetatis*, p. X), possibly penned by L. Cornelius Bocchus.[115] This "Plinian geography" (*Chorographia Pliniana*, as Mommsen called it) must have been composed after the time of Hadrian, as the author Granius Licinianus is cited.[116] Mommsen believed that Solinus took the work of this anonymous author (Mommsen labeled him *homo non indiligens*, "a not undiligent man")[117] and epitomised it. Mommsen further argued that it was this work which was used by Ammianus (i.e., Ammianus did not have Solinus' work to hand). Some years later, Martin Schanz went one step further than Mommsen, and identified the "Plinian geography" with Suetonius' *Roma*.[118] H. A. Sanders, attempting to account for a particular variation between Solinus and Pliny,[119] agreed with Mommsen that Solinus' immediate source drew both on Pliny and on Bocchus, but argued that each of these derived similar, though not identical, information from different works of Varro.[120]

The Italian scholar Gaetano Mario Columba formulated an alternative intermediary theory, postulating that Solinus had a second-century source who, habitually bypassing Pliny, drew on an older geographer who was also one of Pliny's informants.[121] That is to say, rather than Solinus ultimately drawing on Pliny, the two shared a common, older, source. This hypothesis convicts Pliny as well as Solinus of the slavish imitation for which so many have scorned him. One of Columba's principal arguments was that Solinus very rarely alludes to happenings later than A.D. 60, while the *Natural History* is replete with references to events of the Flavian era.

Earlier, F. Rabenald, on a different tack, simplifying the idea of a discrete intermediary source, had theorised that Solinus worked simultaneously from Mela, Pliny, Suetonius and another unknown author.[122] Developing this idea further, Hermann Walter supposed Solinus to have worked from a glossed copy of the *Natural History*.[123] With Walter interest seems to have petered out, and no more theories, weird, wonderful or otherwise, have since been proposed.[124]

We may note, along with Fernández Nieto,[125] that Solinus must have had some species of linear connection with Pliny. So much is inescapable, in view of several references to events or circumstances it is probable Pliny would have been personally privy to. The first of these comes at I §74 (aligned with *NH* VII.80), where Solinus mentions the poet Publius Pomponius Secundus, who was on intimate terms with Pliny. The second is at LIII §8 (aligned with *NH* VI.84), where Solinus describes the Taprobanean embassy to Rome, which Pliny himself probably witnessed first-hand. The third concerns the pearly tunic of Lollia Paulina (LIII §28), which Pliny asserts he had himself seen (*NH* IX.117). This puts paid to the idea of Solinus *exclusively* using (at least for the so-called "Plinian" sections) an older source, and represents a hole in Columba's thesis, though Columba attempted to sidestep this question by admitting the possibility that Solinus' source, his *compilatore soliniano*, gleaned some stray facts from Pliny.

It is likewise certain that Solinus' prevalent *modus operandi* was to lift large sections of text from some (unacknowledged) source[126] and to modify it only superficially. This is clearly apparent from the high degree of similarity between some of Solinus' passages and passages of the *Natural History*. This is a point in favour of the intermediary theories. It nevertheless seems to me unlikely that Solinus, as per various of the above hypotheses, worked from one source alone. Clumsy conflations at several points are an argument in favour of multiple sources. That Solinus was himself the compiler is certainly the more economical view.[127]

Note on the translation

An English translation of the *Polyhistor* has been published only once, although translations into Spanish and German have appeared in recent years.[128] In 1587, Arthur Golding (more famous for his translation of Ovid's *Metamorphoses*) produced a version entitled *The Excellent and Pleasant Worke of Julius Ca. Solinus, containing the Noble Actions of Human Creatures, &c.* While Golding was on occasions misled by Solinus' obscurities, and failed to translate sections which offended his notions of propriety, his version is generally accurate, and, to modern ears, quaint and charming. As W. H. Stahl remarks, there is a certain appropriateness about an Elizabethan rendition of accounts of *mirabilia*.[129] Stahl goes on to predict dire challenges for anyone undertaking a new translation of the *Polyhistor*, an "inexpertly and drastically reduced compilation". If the translator adhered faithfully to the text, he theorised, the results would strike readers as strange, and at times nonsensical. Any attempt to gloss over Solinus' "carelessness and ignorance", he continued, would create a false impression of the author. But this is something of an exaggeration. Solinus was, in the main, not nearly so unskillful a writer as Stahl (and many others) would have us believe. The translated text, as it stands, certainly does not require constant glossing to render it intelligible, though the esoteric nature of certain passages, particularly those describing gemstones (see e.g. XXXIII §18–19) ensures sporadic difficulties. It is true the compilatory nature of the *Polyhistor* compromises ready comprehension at certain junctures. In order to counter this, brief notes have been added to provide context and explanation where necessary. Certain passages do present distractingly contrasting styles (compare, e.g., the two prefatory letters, Chapters I–II, and Chapter XXIV) which may be galling to the modern reader, but I have attempted to preserve these contrasts in an effort to represent the relationship between the author and the text or texts he was abstracting.

For ease of reference I have kept to Mommsen's chapter divisions throughout.

The *Polyhistor*
of Gaius Iulius Solinus

Greetings from Solinus to Adventus:[130]

(1) I realize that you, both in your ears' forbearance and in your devotion to the liberal arts, excel others. I have had much experience of this, and thus cannot believe I rashly anticipate your kindness. Therefore, I thought to give the weighing of this trifling work especially to you. Either your diligence promises a ready judgment, or your generosity ready indulgence.

(2) As far as reason would allow, this book has been designed with a view to brevity; moderately abridged, it has neither a wasteful abundance nor a detrimental beauty of style. If you study it earnestly, you will find it is leavened with knowledge rather than veneered with a gold-leaf of eloquence.

(3) For I confess I have very conscientiously studied a number of excellent books, so I might leave the well-known subjects alone, and devote more attention to those which are less well-known.

Observations of places occupy the majority of it, and nearly all the material is connected with the same. It seemed good to me to recall, in order, the famous sites on land, and the famous features of the seas, preserving the differences in the world.

(4) On the other hand, I have put in a good many other things, though harmoniously, so, if nothing else, the ennui of readers might be assuaged by the very variety. Among these I have included studies on the nature of Man and other animals. I have added some things about strange trees and the appearances of remote tribes, and the unusual rites of far-flung peoples. Also I have included not a few things, worthy of mention, which it seemed negligent to omit.

(5) I would wish you, in your industriousness, to particularly understand that the authority for these things stems from the most accepted writers. For what can we claim as our own, since nothing has been passed over by the diligence of old? What remains untouched up to our own era? Therefore, I beg you not to weigh the credit of this work in the present time, seeing indeed that I, having followed the traces of the old stamps, prefer to choose the universal opinions rather than to innovate.

(6) Thus, if you have a different opinion on something in my work, I wish you would grant indulgence to my foolishness; the consistency of truth is in the power of those whom I have followed.

(7) Those who imitate the shapes of bodies, setting the rest aside, figure the head before determining the lines of the other limbs. You might say they make their beginning at the very citadel of form. So I also will make my beginning with the "head" of the world, that is, the city of Rome, although the most learned authors have left nothing which may be newly spoken in her praise, and it may be almost superfluous to re-travel the course trodden in so many chronicles.

(8) Nevertheless, lest it be altogether ignored, I will pursue its origin with as much faith as I can.

Solinus to Adventus:[131]

Seeing that many people have hurried to snatch up the trifle with which I laboured, more impatiently than studiously, and that they have already assigned it to an obsolete, unpolished mediocrity, I inflict the final form of the unfinished work upon you.

Now, things which were omitted have been added, with greater care, to the incorrect versions (which have been condemned, although, as if approved, they are widely circulated), towards the development of the inquiry. Lest by chance a rough copy, with incomplete content, as though endorsed by me, fall into your hands, I have sent, as you see, this collection, interspersed with my own opinions. I did so because, in the first place, the layout of the work had to be referred to your diligence, and so the betrayal of rough unshapeliness be expunged from the proper edition.

Therefore, the title of the work shall be *Polyhistor*. The title I had designated in the beginning, to wit, *Collection of Marvellous Things*, I have rejected, and I am pleased to assign it to oblivion. So then, when you compare this letter to the one which forms the beginning of my composition, you will understand that you occupy the same place as he to whom I dedicated the culmination of my labour.

CHAPTER I

(1) There are some who would have it that the name "Rome" was first thought of by Evander.[132] Coming across a town there, already built, which the young men called in Latin "Valentia", he paid heed to the meaning of the prior name, and called it in Greek "Rome".[133] And since he and his Arcadians lived on the highest part of the hill, the derivation followed that the safest parts of cities were in later times called *arces*.[134]

(2) But according to Heracleides,[135] after Troy was captured, certain of the Greeks came by way of the Tiber to the place where Rome is now. They were persuaded by Roma, a most noble lady among their captives, who was as a companion to them, to burn their ships. They set up a base, built walls and named the resulting town "Rome" after her.

(3) Agathocles[136] writes that it was not the prisoner Roma, as is said above, but rather the daughter of Ascanius, granddaughter of Aeneas, who was the reason for the name.

(4) Another name, peculiar to Rome, is also recorded. However, it is strictly forbidden to publish it, as it is enunciated along with other secrets during our religious ceremonies. This was agreed upon so that the reverence given to the accepted silence might abolish knowledge of the thing itself.[137] (5) Valerius Soranus, who dared utter this name against the prohibition, was put to death because of his profane talk.

(6) Attendance at the little shrine of Angerona is among our most ancient religious observances: we sacrifice to the goddess seven days before the Kalends of January. She is the protector of Silence itself, and her statue shows her with her mouth gagged and sealed.

(7) Because certain forms of cult were maintained here long before Rome existed, ambiguities arise. Hercules dedicated an altar to his father Inventor, which he had vowed to do after the punishment of Cacus, when he had recovered his lost cattle. (8)This Cacus lived in a place called Salinae, which is today the location of the Porta Trigemina. Gellius reports that he was taken prisoner by Tarchon the Tyrrhenian, to whom he had come as ambassador from King Marsyas, with Megales the Phrygian as his associate. When he broke out of prison he returned from whence he had come, and with a superior number of troops, he seized the country around Vulturnus and Campania. Next, Cacus dared to attack the territory which had been handed over to Arcadian rule. But he was overwhelmed by Hercules, who was by chance present there. (9) Megales was received

again by the Sabines, and he taught them the art of interpreting omens.[138]

(10) Hercules also set up an altar to his own divine spirit, an altar which is held in great reverence by our high priests. He did this after he learned from Nicostrate, mother of Evander, who was called Carmenta because of her prophesying, that he would one day become immortal. He made an enclosure for this altar, and taught the Potitii[139] the rites of worship, which involved the sacrifice of cattle. The sanctuary is in the cattle market, and evidence of his banquets and of his greatness remain there, (11) for, because of divine influence, neither flies nor dogs can enter into the place. This came about, it is said, because when Hercules was performing the public distribution of the sacrificial meat, he invoked the god Myiagrus.[140] Also, he left his club at the entrance, and the dogs fled at its smell. These things have endured to this day.

(12) Hercules' companions also constructed the temple which is now called the Treasury of Saturn. They did this in honour of Saturn, whom, they learned, had been an inhabitant of the region. In addition, they named what is now the Capitoline Hill the Hill of Saturn, (13) and called the gate in the fortifications which they built Saturn's Gate. The name of this gate was later changed to the Porta Pandana.

The lower part of the Capitoline Hill was the dwelling place of Carmenta, now the location of the temple of Carmenta, from which the Porta Carmentalis took its name.

(14) No-one doubts that the Arcadians were the founders of the Palatine. They also first established the town of Pallanteum, which the Aborigines had inhabited for some time. However, because of the inconvenience of the nearby swamp, made by the flowing Tiber, they soon left it behind and set out for Reate.

(15) There are those who think that the name of the Palatine Hill was inspired by the bleating of sheep, and that the name was arrived at by adapting the letters of the word *balatus*.[141] Others think that the name was taken from that of Pales, the pastoral goddess, or, as Silenus[142] shows, from the name of Palantho, the daughter of Hyperboreus, whom Hercules deflowered there.

(16) These things aside, it is at least clear that the glory of the Roman name is indebted to that particular propitious omen[143] which we all know so well, especially since the account of the years makes a hinge for truth.

(**17**) Varro (a very diligent author)[144] asserts that Romulus founded Rome. His parents were Mars and Rhea Silvia, or, as several people believe, Mars and Ilia. At first, Rome was called "Square",[145] because it was set out on the balancing-point.[146] (**18**) It began at the wood which is in the Area Apollinis, and had its end at the top of the Stairway of Cacus, where the cottage of Faustulus was.

Here Romulus stayed overnight, and auspiciously laid down the foundations of the walls when he was eighteen years old, eleven days before the Kalends of May, between the second and third hours, as Lucius Tarruntius, a very notable mathematician, has recorded. Jupiter was in Pisces, Saturn, Venus, Mars and Mercury in Scorpio, the sun in Taurus and the moon in Libra.[147] (**19**) Thereafter it became custom that no victims were sacrificed on this day, the festival of the Parilia, so it should be free from blood. The explanation for this custom, it is believed, is derived from Ilia's progeny.[148]

(**20**) Romulus reigned for thirty-seven years. He held his first triumph over the people of Caenina, and took spoils from their king, Aceron. These he dedicated to Jupiter Feretrius, and called them "choice".[149] His second triumph was over the people of Antemnae, and the third over the people of Veii. He disappeared at the swamp of Capra, on the Nones of July.

(**21**) I will now say where the other kings lived.

Tatius dwelled in the citadel, where the temple of Juno Moneta is now. Tatius was killed by the Laurentes in the fifth year after he had come to the city; this occurred in the 27th Olympiad.

Numa at first lived on the Collis Quirinalis. Later he lived near the temple of Vesta, in the palace which to this day has the same name. Numa reigned for forty-three years and is buried under Janiculum.

(**22**) Tullius Hostilius lived at Velia, where later the shrine of the Penates was made. He reigned for thirty-two years, and died in the 35th Olympiad.

(**23**) Ancus Marcius lived at the uppermost end of the Sacred Way, where the shrine to the Lares is. He reigned for twenty-four years; he died in the 41st Olympiad.

(**24**) Tarquinius Priscus dwelled at the Porta Mugonia, above the top of the New Way. He reigned thirty-seven years.

(**25**) Servius Tullius Esquilinus lived above the Clivus Urbius; he reigned for forty-two years. (**26**) Tarquinius Superbus, as Esquilinus himself, lived above the Clivus Pullius, at the Fagutaline Grove.[150] He reigned for twenty-five years.

(**27**) It pleases Cincius to deem that Rome was founded in the 12th Olympiad. Pictor[151] believes it was during the 8th; Nepos and Lutatius,[152] seconding the opinions of Eratosthenes and Apollodorus, think it was founded in the second year of the 7th Olympiad.[153] Pomponius Atticus and Marcus Tullius[154] hold out for the third year of the 6th Olympiad.[155] After comparing the dates of us Romans with those of the Greeks, I conclude that Rome was founded at the beginning of the 7th Olympiad, 433 years after the capture of Troy. (**28**) To be sure, the Olympic contest (which Hercules proclaimed in honour of Pelops, his maternal ancestor) was discontinued for an interval. Iphitus the Elean renewed it 408 years after the destruction of Troy, and therefore we count the first Olympiad from Iphitus. Thus, allowing six Olympiads (each of which is reckoned at four years) in between, since Rome was founded at the beginning of the 7th, it remains that there were 433 years between the capture of Troy and the foundation of our city.

(**29**) To the latter argument this can be added: when Gaius Pompeius Gallus and Quintus Veranius were consuls, it was the 801st year since the founding of the city, and at the time it was noted down in the public records that it was the 207th Olympiad. Having multiplied 206 by 4, one arrives at an answer of 824 years, to which the first year of the 7th Olympiad must be added. In total, the number of years equals 825. After the 24 years of the six Olympiads which went before are subtracted, it is clear that 801 years remain. (**30**) Therefore, since the 207th Olympiad is reckoned as the 801st year after the founding of the city, it is right to believe that Rome was founded in the first year of the 7th Olympiad.

(**31**) Rome was ruled by kings for 241 years. The Board of Ten was created in the 302nd year. The First Punic War began in the 489th year, the Second in the 535th year, and the Third in the 604th. The war with the Allies began in the 662nd.

(**32**) Aulus Hirtius and C. Pansa became consuls in the 710th year. During their consulship, the 18-year-old Caesar Augustus was himself made consul. His principate was begun in such a way that through his vigilance the Empire remained both untroubled and safe. (**33**) Indeed, this is almost the only time in our history when wars almost ceased and talent could flourish. As the wars were in respite, doubtless this was so the works of virtue should not become weak through the idle holiday.

(**34**) It was at this time, then, that the system of ordering the year, which had been covered in obscurity from the beginning of the world, was first explored. For before Caesar Augustus, the year was reckoned in an uncertain way. Among the Egyptians it was defined as having four months;[156] among the Arcadians three, and among the Arcananians six. In Italy, among the people of Lavinium, it was reckoned as having thirteen. Their year is said to have had 374 days.[157]

(**35**) From the beginning, the Romans reckoned their year with ten months, starting from March. On the first day of the year they kindled fire on the altar of Vesta, and changed their old bay-wreaths for green. The Senate and the people held elections, and the mistresses served dinner to their slaves, just as masters did at the Saturnalia. The mistresses did this so they might encourage better service by the reward; the masters, as it were, did it so they might reward the slaves for completed work. It can be neatly proved that March was the first month: the fifth month from it was called Quintilis, and when the full number was passed through, (**36**) December completed the annual circuit within 304 days. For at that time that number of days finished the year, as six months had 30 days and the remaining four had 31. (**37**) But since this system (which was pre-Numa) differed from the course of the moon, they made the year equal to the lunar reckoning by adding 51 days. (**38**) So they might make up two more months, bringing the total number of months to 12, they took one day from the first six months, and added them to the extra 51 days. The resulting 57 days were divided into two months, one of which was 29 days long, and the other 28. (**39**) Thus the year began to have 355 days.

Later it was by chance perceived that the year was wrongly confined within the boundaries I mentioned above, as the path of the sun clearly did not finish the course of the Zodiac before the 365th day, overflowing even to another quarter of a day. So they added 10 ¼ days, and the year then consisted of 365 ¼ days. They lauded the accuracy of the odd number, which Pythagoras teaches it is fitting to prefer in everything.[158] (**40**) Because of this, it is said that January and March, since they have an odd number of days, are assigned to the Olympian gods, while February, owing to its even number of days, is the province of the gods of the Lower World.

(**41**) When this state of affairs was pleasing to everyone, the quarter was variously inserted by different peoples. However, the times were not made perfectly equal with any certainty.

(42) The Greeks, every eight years, removed 11¼ days from each year, and multiplying this number by eight, they reserved the days to the ninth year. Having produced the number 90, they divided it into three months of 30 days, and restored them to the ninth year, ending up with a total of 444 days, which they called "odd" or "superfluous". (43) At first the Romans approved of this reckoning, but because of the displeasing even number it was neglected, and in a short time, forgotten. The power of the addition was handed over to the priests, who, for a price, mostly acceded to the reasonings of the tax-gatherers, and shortened or lengthened the times as they wished.[159]

(44) When things were thus, the time inserted was sometimes too long, and sometimes too short, or ignored and let pass altogether unnoticed. Sometimes the months which were wont to be in winter came into their time in either summer or autumn.

(45) But Gaius Caesar settled this universal disorder, and brought to an end the confusion of the calendar. So the past error might be remedied, he intercalated 21¼ days. By this means, the months were drawn back to their accustomed times, and the seasons could keep to their appointed order. Therefore, that year alone had 344 days; thereafter, all the others had 365¼.[160] Even then the priests made a mistake. (46) For when they were instructed to insert one day every four years, which ought to have been done at the end of every 4th year before the 5th year began with auspices, they inserted it instead at the beginning of the 4th year. (47) Thus, in 36 years, when only 9 days should have been sufficient, 12 were inserted. This Augustus corrected; he ordered that 12 years pass without addition, so the three days which had been rashly added over the necessary 9 could be reconciled. By this amendment, a system was established for all times after.[161]

(48) Truly, although this and many other things are owed to the times of Augustus, who was almost peerless in his rule, he came upon many great misfortunes in his life. Thus it is not easy to tell whether he was more unhappy or more blessed. (49) Firstly, in his petition to his uncle for the office of Master of Horse, the tribune Lepidus was preferred to him, because of a sign at the taking of the auspices. Soon after, there was the burdensome power of Antony in the Triumvirate, the Battle of Philippi, and the ill-will which arose from the proscriptions. Next there was the renunciation of Postumus Agrippa, after the adoption, and Augustus' subsequent great repentance. Then there were the shipwrecks at Sicily, and his shameful lurking in a cave there, the many seditions of his troops and the anxiety over Perusia. Also there was the detection of

his daughter's adultery and of her wish to murder him. Then there was the disgrace of his granddaughter (no less a shame than the other) and accusations of causing the deaths of her sons. After his own children were lost, there was the grief of childlessness. There was the pestilence in the city, famine in Italy, military difficulties in the Illyrian War, his ill-health, the abusive discord with his step-son Nero, the unfaithful plots of his wife and also of Tiberius, and many other things of the same sort.

(50) Nevertheless, as though the spirit of the age were grieving, scarcity of all crops followed after the death of Augustus. Lest this seem like a mere accident which had befallen, the imminent evil was portended by certain signs. (51) A certain Fausta, a woman of lowly origin, brought forth two sets of twins at one birth: two males and as many females. This monstrous fecundity[162] foreshadowed the future calamity. Howbeit the author Trogus[163] affirms that in Egypt seven were brought forth together at one birth, this is no great miracle. For in that country, the Nile with its fruitful water makes not only the fields on the land thrive, but also the wombs of women. (52) We read that Gnaeus Pompey exhibited a woman from Asia called Eutyche in the theatre with her 20 children, which were known to have been born in three births. Whence, I think it proper to go on from here to examine the begetting of Man.

(53) Indeed, although I am going to treat all living creatures which seem worthy of mention, just as the country of each shall remind me, it is fitting for me to begin with that creature which Nature has placed before all in judgment of feelings and capacity for reasoning.

(54) As the natural philosopher Democritus[164] observes, Woman is the only "monthly" animal. The monthly courses of women, as is observed by many, are justly to be accounted among the marvellous.

(55) The fruit of the earth, stained by menstrual blood, will not sprout; new wine becomes sour, turf dies, trees lose their produce. Iron is attacked by rust, copper becomes black. If any dogs taste it, they become enraged into a frenzy; anyone injured by their bites becomes mad. (56) But these are small things. Bitumen from Judaea, which is produced at Lake Asphaltites,[165] is very sticky, and has a gluey pliability; it cannot be dissipated. It is impossible to divide it—if you wish to break it into parts, the whole will certainly stay together, as it extends as far as it is stretched out. But when the threads are brought near to the polluted blood, they are easily separated. When the noxious fluid is placed near any material, it is dissipated. The sudden division comes about through the tenacity being joined to the contagion.

(57) To be sure, the substance does have one beneficial property: it averts the Star of Helen,[166] most pernicious to sailors.

(58) For the rest, women themselves, whose functions are a necessity, do not possess harmless glances during the period they are subject to this natural law of theirs. The brightness of mirrors is spoiled by their aspect; the mirror becomes dulled, and no longer reflects faces as it is wont to do. The beauty of the gloss becomes obscured by darkness.

(59) Some women are always barren. Others, by dint of changing husbands, are able to leave sterility behind. Some bear only once; others bear only males or only females. By the age of 50, the fertility of all women is stilled, but men in the 80th year can still procreate, as in the case of King Masinissa.[167] He begot his son Mathumannus in his 76th year. Cato,[168] when he had past 80 years of age, begot the grandfather of the Cato of Utica with the daughter of his client Salo.

(60) It is also known that when two children are conceived within a short time of one another, both settle in the womb, as did Hercules and Iphicles, who were carried in the same pregnancy. Nevertheless, it seems that these two were born at the same interval at which they were conceived.

(61) Then there is the case of the slave-girl from Proconnesus, who brought forth twins from her two-fold adultery, each similar to his father.

This Iphicles fathered Iolaus, who, after he went to Sardinia, and by blandishments persuaded the fearful minds of the inhabitants into concordance, built Olbia and other Greek towns. His descendants, called the Iolenses, bestowed a temple on his tomb, because, in imitation of his uncle's virtue, he had freed Sardinia from many evils.

(62) Above all, women wanting children should beware of sneezing after sexual union, lest the sudden shock reject the semen before the paternal fluid can penetrate to the mother's inner parts.

If natural processes prevail, the pregnant mother will be troubled by pain on the tenth day from conception. From this time she will become restless in mind, and her sight will dim with darkness. Also the desire of her stomach lessens and she begins to loathe food.

All agree that it is the heart which is first formed of all the flesh. It grows until the 65th day, and then diminishes. First of all the bones is the backbone. Because of this, it endangers life if either of these parts are harmed.

(63) If the little body is being fashioned into a male child, the colour of the mother is better, and the birth is easier. Also the baby begins to stir from the 40th day. A female first quivers after the 96th day. The conception of a female dyes the countenance of the pregnant mother with pallor. Also it hinders her legs with a faint lethargy.

(64) In both sexes, when the hair starts to grow, the mother becomes more troubled. The sickness is exacerbated when the moon is full; this time is always harmful until the birth happens.

If the pregnant mother eats rather salty food, the child is born without nails.

When the proper time for the birth draws near, it best suits the woman in labour to hold her breath, since yawning causes a lethal delay, suspending the birth.

(65) It is against nature for children to be born feet first. Just like other children brought forth with difficulty, those who are born thus are called "Agrippa".[169] These same mostly lead unfortunate lives, and die young. (66) Only in one man, Marcus Agrippa, was it a sign of felicity. Nevertheless, one could hardly say he was completely untouched by hardship. It is rather that he had less of adversity than of good fortune. By the wretched pain of his feet,[170] by the open adultery of his wife and by several other unhappinesses he paid for the foretoken of his inverted birth.

(67) For female babies, there is another unpropitious manner of birth. This is when the child is born with the vulva grown together. In this way were the genitalia of Cornelia, mother of the Gracchi: she atoned for the portent by the unlucky death of her children.[171]

(68) A birth is more auspicious if the mother dies of it, as in the case of the first Scipio Africanus. His mother died, and because he was born by being cut from her womb, he was the first Roman to be called "Caesar".

(69) On the subject of twins, if one of the two perishes by being prematurely born, the one that survives and is born at the proper time is called "Vopiscus".

(70) When people are born with teeth, as were Gnaeus Papirius Carbo and Manius Curius, they are given the surname "Dentatus".[172] Some in

turn are armed with solid teeth which form one continuous bone, such as the son of King Prusias of Bithynia. (**71**) The sex of the child determines the number of teeth, since males have more and females fewer.[173] In those who have pairs of projecting teeth, if the double is on the right side, it gives hope of good fortune. In those whom the double is on the left, it is the opposite.

(**72**) The first sound made by newborns is screaming; the emotion of happiness is delayed until the 40th day. I know of only one who laughed in the same hour as he was born, namely, Zoroaster, who became extremely skilled in the arts. But Crassus, the grandfather of the Crassus who was violently seized in the Parthian War, used to be surnamed "Agelastus", because he never laughed.[174] (**73**) Among the other extraordinary things we are told about Socrates, it is a celebrated fact that his face kept the same expression, even when he was troubled by misfortune. Heraclitus and Diogenes the Cynic never yielded from their hardness of spirit. Trampling upon the whirlwind of fortune, they continued unchanged in their purpose against all sorrow and compassion.

(**74**) It is said that Pomponius, the poet and consul, was a man who never burped. Among other examples is that of Antonia, wife of Drusus, who did not succumb to enticements to spit.

I have heard of several born with hardened bones, who were not accustomed either to sweat or to thirst. Lygdamis the Syracusan is said to have been of such a sort. He was the first, in the 33rd Olympiad, to carry away the crown for the *pancratium*.[175] His bones were found to have no marrow in them.

(**75**) It is certain that the sinews make the greatest contribution to human strength. The thicker they are, strength is all the more ready to grow. Varro, in his report about unnatural strength, notes that there was a gladiator called Tritannus, who wore the Samnite armour,[176] who had sinews both straight across and athwart his hands and arms, as well as his breast, like lattice. In conflicts, he conquered all his adversaries with a light touch, almost carelessly. (**76**) Varro also writes about this man's son, a soldier of Gnaeus Pompey, who was born in a similar way. He fought an enemy who challenged him, overcame him with his unarmed right hand and with one finger carried him back as a captive to the camp of his own general.

(**77**) Milo of Croton is also reported to have done many things above the power of humans. It is even said that he felled a bull at a blow from his bare hands, and that he willingly consumed the entire victim on the day which he had killed it. Of this there is no doubt, for there exists an inscription in witness of the deed. He died the victor of all competitions.[177]

It is reported that there is a use for *alectoria*, which has the appearance of a crystal in the shape of a bean. It is found in the bellies of fowls: they say it is suitable for fighting cocks.[178]

Milo shone in the age of Tarquinius Priscus.

(**78**) Now, the reader who presses on after his mind has been turned to other things, to the causes of likeness, will discover how great is the talent of cunning Nature!

Sometimes we observe likenesses between relatives. The passage of time, by means of offspring, makes them in families, just as small children frequently bear moles or scars, or some other mark of their ancestors.

This was so among the Lepidi, of whom three from the same house (although not in direct succession) were found to have been born with a membrane drawn across the eye. (**79**) There is also the famous boxer of Byzantium. He had a mother who was the daughter of a bastard Ethiopian, and although she in no way resembled her father, he himself begot children in the likeness of his Ethiopian grandfather.

(**80**) But this is not so amazing if we consider the likenesses which have been observed between complete strangers. A certain Artemon, a low-born Syrian, is said to have had a similar appearance to King Antiochus. It is further said that Antiochus' royal wife Laudice, by showing this base fellow to the people, was able to conceal her husband's death for a long time, until a successor of her choice was arranged for the kingdom.

(**81**) Such was the uncertainty due to the similarity of Gnaeus Pompey and Gaius Vibius, a man of low origins, that the Romans called Vibius by the name of Pompey and Pompey by the name of Vibius.

The actor Rubrius so resembled the orator Lucius Plancus that he was even called Plancus by the people.

(**82**) Armentarius, a gladiator of the *murmillo* type,[179] and the orator Cassius Severus did so resemble one another that if at any time they were seen together, no-one was able to tell them apart unless their dress betrayed the difference.

Marcus Messala, who had been a Censor, and one Menogenes, who was from the commonplace dregs of society, were so similar in appearance that no matter which was seen, people thought Messala to be none other than Menogenes, and Menogenes to be none other than Messala.

(83) A fisherman from Sicily was compared to the proconsul Sura, because (among other things) of his open-mouthed expression. They resembled one another in the same impediment of speech, namely, in the natural obstacle of slowness in bringing forth words.

(84) It is a marvel to see indistinguishable faces not only among strangers, but also among people drawn together from the furthest parts of the world. When a certain Toranius sold two boys of extraordinary beauty as twins to the triumvir Antonius for 300,000 sestertii, he had acquired one from Transalpine Gaul and the other from Asia. Indeed, they might have been believed to be twins, had not their speech betrayed them. (85) Antonius was angry at being deceived, but Toranius not unreasonably remonstrated that the thing he as a buyer took such exception to was actually of great worth. It was, he said, no marvel for real twins to be alike, but that these two could be born more alike than twins, with such a great distance separating them, could not be priced at any value. (86) Indeed, Antonius was mollified by this answer, and thereafter he would tell people that there was nothing among his possessions that he held more dearly.

(87) Now, if we investigate the very shapes of men, it is clearly evident that Antiquity proclaimed nothing falsely, but that the progeny of our time, corrupted by degenerate successors, and through the gradual dwindling of the children now born, has lost the grace of the old beauty.

(88) Although the majority assert that no man can exceed a height of seven foot, which was the very measure of Hercules, it was found that in the time of the Romans under the divine Augustus that Pusio and Secundilla[180] were ten feet high and more. Their remains are yet to be seen in the sepulchre of the Sallusts. (89) Later, in the principate of the divine Claudius, there was a man brought from Arabia, by name Gabbara, who was nine feet and as many inches high. But 1000 years before Augustus, no-one of such a sort appeared, just as after Claudius, no-one of a like sort was seen. (90) For who in this age is not born lesser than his parents were?

Orestes' remains testify as to the bulk of the men of old. His bones (they were discovered in Tegea in the 58th Olympiad by the Spartans, who had been advised by an oracle) were seven cubits long. Also, writings summon faithful memories from antiquity of an incident in the Cretan war. **(91)** The rivers were swollen with more violence than is usual, and had broken up the ground; when the flood departed, among the many cracks in the earth a human body 33 cubits long was discovered. Lucius Flaccus the legate and even Metellus himself desired to see it. People refuted the marvel as hearsay, but they saw it with their own eyes.[181]

(92) I must not omit that the son of Euthymenes of Salamis grew to three cubits high in three years. However, he was slow of gait, dull-witted, and boisterous of voice; he matured too soon and was immediately beset by many ills. He paid for his swift growth by falling prey to all manner of sicknesses.

(93) Man's system of measurements has a two-fold harmony, for the measure between the two longest fingers, the arms being stretched out, is as much as is between the sole of the foot and the top of the head. Therefore, the natural philosophers judge Man to be a little world.

(94) More maneuverable movement is ascribed to the right hand, and greater firmness to the left. Whence, one is more suitable for gesticulating, and the other is more suited to bearing burdens.

(95) Nature has devised a method of modesty even between dead bodies. If ever the bodies of those killed are borne up by the waves, those of men float face up and those of women float face down.

(96) Now we may pass to the title of swiftness. A certain Ladas gained the first award for speed. He was accustomed to run so fast above loose dust that the sand still hovered, and there was no evidence of his footprints.

(97) When Polymestor, a Milesian boy, had been directed by his mother to feed the goats, he chased a hare for sport and caught it. Because of this, he was immediately induced by the master of his flock to compete in the 46th Olympiad, as the author Bocchus[182] reports. He was victor in the race, and won the crown.

(98) Philippides, in the space of two days, ran the 1240 stades from Athens to Lacedaemon.

Anystis the Laconian and Philonides, couriers of Alexander the Great, ran the 1200 stades from Sicyon to Elis in one day, without halt.

In the year that Fonteius and Vispanus were consuls, an eight-year-old boy in Italy ran 65 miles between noon and evening.

(99) Next, Varro mentions one Strabo, who, having the clearest sight, could see over 135 miles. From the watch tower at Lilybaeum he was able to accurately note the number of ships in the Punic fleet which had just left Carthage.

(100) Cicero reports that the whole Iliad was so finely written on vellum it could be enclosed within the shell of a nut.

Callicrates carved some ants out of ivory; it was not possible to distinguish them from the real ones in the portico.

(101) Apollonides[183] mentions some women called the Bitiae, who live in Scythia. They have twin pupils in their eyes, and if they look angrily at someone, they can kill by a glance. They also live in Sardinia.

(102) Among the Romans, Lucius Sicinius Dentatus is shown to have been the most courageous by the number of his titles. He was Tribune of the Plebs a little while after the expulsion of the kings, when Spurius Tarpeius and Aulus Arterius were consuls. He, eight times victor in challenges, had 45 scars in front, and no mark on his back. (103) He captured spoils from the enemy 34 times. He earned 312 gifts of *phalerae*,[184] ceremonial spears, bracelets and crowns. He followed nine other generals in their triumphs; they had conquered because of his work.

(104) After Sicinius comes Marcus Sergius, who served twice in the military. The first time he was wounded 32 times in front; the second time he lost his right hand in battle. Because of this, he afterwards made himself an iron hand, and although neither hand was much use for fighting, he fought four times in one day and conquered with the left hand. He had two horses slain under him. (105) He escaped twice when captured by Hannibal. During the 20 months when he endured the fate of bondage, he was not for one moment without shackles and chains. He was rewarded with military honours in all the harshest battles the Romans experienced in those times. He carried away civil crowns from Trasimene, Trebia and Ticinus; also from Cannae, from which it was accounted an extraordinary feat merely to have escaped. He alone received a crown. Surely blessed would he be, with so many votes of glory, had not his heir Cataline, in the succession of his posterity, darkened his prizes with his hated name.[185]

(106) As much as Sicinius and Sergius shone among the soldiers, among leaders (indeed, I may with more truth say among all men) shone Caesar the dictator. Under his command, 1,192,000 of the enemy were slain. He was unwilling to note how many he routed during the Civil Wars. He fought 52 times in pitched battles. (107) He alone surmounts Marcus Marcellus who fought 39 times. Besides this, no-one wrote more swiftly, no-one read more quickly; he could dictate four letters at once. He was even endowed with kindness: those whom he had defeated in battle were further conquered by his clemency. (108) Cyrus was famous for the gift of memory. In the army which he captained, which was most numerous, he could address each man by name. Lucius Scipio did the same thing among the Romans. (109) But we may believe that Cyrus and Scipio did it out of habit, while Cineas, the ambassador of Pyrrhus, greeted both the Equestrian order and the Senate by their own names on the day after he had come to Rome.

Mithridates, the Pontic king, ministered justice without an interpreter to the 22 nations he governed.

Plainly, memory is governed by practice, as we see in the case of Metrodorus the philosopher, who lived in the time of Diogenes the Cynic. He carried himself forward so much by regular practicing that he not only remembered the speech of many people speaking at once, but also the order of the words.

(110) Nothing, however, it is often seen in men, can be so easily lost as memory, whether by fear, or falling, or sickness. I heard that someone struck by a stone forgot how to read. Certainly, Messala Corvinus, after an illness which he endured, was stricken to forgetfulness of his own name, notwithstanding how much his senses throve previously. (111) Fear destroys memory. Fear is in turn sometimes a stimulant for speech. Not only does fear incite speech in normal circumstances, but it can also wrench speech from those who were formerly dumb.

(112) When in the 58th Olympiad, the victorious Cyrus had eventually entered the Asian town of Sardis, where Croesus was lying hidden, Atys, the king's son, mute up to this time, erupted into speech at the violence of his dread. For it is said that he shouted out: "Spare my father, O Cyrus, and learn from our plight that you are a man".

(113) It now remains to hold forth on men's characters. Excellence stands out the most in two cases. Firstly, in the case of Cato, founder of the Porcia clan, who was an excellent senator, orator and general. He was

arraigned 44 times, because he had striven in the hostile rivalry of hatred, but he was always acquitted.

(114) Second, there is Scipio Aemilianus. It is easier to praise this man: going beyond those things for which Cato was famous, also excelled in public favour.

(115) Scipio Nasica, an excellent man, was judged to be so not only by private testimony but also by a guarantee of the Senate. Of course, none could be found worthier than he to be entrusted with the office of special religion, since the oracle warned that the sacred ceremonies of the mother of the Gods should be brought from Pessinus.[186]

(116) Among the Romans many flourished in eloquence, but this good gift was never hereditary, except in the Curio family. Among them were three orators in succession. (117) Certainly it was a great thing in those times, when eloquence was especially marveled at both in men and in gods.

Apollo exposed the murderers of the poet Archilochus.[187] The crimes of robbers were also detected by the accusing God.

(118) And when Lysander the Lacedaemonian besieged Athens, where the unburied body of the tragedian Sophocles was lying, father Liber continually warned Lysander in his sleep to allow his darling to be buried. (119) He did not stop until Lysander, learning who had died and which god was commanding him, instituted a truce to allow the great man to be buried accordingly.

(120) Castor and Pollux, who were standing outside a dinner-party, called to Pindar the lyric poet when he was threatened with catastrophe, lest he perish with the rest. By this ploy alone Pindar escaped the impending danger.

(121) Gnaeus Pompey Magnus must be counted next after these gods. When he was about to enter the house of Poseidonius, then the most famous teacher of wisdom, he forbade the lictor to strike on the door, as the custom was. Lowering the *fasces*,[188] although he was victorious in the East and had subdued Mithridates, he yielded of his own will to the door of learning.

(122) Scipio Africanus earlier ordered a statue of Quintus Ennius to be put in his tomb.

Cato of Utica brought one philosopher to Rome when he was a military tribune, and another when he was ambassador to Cyprus. He declared that by these deeds he had bestowed much on the Senate and the people, even if his ancestor had very often recommended that the Greeks should be driven from the city.

(123) The tyrant Dionysius sent ships decorated with ribbons to greet Plato, and he himself honoured him by coming to meet him as he stepped onto the shore, in a chariot drawn by four white horses.

Complete wisdom was imputed to Socrates alone by the Delphic oracle.

(124) A well-respected example of piety shines forth from the house of the Metelli,[189] but the most prominent is found in the case of a plebeian woman who had lately had a child. This woman was of low birth, and therefore of obscure fame. When she was allowed to go to her father (who was confined in prison, as a punishment) she was searched many times by the gaolers, lest she by chance had brought food for him. But later she was discovered feeding him from her breasts.

(125) Both the place and the deed were consecrated. For the father, who was condemned to death, was spared because he was given a memory of such praise by his daughter. The place was set aside as a shrine to the god of Piety.

(126) The Crown of Modesty was bestowed on Claudia by the ship which bore the sacred mysteries from Phrygia, and she followed it with the ribbons of Chastity.[190]

But Sulpicia, daughter of Paterculus and wife of Marcus Fulvius Flaccus, was chosen (she was carefully selected by the matrons, from the hundred most esteemed women) to dedicate the image of Venus, as the Sybilline Books advised.

(127) As touching happiness, a man has not been found who ought to be justly deemed happy. Cornelius Sulla was said to have been happier than he actually was.[191]

The Delphic Oracle judged one Aglaus alone to be blessed; he was the owner of a meagre plot in the narrowest niche in Arcadia, and he was never found to have gone forth from the boundaries of his ancestral ground.

About Man I have said enough.

CHAPTER II

(1) Now, in order to return to my resolve, I must steer my pen towards the commemoration of places. First, I will visit Italy, the splendour of which I have already touched upon in writing of the city of Rome. **(2)** But as Italy has already been discussed with such care by everyone, especially by Marcus Cato,[192] there is nothing now to be found which the old authors' diligence did not anticipate. As material is plentifully at hand for the praise of this excellent land, the most pre-eminent authors have reflected upon many things: the salubriousness of Italy's regions, the temperateness of the climate, the fertility of the soils, the sunny places on the hillsides, the shady groves, the benign passes, the successes of the vines and olives, the noble herds, the many rivers, the great lakes, and the violet beds that flower twice a year. **(3)** Then there is Vesuvius, heated with the breath of a fiery spirit; Baiae, warm with springs; the many colonies; the constant beauty of new cities. There is the famed glory of the old towns, built by the Aborigines, the Aurunci, the Pelasgians, the Arcadians, the Sicilians, then by migrants from all over Greece, and lastly by the victorious Romans. Besides this, Italy's coasts are full of havens; the coasts, with their open bays, are suitable for trading with the whole world.

(4) However, lest it appear as though I have left Italy entirely untouched, it seems by no means absurd for me to exert my mind about those things which are less familiar, and to travel through those areas which have been more sparingly investigated. **(5)** For who does not know that Janiculum was either named or founded by Janus? That Latium and Saturnia were founded by Saturn, Ardea by Danae, and Polycle by the companions of Hercules?[193] Who does not know that Pompeii was founded in Campania by Hercules himself, because thence, after his victories in Spain, he had led his procession of cattle? **(6)** Who does not know of the stony plains in Liguria, where the stones are believed to have been rained down when he was fighting there? Or that Ionia takes its name from Ione, the daughter of Aulochus, whom they say Hercules slew, as she impudently sat down in the road? Or that Archippe was founded by Marsyas, king of the Lydians, and was destroyed by being swallowed up into an opening in the ground, into the Fucine Lake? **(7)** Or that the temple of Argive Juno was founded by Jason, or Pisae by the Pelopidae? Who does not know that the Daunii were named by Cleolaus, son of Minos; that the Iapygians were named for Iapyx, son of Daedalus; the Tyrrhenians for Tyrrhenus, king of Lydia; Cora by Dardanus; Agylla by the Pelasgians, who first brought letters into Latium; Falisca by the Argive Halesus; Falerii by the Argive Falerius, and Fescenninum also by the Argives? Who does not know that the port of Parthenius was founded by the Phocians? That Tibur, as Cato gives testimony, by Catillus the Arcadian, prefect of Evander's fleet, or, as Sextius has it, by the youth of Argos? **(8)** Catillus was the son of Amphiaraus. After the portentous death of his father at Thebes, he, the sacrifice of the spring-born, was sent forth on his grandfather Oecleus' orders, with all his children. In Italy he begot three more children: Tibertus, Coras and Catillus; he expelled from Sicilia the old inhabitants of the town, the Sicani, and called it by the name of the eldest brother, Tibertus. Soon after, the temple of Minerva in Bruttium was built by Ulysses.

(9) The island of Ligea is called so because the body of a Siren named thus was cast ashore there. Parthenope, which Augustus later preferred to be called Neapolis, took its name from the tomb of the Siren Parthenopa situated in that place. Praeneste, as Zenodotus[194] writes, was named after Praenestus, grandson of Ulysses and son of Latinus. On the other hand, the books of the Praenestians say the city was founded by Caeculus, whom, as the tale goes, the sisters of the Digidii came upon hard by a fortuitous fire.[195]

(10) It has been noted that Petilia was established by Philoctetes, Arpi and Beneventum by Diomedes, Patavium by Antenor, Metapontum by the Pylians and Scylaceum by the Athenians. Sybaris was founded by Sagaris, the son of Locrian Ajax, and the Troezenians; the country of the Sallentines was established by the Lyctians, Ancona by the Sicilians, and Gabii was founded by the Sicilian brothers Galatius and Bius; Tarentum was founded by the Heraclidii, the island of Tempsa by the Ionians, Paestum by the Dorians, Croton by the Achaean Myscellus, Regium by the Chalcidians, Caulonia and Terina by the Crotonians, and Locri by the Naricii. Eretum was founded by the Greeks in honour of Hera (for thus the Greeks call Juno). Aricia was founded by Archilochus the Sicilian, from whom, as it pleases Hemina[196] to say, the name was derived. **(11)** In this place Orestes, who had been advised by an oracle, consecrated the image of Scythian Diana, which he had carried out of Taurica before he made for Argos.

Metaurum was established by the Zanclenses; Metapontum, which, as Bocchus asserts, is now Vibo, was established by the Locrians.

Marcus Antonius reports that the Umbrians are descended from the ancient Gauls; the Gauls, because in the time of the calamitous flood they survived the rains, were called "Umbrians" by the Greeks.[197]

(12) It pleases Licinianus[198] to say that the name "Messapia" was originally given by the Greek Messapus to the area afterwards called Calabria; in the beginning, Peucetius, brother of Oenotrus, had named it Peucetia.

(13) Everyone agrees that Palinurus was named after Aeneas' helmsman, Misenum after his trumpeter, and the island Leucosia after his first cousin on his mother's side. Caieta was named after Aeneas' nurse, and Lavinium, which, as Cosconius[199] holds, was built four years after the destruction of Troy, after his wife.

(14) It must not be omitted that Aeneas landed on Italian shores in the second year after Troy was captured, with not more than 600 companions, as Hemina asserts. He pitched his camp in a Laurentine field. Here he dedicated an image, which he had carried out of Sicily, to his mother Venus, who is called Frutis, and received the Palladium from Diomedes. Next, he accepted 500 *iugera*[200] from Latinus, and reigned for three years in conjunction with him. (15) After Latinus' death, Aeneas ruled alone for a period of two years, and then, in the seventh year, disappeared at the River Numicius. The name Father Indiges was given to him. (16) After this, Ascanius founded Alba Longa, Fidenae and Aricia; the Tyrians founded Nola, and the Euboeans Cumae. In Cumae is the shrine of the Sibyl who was involved in Roman affairs in the 50th Olympiad, and whose Book was consulted by our priests up until the time of Cornelius Sulla. (17) At that time the Book — along with the Capitol — was consumed by fire. The two previous Books the Sibyl had herself burned, as Tarquinius Superbus had offered her a meaner price than she asked for them.[201] Her tomb remains in Sicily to this day. (18) Bocchus asserts that the Delphic Sibyl prophesied before the Trojan Wars, and he declares that Homer inserted many of her verses into his work. Several years after her came Herophile of Erythrae, who was also called Sibyl, because of the similarity of her talents. Among other magnificent things, she forewarned that the Lesbians would lose dominion of the sea, long before it came to pass. Thus the sequence of time itself shows that the Cumaean Sybil was the third.

(19) Italy as a whole — ancient Latium, formerly, reached from the mouth of the Tiber all the way to the River Liris — springs from the ridge of the Alps and stretches to the promontory of Rhegium and the shores of the Bruttii, where it extends southwards into the sea. (20) Thence it proceeds, raising itself by degrees to the Apennine range. It extends between the Tuscan and the Adriatic, that is, between the upper and lower seas. In shape it is similar to an oak-leaf, namely, wider in length than in breadth.[202] (21) Further off, where it disappears, Italy is split into two horns, one of which watches the Ionian Sea, and the other the Sicilian. One shore does not receive the onset of the sea which insinuates between

these projections; the open sea is admitted separated by spurs, which jut out like projecting tongues.[203] **(22)** Along the way, we might note things here and there: the citadels of Tarentum, the region of Scylacea with the town Scyllaeum, and the River Crateis — Scylla's mother, as antiquity has fabled. Then there are the gladed woodlands of Rhegium, the valleys of Paestum, the rocks of the Sirens, the charming tracts of Campania, and the Phlegraean plains. There is Terracina, and the house of Circe, once an island encircled by the boundless sea, but now, in the fullness of time, attached to the mainland. It experienced the opposite fortune to the people of Rhegium, whom the sea, by insinuating itself between, violently separated from the Sicilians. Also there is Formiae, which was inhabited by the Laestrygones, and much more beside, which I thought best to pass over, rather than taking the risk of pursuing in an unsatisfactory fashion.

(23) The length of Italy, which extends from Augusta Praetoria through the city and Capua all the way to the town of Rhegium, adds up to 1020 miles. The breadth, at the widest point, is 410 miles, and at the narrowest point, 136 miles. The narrowest part is actually near the port which is called "Hannibal's Camp", for there it does not exceed 40 miles. The centre of Italy, as Varro set forth, is in the Reatine fields. The circumference of the whole is 2049 miles. **(24)** In this circuit, the first gulf of Europe, having begun from Gades, has its end looking towards the beginning of the country of the Locrenses. The second, having begun from Lacinium, has its end at Acroceraunium.[204]

(25) Italy is famous for the River Padus, which Vesulus, the highest mountain, pours out of his bosom among the ridges of the Alps. The Padus first hurls itself forward from this spring, which can be seen on the borders of Liguria; after being submerged in an underground tunnel, it rises in the fields of Vibo. Padus is not lesser in fame than any river, and is called Eridanus by the Greeks. It becomes swollen at its source at the rising of the Dog Star,[205] with the melting snows and dissolving hoar-frosts of winter, and is augmented by the inflow of other waters. Padus carries 30 rivers into the Adriatic Sea.

(26) Among other things worthy of remembrance, celebrated and conspicuously talked of by everyone, is this. There are a very few families in the fields of the Falisci who are called "Hirpus". They make a yearly sacrifice to Apollo on Mount Soracte, in the course of which they dance with impunity in burning heaps of wood, making religious gestures. The flames yield in honour of the divinity. The Senate have honoured their devotion magnificently; the Hirpi were given perpetual freedom from all services.

(**27**) It is not to be wondered at that the Marsi people are resistant to the bites of serpents. They regard their family as being descended from the son of Circe; because of this ancestral power, they know that they ought to hold poisons in servitude. For this reason, they disdain poisons.

(**28**) Gaius Coelius[206] says that Aeetes had three daughters: Angitia, Medea and Circe. Circe settled in the Circean mountains, and there with sorceries invented sundry contrivances to do with charms and phantoms. (**29**) Angitia lived in the neighbourhood of Fucinus, and spent her life pursuing the wholesome science of disease prevention. Since she gave her life to men, she is regarded as a goddess. (**30**) Medea was buried by Jason at Buthrotum, and her son ruled among the Marsi.

(**31**) But although Italy has this defence, it is not completely free from serpents. (**32**) In fact, the inhabitants of Amunclae, which the Greeks from Amyclae built, were driven forth from their town by serpents.[207]

There are numerous vipers with incurable bites in Italy. They are shorter than those which are found in other parts of the world; they harm all the more easily when, for this reason, they are deemed contemptible.

(**33**) Calabria swarms with water-snakes, and gives birth to the boa, which is a kind of snake said to grow to an immense size. First, the boa hunts herds of cattle, and he fastens himself to the udder of whichever cow is watered with the most milk. Fattened by continual sucking, he swells to such a state of satiety that no force is able to withstand his magnitude. Having plundered the animals, he brings the regions which he takes possession of to desolation. (**34**) In the reign of Claudius, a whole child was seen in the belly of a boa slaughtered in the Vatican field.

(**35**) Italy has wolves which are different to others; when one of these wolves sees a man before the man sees the wolf, the man is stricken dumb. Regarded by a baleful gaze, he does not have the use of his voice, even though he may wish to shout. (**36**) I pass over much I know about wolves, and include this as the most worthy of observance: a very small tuft of hair in the tail of this animal procures love. When he fears to be caught after being injured, the wolf willingly casts away this tuft, but it does not have the power unless it is pulled from the wolf while he is alive. Wolves do not breed on more than twelve days per year in total. In famines, they feed on the earth.

(**37**) When those creatures who are called deer-wolves,[208] after long hunger, light on flesh, they painfully begin to chew, but they forget their food if by chance they gaze on something else. Heedless of the present abundance, they go searching for the satiety they left behind.

(38) Lynxes are to be numbered among this kind of animal. The urine of the lynx is said to collect and harden into precious stones by those who have narrowly investigated the nature of stones. That this is known to the lynxes themselves is proved by this example: when they discharge liquid, they immediately cover it, as much as they are able, with hillocks of sand. No doubt they do this from spite, lest such matter as issues from them be useful to us. As Theophrastus holds, these stones are the colour of amber. The substance attracts by a breath things that are near at hand. It cures diseases of the kidneys and assuages the jaundice; it is called *luncurium.*[209]

(40) At Rhegium, and nowhere else, the cicadas are silent. This silence is a marvel, and not to be deplored, since the neighbouring Locrensian cicadas make more noise than all the rest. Granius[210] relates the reason for their silence: when they were murmuring in protest at Hercules, who was resting there, the god ordered them not to make such a loud noise. From that day, the silence which then began has remained.

(41) The Ligurian Sea produces shrubs, which, however long they have been in the depths of the water, are lush and flesh-like to the touch. When they are removed from their origins and finally raised into the upper world, they become as rocks. Not only their quality but also their colour is altered, for they immediately blush crimson. Their little branches are such as we see on trees, mostly half a foot long. It is rare to find one a foot long. From these plants are fashioned many things for the adornment of the body. (42) As Zoroaster says, this substance actually has a kind of power. For this reason, whatever may come from it, it is deemed wholesome. (43) Metrodorus[211] calls it *gorgia*; others call it "coral". Metrodorus also affirms that it resists typhoons and lightning bolts.

In a part of Lucania a gemstone with a very beautiful appearance may be dug up. It is saffron in colour, and it has stars inside it, which are dim, as though shining under a cloud. Since it was first discovered on the shores of the Syrtes, it is called the Syrtian stone. (44) There is also the Veiian stone, called so from the place where it is found. Its colour is black, which, with beautiful contrast, is intersected by white tracks and marks.

(45) There is an island which watches the shore of Apulia which is famous for the tomb and shrine of Diomedes. Also, here alone nest Diomedes' birds; these birds cannot be found anywhere else, which can be judged remarkable. Their shape is almost the same as that of a coot; they are

white in colour, their eyes are fiery, and they have toothed bills. (46) They fly about in flocks, which, for purposes of proceeding efficiently, are not without order. There are two leaders who rule the onrush: one goes in front of the column and the other brings up the rear — the former that he might lead a direct route and the latter that he might urge on the tardy. This is the discipline of their traveling. (47) When the time for fructifying comes upon them, they dig trenches with their bills, and stretch shoots over the top, imitating the framework of a basket. Thus they cover up the space hollowed out underneath. Lest these lids be found wanting, and the wooden hollows carried away by chance winds, the birds press down the pile with the earth they dug out when constructing their wells. (48) They build their nests with double entrances. It is not done fortuitously—they mark out the entrances and exits according to the regions of the heavens. The opening that dismisses them to the feeding grounds is open to the east, and that which receives them is situated towards the west; thus, light rouses them, and does not deny them for their retreat. For the relieving of their bellies, they fly upwards in adverse winds, so their bodily discharges may be blown further away from them. (49) They discriminate between visitors. Those who are Greek they permit to approach, and as far as it is to be understood, they fawn coaxingly upon them as countrymen. If they are of another race, they rush upon them and attack. They frequent the sacred shrine every day, and their zeal takes this form: they wet their feathers with water, and they flock together with thoroughly soaked and dewy wings. By shaking off the moisture, they purify the shrine. Then they clap their wings and depart, as though they have completed their worship. (50) Because of this, the birds are said to have been Diomedes' companions. Certainly, before the advent of the Aetolian leader, they did not go by the name of Diomedes, but thenceforth they have been called thus.

(51) Italy runs as far as the land of the Liburnians, who are an Asiatic race, to the foot of Dalmatia. Dalmatia extends to the Illyrian border, on which coast the Dardanians have their home. These men have been brutalized from their Trojan lineage into barbarous customs.

(52) But from the other side it proceeds down the Ligurian coast into the province of Narbo. Here the Phocaeans, having at one time been driven into exile by the advent of the Persians, built the city of Massilia in the 45th Olympiad. (53) Gaius Marius, in the war with the Cimbrians, let the sea into canals, and so assuaged the danger of sailing on the swollen river Rodanus.[212] This river, cast down from the Alps, first runs through the territory of the Helvetii, dragging streams of running waters with it. It increases by a great amount, and becomes more turbulent than the

sea itself, which it invades, except when the sea is raised. Rodanus rages even when the weather is calm, and for this reason it is reckoned one of the three greatest rivers of Europe. (**54**) The Aquae Sextiae also became famous there. Once they were the winter quarters of a consul, and later they were improved by walls. Their heat, which once breathed out sharply, evaporated over time, and now they do not enjoy their prior fame.

If we wish [now] to turn to the Greeks, it is best to go to the Tarentine coast. Thence, from that promontory which they call Acra Iapygia, is the shortest voyage to Achaia.

CHAPTER III

(1) From here, my pen must change its course. Other lands call on me, and it would be tedious to travel slowly along the shores of all the islands which face the promontories of Italy. These islands are scattered in the most delightful nooks, and seem arranged by Nature as a show lest they be omitted. (2) But how long would I tarry, if, through idleness, I delayed treating the important things, and spoke of Pandateria, or Prochyta, or Ilva, fertile with iron, or Capraria, which the Greeks call Aegilon, or Planasia, called thus because of its plain-like appearance, or from the wanderings of Ulysses?[213] Or Columbaria, mother of the birds which bear this name,[214] or Ilhacesia, Ulysses' watchtower, or Aenaria, named Inarime by Homer, and of others just as pleasing?

Among these islands is Corsica, of which many have written fairly extensively, after having travelled around it. They have completed their narratives with the fullest diligence, and nothing has been omitted which it would not be superfluous to undertake anew. (3) They describe how the Ligurians gave a beginning to the inhabitants, how towns were built, how Marius and Sulla led colonists there, and how the level waters of the Ligurian Sea lap upon it. But let these things pass.

(4) Corsica alone brings forth the stone which they call *catochitis*, which is most worthy to be spoken of, as it is a unique thing. It is larger than other stones used for decorative purposes, and is not so much a gemstone as a common rock. It holds down hands placed upon it, attaching itself to adjoining bodies in such a way that those which it touches stick to it. There is in it I know not what—a kind of very sticky glue, like gum. (5) I have heard that Democritus of Abdera often used this little stone to prove the hidden power of nature in disputes he had against magicians.

CHAPTER IV

(1) As for Sardinia (which we read about in Timaeus by the name Sandaliotis,[215] and in Crispus[216] by the name Ichnusa), in what sea it lies, and who the ancestors of the inhabitants were, has been sufficiently celebrated. It is to no purpose, therefore, to write that Sardus was begotten by Hercules, Norax by Mercury, and that the one travelled into this country from Libya, and the other all the way from Tartessus in Spain. Or that the name was given to the land by Sardus, and to the town Nora by Norax. (2) Or that soon after, Aristeus, by ruling in the city of Caralis, which he himself, joining the people of each blood, had founded, united the separate tribes under one custom, they nothing scorning his rule because of its strangeness.

So we may pass over these things, as well as Iolaus, who settled the land in those regions, and also the Ilienses and Locrenses, let us note that Sardinia is truly without serpents. (3) But what brings serpents to other places brings the *solifuga* to the fields of Sardinia. This is a very small creature with the shape of a spider, and it is called by this name because it flees daylight. It is found mostly in silver-mines (for the soil of Sardinia is rich in silver); it crawls secretly, and calls down pestilence on those who sit upon it unawares.

(4) To this mischief is added the herb sardonia, which prospers quite plentifully in places where springs flow forth. If eaten by people who are ignorant of it, it tightens the muscles and divides the mouth into a rictus, so that those who thus meet death die with the appearance of laughter.[217]

(5) On the other hand, the waters of Sardinia have various benefits. The lakes have a great abundance of fish. The winter showers are saved for the summer scarcity, for the Sardinian man has much wealth as regards rainy skies. They consume collected water,[218] and it suffices for use where there are no bubbling rills. Springs, hot and wholesome, well up in many places. (6) They offer a cure for broken bones, and for the dispelling of poison inserted by *solifugae*, and also for the curing of eye diseases. (7) But what cures eyes is also powerful for discovering thieves. For whosoever denies a theft with an oath, and washes his eyes with these waters sees more clearly if he has not perjured himself. If a man falsely denies perfidy, his crime is revealed by blindness; captured by his eyes, he is driven to confess.

CHAPTER V

(1) If we were to pay respect to the progression of history, or of places, after Sardinia, Sicily would call us, firstly because both islands, brought under Roman jurisdiction, were made provinces at the same time, since in the same year Marcus Valerius was appointed praetor of Sardinia, and Gaius Flaminius the praetor of the other. Say in addition that when you come out of the Sicilian Straits the sea bears the name "Sardinian".

(2) Sicily—this thing must be especially noted—is shaped like a triangle, by reason of its far-flung promontories. Pachynus guides its view towards the Peloponnese and the southern region; Pelorias, facing the west, watches Italy, and Lilybaeum stretches out towards Africa. Of these, Pelorias stands forth; it is praised for the unparalleled moderation of its soil, which is neither turned into mud by the moisture of swamps, nor cracked open into dust by drought.

(3) Where Pelorias retreats inland and spreads out in width, there are three lakes. That the first of these is abundant in fish, I do not, for my part, consider marvellous. But near to the lake, the land is thick with trees, and the groves of brushwood nurture wild beasts. Hunters and others on foot are given access by means of paths. Thus the lake offers the double pleasure of fishing and hunting, and can be numbered among the admirable features of this land.

(4) The holiness of the third lake is proved by an altar which stands in the middle of it and divides the shallows from the deeps. Upon the way proceeding to it, the water is leg-deep. What is beyond it is neither permitted to explore nor touch. He who dares to do so is punished by misfortune, and how quickly he goes to ruin is gauged by how much of himself he immerses in the water. They say that a certain man threw a line as far as he could into these depths, and when he assuaged the labour of recovering it by dipping his arm into the water, his hand became rotten.

(5) The Pelorian shore is inhabited by the colony Tauromenium, which the men of old called Naxus. The town Messana is placed opposite to Rhegium in Italy. The Greeks called Rhegium Ῥήγιον, on account of the division.[219]

(6) There is a great abundance of tuna fish at Pachynus, and because of this, the catch there is always large.

(7) The town of Lilybaeum dignifies the Lilybaean tomb of the Sibyl.

A long time before the Trojan war, Sicanus the king arrived here with a very large band of Spaniards, and named the place "Sicania", after himself. After this, Siculus, son of Neptune, named the land "Sicily". (8) Very many Corinthians, Argives, Ilienses, Dorians and Cretans flocked here. Among them was Daedalus, the expert craftsman.

Sicily has its chief city in Syracuse, where the weather is tranquil even when it is winter, and there is no day without sun. Add to this that the spring of Arethusa is in this city.

(9) Aetna and Eryx are the highest of the mountains. Aetna is sacred to Vulcan, and Eryx to Venus. There are two gaps in Aetna's summit, called craters, through which vapour erupts after being noisily discharged. Loud noises precede it, rolled in different directions, with extended roaring, through the seething hiding-places of the caverns, in the bowels of the earth. Balls of fire do not lift themselves on high before internal uproar has occurred. (10) This is a marvel; and it is not less marvellous that in the burning heat of Aetna, the stubbornness of nature displays snow mingled with the flames. (11) Although Aetna exudes monstrous heat, the summit is perpetually white, holding on to the appearance of winter. There is an unconquerable violence in both: the heat is not mitigated by the cold, nor the cold melted by the heat.

(12) Two other mountains, Nebrodes and the Neptunian, are praised. On the Neptunian is a watchtower which looks into the Tuscan and Adriatic seas. Nebrodes takes its name from the fallow deer and fawns which wander there in flocks.[220]

(13) What Sicily produces (whether from the soil or by the genius of man) we may judge as approaching the best. The fruits of the earth are excelled by the saffron of Centuripe.

Comedy was first invented here, and here the badinage of mimicry remained on the stage.[221] The house of Archimedes is here. He, familiar with the science of the stars, was an engineer and a maker of siege engines. Here was Lais, the woman who preferred to choose her country rather than to confess.[222]

(14) The huge caves bear witness to the race of the Cyclops; the settlements of the Laestrygones are named thus to this day. Of this country was Ceres, the teacher of cultivation and fruit-nurturing. In the same place is the Field of Henna, which is always in flower, and vernal every day. (15) Near to it is the sunken hole out of which Father Dis, as

the tale goes, having swallowed the light, came forth to abduct Libera.

Between Catina and Syracuse there is rivalry concerning the story of some famous brothers. The two sides choose the brothers' names to suit themselves: if we listen to the Catinenses, the names were Anapius and Amphinomus; if we were to prefer the Syracusan version, we would believe they were Emantia and Crito. Nevertheless, the locality gives the cause of the deed to the Catinenses. When the fires of Aetna burst out, the two young men lifted up their parents and carried them through the flames, unhurt by the conflagration. Their memory was given to posterity, as the place where their tombs are was named the Field of Piety.

(16) As far as Arethusa and Alpheus are concerned, it is true that the spring and the river come together.[223]

The marvels of Sicily's rivers are exceedingly various. If someone who has lived unchastely drinks from Diana's river, which flows into Camerina, the liquid of the wine and the liquid of the water will not join into one substance.[224]

(17) The River Helbesus, which is in the country of the Segestans, grows hot in the middle of its stream with sudden boilings. The river Acis, although it comes down from Aetna, is colder than all.

The zones of the heavens change the River Himera; it is bitter when it flows into the north, and it is sweet when it curls towards the south.

(18) There is as much strangeness in the salt-mines as is in the waters. If you put salt from Agrigentum in the fire, it is dissolved by the burning; if water draws near, it crackles as though it is being burned.[225] Aetna produces salt of a dark red colour; that found at Pachynus is transparent.

(19) Other salt-mines, near to Agrigentum and Centuripe, do the work of quarries, for there statues are carved into the likenesses of gods and men.

In the place where the hot springs are is an island with an abundance of reeds. They are very good for producing the sounds of all *tibiae*[226]—whether you make *praecentoriae*, which are for playing before the couches of the gods, or *vascae*, which have more holes than *praecentoriae*, or maiden-pipes, which are called so because of their clear sound, or *gingrinae*, which, although they are shorter, nevertheless produce a finer sound, or *milvinae*, which issue the sharpest sound. These reeds are likewise good for making the Lydian pipes, which are also called *turariae*, or the Corinthian, or the

Aegyptian, or others, which musicians differentiate by function and name.

(20) In the district of Halesa is a spring which, when the environs are silent, is quiet and tranquil. If pipes are sounded, it rises up, exulting at the singing; it swells beyond its banks as though marveling at the sweetness of the voice.

(21) The Gelonian Lake, with its foul stench, drives away those who draw near. Also in that place are two springs. If a barren woman drinks of one of these, she is made fertile; the other, if a fertile woman drinks of it, she becomes sterile.

(22) The lake at Petra is noxious to serpents and healthful to men.

Oil floats on the surface of the Agrigentine Lake. Because of their constant wallowing therein, the fat sticks to the foliage of the reeds. From the reeds' hair-like fibres is gathered a medicinal ointment for use against the diseases of herdsmen.

(23) Not far from there is Vulcan's Hill. Men who are sacrificing to the god go there and strew vine wood upon the altar. Fire is not placed near the heap. If the god is present when they carry in the carved meat, and the sacrifice is approved, the twigs, although green, catch fire. The kindling is done by the deity himself, without any burning breath. **(24)** When they are dining sumptuously, the flame frolics; it wanders on sinuous paths, and he whom it touches is not scorched. It is nothing less than an image, a message that the rite has been correctly and completely performed.

In the same Agrigentine field, muddy springs violently well up.[227] The veins of the springs provide water to the streams; thus, in this part of Sicily, the soil is never deficient. The land vomits out land with eternal rejections.

(25) From Sicily came the first agate stone, found on the banks of the river Achates. Agate is of no small value if it is found there, for the intersecting veins inscribe natural shapes upon it. When it is the best, the images of many things are displayed. The ring of King Pyrrhus (who waged war against the Romans), which was not of obscure fame, came from there. Its gem was an agate, in which the nine Muses, with their distinguishing marks, and Apollo, holding his cithara, could be seen. The figures were not stamped there, but were made by nature. **(26)** Now agate is found in other places. Crete yields what they call coral agate, which is similar to coral, but is smeared all over with specks that sparkle like gold, and it resists the attacks of scorpions. India gives agates which are good for the eyes to look at. They have in them now the shapes of groves, now of animals. If these stones are taken into the mouth, they allay thirst. **(27)** There are also agates which, after they have been burned, are redolent of myrrh. Blood agates are red with blood-like spots. But the agates which are most sought after, such as the Cyprian ones, have a clearness resembling that of glass; those which have a waxy appearance are abundant and are commonly ignored.

The circuit of this entire island is completed in 3000 stadia.

CHAPTER VI

(1) In the Sicilian straits are Hephaestus' Isles,[228] which are twenty-five miles distant from Italy. The Italians call them Vulcan's Isles, for their earth burns by its very nature. The fires are either borrowed from Aetna, or supplied through some hidden trade. This place was consecrated as the seat of the God of Fire.

The islands are seven in number. (2) Lipara is named after King Liparus, who ruled there before Aeolus. They call another of the islands Hiera. It is especially sacred to Vulcan, and it has an exceedingly high hill which blazes most at night.

(3) The third is Strongyle, the home of Aeolus. It faces towards the sunrise; it is the least angular island, and its flames appear more liquid than those of the rest. Chiefly from the smoke, the inhabitants know three days beforehand which winds will blow; for this reason, Aeolus was believed king of the winds. The others, Didyme, Eriphusa, Phoenicusa and Euonymon are so similar, I have to all intents and purposes described them already.

CHAPTER VII

(1) The third gulf of Europe commences at the Ceraunian mountains, and ends at the Hellespont. On this coast, in the country of the Molossians, where the temple of Dodonaean Jupiter is, is Mount Tomaros. It is famous, as Theopompus[229] asserts, for the hundred springs around its roots.

(2) In Epirus there is a sacred spring which is cold beyond all other waters, and which is observably unique. For if a burning torch is immersed in it, the torch is extinguished, but if you remove the torch to a distance, it rekindles of its own accord.

(3) Mount Tomaros at Dodona is lofty. Delphi is celebrated for the river Cephisos, for the spring Castalia, and for Mount Parnassus. Acarnania is famous for Mount Aracynthus. The mountain Pindus divides this country from Aetolia, and gives birth to the river Achelous, gifted of old with renown as being among the chief rivers of Greece. This is not unworthy praise, since *galactitis*[230] is found among the pebbles which glitter on its banks. *Galactitis* is a little black stone; if it is rubbed, it exudes a white juice tasting of milk. (4) If it is worn by women who are breast-feeding, their breasts become more fruitful. If it is bound to children, it causes them to swallow more saliva, and if taken into the mouth, it melts. When, however, it is spat out, it kills the gift of memory. Besides by the Nile, this stone is given only by Achelous, and not by any other.

(5) Near to the town Patrae is a place called Scioessa, which nine hills overshadow with darkness. It is renowned for no other reason than it is almost inaccessible to the rays of the sun.

(6) In Laconia is the vent called Taenaron. Taenaron is also the name of a promontory facing Africa. Here the shrine of Arion of Methymna is situated. Arion, as his brazen image is witness, was carried hither by a dolphin. The image shows the likeness of his plight and of his true exploit.[231] In addition, the time is designated on the statue. It is the 29th Olympiad, in which the same Arion is written as victor at the Sicilian contest. So the deed itself is proven. (7) There is also a town of renowned antiquity called Taenaron. There are several other cities in Laconia. Among them is Leuctra, which is today not unheard of, owing to the disgraceful end the Lacedaemonians made there in times gone by.[232] (8) There is Amyclae, ruined through its own silence;[233] Sparta, notable for the temple of Castor and Pollux, and also for the monuments of that illustrious man Othryades; Therapne, whence first came the cult of Diana; Pitane, which Arcesilaus the Stoic (who was born there) brought

into the light by the merit of his own wisdom;[234] Anthia and Cardamyle.

(9) Where Thyrae is now said to have been is the place where, in the 17th year of Romulus' reign, a memorable war was fought between the Lacedaemonians and the Argives.[235] Mount Taygetus and the river Eurotas are so well known they do not require a written description.

(10) Inachus, a river in Achaea, bisects the Argive regions. King Inachus named it after himself. He was the founder of the Argive nobility. Epidaurus's distinction is the shrine of Aesculapius; those who lie in it obtain remedies for their ills through advice given in dreams.

(11) In Arcadia is a town called Pallanteum. It is enough to remember that it gave the name to our own Palatine through Evander the Arcadian.

In Arcadia also are the mountains Cyllene and Lycaeus. Then there is Maenalus, illuminated by the gods who were nursed there. Mount Erymanthus is not obscure. Among the rivers is Erymanthus, which is cast down from Mount Erymanthus, and Ladon, the former famous because of a fight of Hercules, and the latter because of Pan.[236]

(12) Varro holds that there is a spring in Arcadia whose draught is death. There is something worth relating about the birds in this same place. Although in other places, blackbirds are dusky, around Cyllene they are a very bright white.

(13) We should not scorn a rock which Arcadia yields. Its name is asbestos, and it is the colour of iron. If it is set on fire, it cannot be quenched.

(14) The Isthmus sprouts into the bay of Megara. The Isthmus is famous for the four-yearly games and the temple of Neptune. These games, they say, were instituted in remembrance of the five coasts of the Peloponnese, washed against by five seas: the Ionian in the north, the Sicilian in the west, the Aegean in the south-east, the Myrtoan in the north-east, and the Cretan in the south. The games were stopped by the tyrant Cypselus, but were restored to their former solemnity by the Corinthians in the 49th Olympiad.

(15) For the rest, the name provides the evidence that the Peloponnesus was ruled by Pelops. It is fashioned like the leaf of a plane-tree, with recesses and promontories. It makes a point of separation between the Ionian and Aegean seas, called the Isthmus because of its narrowness; the thin walk between either shore is not more than four miles.

(**16**) Here begins Hellas, which people rightly consider the true Greece. What is now called Attica was previously known as Acte. Athens is situated here. The Rocks of Sciron are close to this city. They extend for six miles, and were thus named in honour of Theseus the Avenger and the notable punishment.[237] (**17**) Ino cast herself and her son Palaemon headlong from these cliffs into the depths, and increased the gods of the sea.

(**18**) We will not pass over the mountains of Attica. There are Icarius, Brilessus, Lycabettus and Aegilaus, but first place is by right given, and deservedly, to Hymettus. This is because it is especially abundant in flowers, and the excellent taste of its honey conquers that of all the honeys from its own and other lands.

(**19**) The spring Callirhoe is said to be miraculous, yet the waters of another spring, Crunesos, are numbered among the things of no account. The place of judgement for the Athenians is in the Areopagus. The plain of Marathon was made famous by report of a most bloody battle fought there.

(**20**) Many islands lie opposite to the Attic mainland. Salamis, Sunium, Ceos and Cos are almost suburbs of the city.[238] Cos, as Varro testifies, was the first to make fine garments for women by the science of spinning.

(**21**) Boeotia is celebrated for the city of Thebes. Amphion founded Thebes, not by commanding the stones with his lyre (for it is not likely that the deed should be done thus), but by coaxing the wild inhabitants of the rocks (who had uncouth customs) with sweet speech, towards the discipline of civil allegiance. (**22**) This city was glorified by the birth of gods within its walls, as is told by those who celebrate Hercules and Liber in sacred songs. In Thebes is the grove Helicon, the forest Cithaeron, the river Ismenus, and the springs Arethusa, Oedipodia, Psamanthe and Dirce. But before the other springs are Aganippe and Hippucrene. (**23**) Cadmus, the first inventor of letters, discovered them when he was exploring on horseback, while he was searching out the regions he was taking possession of. The liberty of the poets was thus kindled: in their writings it is set down that one of these springs was opened by the hoof of the winged horse, and that the other, when drunk, gave literary inspiration.

(**24**) The island of Euboea makes the haven of Aulis by casting out its coast. This haven is recounted over the ages as the memorial to the Greek confederacy.

(**25**) The Boeotians used to be known as the Leleges. The river Cephisos flows through their territory and pours itself into the sea.

(**26**) In this land is the Opuntian Bay, the town Larissa, and Delphi. There is also Ramne, in which is the shrine of Amphiaraus and the image of Diana made by Phidias.

(**27**) Varro asserts that there are two rivers in Boeotia, which, although they are separated by nature, do not differ in wonderfulness. If a herd of sheep drinks from one of them, their fleeces become coloured. If a herd drinks from the other, any dark fleeces become white. (**28**) He says in addition that there is an unwholesome well there, whose liquid is death.

Whereas the partridges everywhere are certainly free, as are all birds, in Boeotia they are not. They cannot fly where they will, but have boundaries in the very air which they do not dare to cross. They never fly forth from their borders, and thus do not traverse Attic soil. (**29**) This is peculiarly Boeotian. What is common to all partridges, we will now pursue. Partridges make nests with clever defences. They clothe the exits of the nests with thorny bushes, so the animals which harass them are warded off by the harsh prongs. (**30**) They cover the eggs with dust, and return to them secretly, lest their frequent comings and goings betray where they are. The females repeatedly move the eggs about to cheat the males, who often crush them with their impatient fluttering. The males fight for mates, and it is believed that the losers have to let the victors treat them like females. The females are so agitated by sexual lust, that if a breeze blows from the males, they are made pregnant by the smell. (**31**) If a man draws near where they nest, the mothers come out voluntarily and offer themselves to whoever is approaching. They assume a weakness of foot or wing (seeming as though they might by and by be caught) and counterfeit a limping walk. This fraud incites their enemies, and baffles them, until, enticed for a long while, they are diverted from the nests. (**32**) Nor are the chicks more torpid in the art of defensive action. When they begin to perceive that they themselves are seen, they cast themselves on their backs, and lift little clods of earth with their feet. They are so cleverly concealed by these that they escape notice even when seized.

CHAPTER VIII

(**1**) Thessaly is also known as Haemonia; Homer calls it Pelasgian Argos. Hellen, the king for whom the Hellenes were named, was born here.

Pieria extends from the back of this country to Macedonia. Pieria, after it was conquered, came under the yoke of the Macedonians. There are many towns and rivers there.

(**2**) The notable towns are Phthia, Thessalian Larissa, and Thebes. Among the rivers, Peneus is notable. It runs past Ossa and Olympus, and makes Thessalian Tempe, a wooded vale with gently rising hills on either hand. Flowing between Magnesia and Macedonia, wide and wavy, it falls into the Thermaean gulf.

(**3**) The Pharsalian plains belong to Thessaly. The storms of civil war thundered in this place.[239]

We will leave the famous mountains to others—let those who seek the origin of the Lapiths pursue Pindus and Othrys, and let those to whom it is a delight to devote attention to the dwellings of the centaurs pursue Ossa.[240] (**4**) Pelium has been given such celebrity by the wedding feast of Thetis and Peleus, that it would be more amazing in me to keep silent on the subject than to discuss it.

(**5**) The things that are to be seen at Olympus show that Homer did not celebrate it rashly. First, it rises so high, with a pre-eminent peak, that the inhabitants call the top of it heaven. (**6**) On the summit is an altar dedicated to Jupiter. If burned offerings of entrails are brought to it, they are neither blown off by windy breath nor washed away by rain, but as the year rolls on, whatever is left there is discovered unchanged; what is consecrated to the god triumphs over time and the corruption of the air. Letters written in the ashes remain until the next year's ceremony.

(**7**) In the country of Magnesia is the town Mothona. When Philip, father of Alexander the Great of Macedonia, blockaded it, he was wounded in the eye by an arrow.[241] The arrow was fired by a townsman named Aster; the arrow was inscribed with his own name, the place of the wound, and the name of whom he attacked. That these people are skilled in the art of archery we can well believe, as Philoctetes came from here[242]—Meliboea is reckoned in the foot of this country. If I went no further on this subject, I would still have the help of the poets. The fountain Libethrius itself is also in Magnesia.

CHAPTER IX

(1) The people who were once known as the Edonii, the land which was once known as Mygdonia, and the Pierian and Emathian territories, are now all called by the uniform name of Macedonia. The divisions which, formerly, were made individually, were united and made into one body under this name. (2) Macedonia is therefore bounded by the Thracian marches. In the south, the Epirotes hold the country of Thessaly, and in the western region are the Dardanians and Illyrians. In the north, Macedonia is beaten by the cold north winds cast down from the mountainous borders. Here Pelagonia and Paeonia protect the country from the Triballi.

(3) The river Strymon, which runs down from the ridge of Haemus, makes the boundary between Macedonia and Thrace. In order not to speak either of Rhodope (a Mygdonian mountain), or of Athos (which was cut off from the mainland by a distance of a mile and a half, so the Persian fleet could sail through)[243], or of the veins of gold and silver (many of these, of the best quality, are dug up in the fields of Macedonia), I will treat the country of Orestis. (4) People here are called the "Orestae" because of the following tale. After Orestes had fled from Mycenae because of his matricide,[244] he was determined to go far away. So he commanded that his son, who had been born in Emathia from Hermiona, with whom he had associated as a companion during all his adventures, be hidden there. (5) The boy grew up with the air of one of royal blood, bearing anew his father's name. Having seized the area which extends to the Macedonian Gulf and the Adriatic Sea, he called the land which he had conquered "Orestis".

(6) Phlegra (before the town was built it is said that the soldiery of heaven fought there with the giants) reminds us, as we thoroughly pursue such great proofs of sovereignty, that evidence of divine wars perseveres into this age. (7) If at any time here (as does bechance), the torrents become swollen with rain, and they break their banks with the increased weight of water, throwing themselves into the plain, bones are said to be even now uncovered by the inundation. These bones are in the form of human bones, but larger. Because of their immense size, it is said that they are from the bodies of that monstrous army. This argument is strengthened by the evidence of huge rocks, with which it is believed heaven was assaulted.

(8) Let us proceed to the remainder of Macedonia, which extends to Thessaly and Athamania. The mountainous heights here are lifted higher than anywhere. There is nothing in any other land which can worthily be

compared to such prominences. The assault of the Flood,[245] which covered everything else with moist stagnation, did not reach this inaccessible soil. (**9**) That these places were above the Flood is made apparent by traces of no small authority which endure here. In the caves hidden in the cliffs, which were eroded by the violence of the water, remnants of shellfish were left behind, and of the many other things which were copiously spat out by the enraged sea. Thus, although this place is inland, it nevertheless has all the appearance of the sea-shore.

(**10**) Now I will return to the inhabitants. Emathius, who was the first to obtain leadership in Emathia (whether because the truth about his origins has perished, or because it is indeed so) is thought to have been born from the earth. (**11**) After him, the name Emathia, having started with him, endured in Macedonia. But Macedo, the maternal grandson of Deucalion, who alone with the family of his house survived the massacre,[246] changed the name and called it Macedonia after himself.

(**12**) Caranus, the leader of the Peloponnesian army, followed Macedo. In accord with an oracle, he built a city where he had seen a herd of goats rest, and called it Aegae. It was the custom for the kings to be buried here; another place was not given for the tombs of the more distinguished men among the ancient Macedonians.

(**13**) After Caranus, in the 22nd Olympiad, came Perdiccas. He was the first to be named the king of Macedonia. After him was Alexander, son of Amyntas, who was reckoned rich, not without cause. He had so many successes that first of all men he sent gold statues as gifts to Apollo at Delphi and to Jupiter in Elis. (**14**) He was most indulgently given over to the pleasures of music, so much so that he held by his side with generous gifts many who were skillful instrumentalists. He did this while he lived for the sake of his delight. Pindar the lyric poet was among them.

(**15**) Thence followed the reign of Archelaus, who was skilled in war. He was also a pioneer of naval battles. This Archelaus was so great a lover of learning that he entrusted the highest of his confidences to Euripides the tragedian. At his death, Archelaus was not content to bear the cost of the funeral, but shore his hair and showed everyone on his face the sorrow he had conceived in his heart. (**16**) He won the prizes for the four-horse chariot at the Pythian and the Olympic games. He bore that glory rather with the soul of a Greek than with a royal one.

(**17**) After Archelaus, Macedonia was disturbed by dissension, but came to rest during the reign of Amyntas, who had three sons. Alexander succeeded his father, but he was removed, and the wealth of that very ample power which had to be overtaken was first given to Perdiccas. Dying, he left the kingdom to his brother Philip who (as I have said above) lost his right eye at Mothona. This debility was preceded by an omen. For when Philip got married, it is reported that the *tibia*-players brought from abroad sang of the Cyclops as though in sport.

(**18**) This Philip begot Alexander the Great, however much Olympias, his mother, desiring to gain a nobler father for him, claimed that she had been fertilised by a serpent. Nevertheless, Alexander himself behaved in such a way that he was believed to have been born from a god. (**19**) He travelled over every part of the world, making use of his teachers Aristotle and Callisthenes. He conquered Asia, Armenia, Hiberia, Albania, Cappadocia, Syria, and Egypt. He crossed Mount Taurus and the Caucasus; he subdued the Bactrians. He ruled the Medes and the Persians; he captured India and passed beyond everything which Liber and Hercules had approached. (**20**) In appearance he was dignified beyond all men, with a long neck, cheerful, shining eyes, and cheeks pleasantly flushed. The rest of his body was not without a certain graceful majesty.

This conqueror of all men was nevertheless himself conquered by wine and by temper. In this way, he was carried off in Babylon by the disease of drunkenness, a more humble fate than he had lived.

(**21**) We find that those who came after him were born more for the profit of Roman glory than to the inheritance of so great a name.

(**22**) Macedonia produces a stone which is called *paeanitis*. It is commonly said that this stone brings aid to child-bearing women, both in conceiving and giving birth.

CHAPTER X

(**1**) Now let us proceed to Thrace, setting sail for the most powerful nations of Europe. Those who sedulously wish to learn of the barbarian Thracians will easily discover that there is disregard of life among them. This is the result of their system of beliefs. (**2**) Every one of them agrees to a voluntary death, while not a few of them think that their souls return. Others think that their souls are not destroyed by death but become more blessed. Most of them deem childbirths to be sorrowful. Indeed, those who are newly parents receive the birth with weeping. (**3**) On the contrary, funerals are happy occasions, to such a degree that the deceased are escorted to the pyre with gladness.

The men boast about the number of wives they have, and judge many marriages to be an honour. The women hold fast to their modesty. They throw themselves on the funeral pyres of their dead husbands, and, which is held to be the greatest mark of chastity, walk headlong into the flames. (**4**) Women of marriageable age do not have their husbands chosen by their parents. Those who are most beautiful prefer to be auctioned off, and with the liberty of appraisal permitted them, do not marry the man of the highest morals, but the man with the most gifts. Those women who are hindered in this by a repulsive appearance obtain dowries, which they use to get a husband.

(**5**) When they feast, both the men and the women roam about the hearths, casting the seeds of their herbs above the flames. The fumes overpower them; their senses are impaired, and in an imitation of drunkenness, they have good sport.

(**6**) So much for the customs. Examination of the places and peoples will follow. The Denseletae live near the Strymon, on its right side. Here also, up to the river Mestus, are many tribes of the Bessi. The Mestus runs around the roots of Mount Pangaeus.

(**7**) The soil of the Odrysians pours forth the river Hebrus, which runs among the Priantae, the Dolongi, the Thyni, the Corpili, and many other barbarians. It also touches the territory of the Ciconae. Next comes Haemus, six miles high. The Moesians, Getae, Sarmatians, Scythians and many other peoples inhabit its hinder part.

(**8**) The Sithonians occupy the Pontic shore; the Sithonians are judged among the foremost peoples as Orpheus the poet was born there. They report that he practised secrets (either religious rites or songs) on the promontory Sperchivum. Nearby is the Bistonian lake. (9) Not far from this lake is the Maronian country, in which is the town Tirida. In Tirida were the stables of Diomedes' horses,[247] but they have yielded to time, and only traces of the tower endure. (10) Abdera, which Diomedes' sister both founded and named after herself, is not far from there. Later it was the home of Democritus the natural philosopher; therefore (to say truth) it is the more renowned. Abdera became decayed with age, and was restored to even greater beauty in the 31st Olympiad by the Clazomenians from Asia, who claimed what had gone before, and was obliterated, for their own name.

(11) The advent of Xerxes made Doriscos famous, because the sum of his soldiers were mustered there.

Aenus has the tumulus of Polydorus, in the region held by the Aroteres Scythians. A certain city called Gerania (the barbarians call it Cathizon) there is celebrated. They say that the Pygmies were expelled from it by cranes.

(12) It is indeed obvious that in winter cranes congregate in great numbers in this northern region. It will not grieve me to recall how they direct their journeys. They go forward like a military company under a standard. Lest the strength of the breeze blow them off course, they consume sand, and ballast themselves with small stones to a moderate weight. (13) Then they hasten aloft, so they can mark the lands they are making for, as if from a tall watchtower. A bird confident of the course goes in front of the flock. She castigates idleness of flight with her voice, which gathers the troop together. When she has grown hoarse, another takes her place. (14) Preparing to cross Pontus, they aim for the narrowest passage. This (it is easy to discern by looking) is between Taurica and Paphlagonia—that is, between Carambis and Criumetopon. When they know themselves to have passed the middle of the channel, their feet drop the bundles of small stones. (15) Sailors report that from this circumstance they are often rained upon with stony showers. The cranes do not bring up the sand again before they are settled as securely as possible.

The birds are of one mind in caring for those who become weary; indeed, if some falter, they all flock together and continuously bear up the exhausted ones until they recover their strength by resting. They are not less zealous on land. (16) They divide the night watches so that at any one time ten of them are wakeful. The watchers clasp little weights in their claws, which if by chance are let fall, convict them of slackness. When they perceive something to take precautions against, they make a clamour. Their colour reveals their age: they grow dark with old age.

(**17**) Let us go to the promontory the Golden Horn, famous for the town Byzantium, formerly called Lygos. The town is 711 miles away from Dyrrhachium, for the Adriatic and Propontic Seas extend such a distance.

(**18**) In the Ceniensian region, not far from the colony Flaviopolis, is the town Bizye, formerly the territory of king Tereus. It is hateful to swallows, and in turn inaccessible to them. Swallows also refuse to go to Thebes, because its walls have very often been captured. (**19**) Among other things, swallows have a certain foreknowledge which is thus proved: they do not make for roofs about to fall and scorn houses about to perish. They are certainly not attacked by fearful birds and are not ever prey. Thus, they are sacred. They do not take up food standing, but capture and swallow it in the air.

(**20**) There is another isthmus in Thrace, which, by the art of the sea, has a similar narrow passage, and is of equal width.

Pactye marks the Propontic shore, and Cardia the bay of Melas. This last was called "Cardia" because it is built in a heart-shape.

(**21**) Here is, moreover, the great Hellespont, which is drawn together to a distance of seven stadia, and divides Europe from the Asiatic regions.

Here also are two cities: Abydos on the Asian shore, Sestos on the European.

(**22**) Next, there are two opposing promontories: Mastusia of the Chersonese, where the third gulf of Europe finishes, and Sigeum of Asia, where the tumulus Cynossema is, which is called the tomb of Hecuba. There is also the tower of Protesilaus, used as a sanctuary.

(**23**) On the northern marches of Thrace the Ister[248] is spread. In the east is Pontus and Propontis and in the south, the Aegean Sea.

CHAPTER XI

(1) There is a rock (it more truly merits to be called a rock than an island) between Tenedus[249] and Chios, whence the Aegean gulf spreads out. It is on the right as people sail to Antandrus. Because, from a distance, it looks similar in shape to a goat, the Greeks call it "Aega". The Aegean gulf takes its name from this rock. (2) A rock in the shape of a ship projects from Phalarium, a promontory of Corcyra, into which, they believe, Ulysses' ship was transformed.

Cythera, which is five miles away from Malea, went by the name of Porphyris in former times.

(3) It is easier to speak of the land of Crete than to conclude in which sea it lies. For the Greeks have mixed up the names of the surrounding waters. Some names have been put in place over the top of others, so almost everything has been obscured. Nevertheless, I will arrange my work with a view to clarity as much as I can, lest uncertainties arise.

(4) East and west, Crete extends in a very long tract. Greece lies on one side, and Cyrene on the other. On the northern side, Crete is lashed by its own part of the seething Aegean— that is to say, by the Cretan Sea. On the southern side, it is bathed by Libyan and Aegyptian waves. It is not crowded with one hundred cities, as reported by those who prodigally give tongue, but it has great and ambitious towns, the chief of which are Gortyna, Cydonea, Knossos, Therapnae and Cylissos.

(5) Dosiades[250] reports that Crete was named after a young maiden called Creta, who was daughter to the Hesperides. Anaximander[251] is of the opinion that it was named after a Cretan king of the Curetes, and Crates[252] holds the view that it was first called Aeria, and soon after Curetus. Not a few also record that it was named Macaronnesus because of the mildness of the climate. Crete was the first to gain power through oars and arrows, and was the first to write down its laws. Crete first taught (the inventor was Pyrrhichos) cavalry squadrons to interweave with mischievous whirlings.[253] From this discipline came military practice.

(6) The study of music has its origins in Crete, when the Idaean Dactyls changed little measures into the order of verse. They were led to this by the rattling and clanging of bronze.[254]

(7) Because of the mountain chains Dictynnaeus and Cadistus, Crete appears white. These mountains glisten so that people sailing far off suppose them to be clouds.

Ida stands before the others: it sees the sun before the sunrise. Varro, in his work about the shores, affirms that in his time, the tomb of Jupiter was to be visited there.

(8) The Cretans are very devout in their worship of Diana. In their native language they name her Britomartis, which in our language sounds like "sweet maiden".[255] No-one is allowed to enter the shrine of this deity unless bare-footed. The shrine displays the work of Daedalus.

(9) The river Lenaeus flows past Gortyna, where, the Gortynians say, Europa was carried away on the back of a bull. The Gortynians also honour Europa's brother Adymnus. They say that he is seen thereabouts, and runs to meet people, but that when the day draws towards evening, he offers himself to view with a more majestic appearance.

(10) The Knossians number the goddess Minerva among their citizens, and rashly contend with the Atticans that grain was first sown among them.

(11) The Ager Creticus has many wild goats, but no deer. It has never nourished wolves, foxes or other noxious quadrupeds.

(12) There are no serpents in Crete. There is an abundance of vines there, and the soil is wondrously kind. Produce from trees is copious. In one part of the island, cypress trees which have been cut down send forth new growth.

There is a Cretan herb called *alimos*, which, if chewed, prevents hunger for a day.

(13) There is also a kind of spider called *phalangium*. If you research its strength, you will find that it has no vigour of body, but if you research what power it has, you will discover that it can kill a man with its poison.

(14) The Idaean finger stone is also said to be native to this island. It is the colour of iron, and similar in shape to a human thumb.

Crete has no night-owls. If one is imported, it perishes.

(15) Carystos has hot springs, called the Ellopiae. It has birds called "Carystiae", which fly through flames with impunity. It also has linen which remains strong in fire.

This same place was called Chalcis by men of old, as the author Callidemus details, because bronze was first discovered there.

(**16**) The religious rites make it clear that the Titans ruled there a very long time ago, for the Carystians make divine observances in honour of Briareus, as the Chalcidians do for Aegaeon. The Titans' kingdom comprised almost all of Euboea.[256]

(**17**) They say that the Cyclades are so called because they are situated in a circle around Delos (although some jut out further than others), and the Greek word for circle is "cyclos". Chios, because it has the tomb of Homer, surpasses the others.

(**18**) It is suitable to observe here that after the first flood, noted to have been in the time of Ogyges, when continual night overshadowed the days for nine months together, Delos, first of all lands, was illuminated by the sun's beams. Because Delos was the first to be restored to light, the name "Delos" was appointed.[257] (**19**) The time between Ogyges and Deucalion is given as 600 years.

Delos is also known as Ortygia. The most famous of the Cyclades, it is also variously named Asteria (from the cult of Apollo), Lagia or Cynetho (because of the hunting to be had there), and Pyrpile, since both fire-instruments and fire itself were discovered there.

(**20**) On this island, quails were first seen. The Greeks call them "ortygae". These birds are thought to be appointed to the guardianship of Latona. They are not seen in all seasons: they arrive when summer is drawing to a close. When they cross the sea, they put off making an effort through fear of a longer journey; they nourish their strength through slowness of movement. (**21**) When they can clearly see the land, they gather in large flocks and move more vigorously. Their haste often brings destruction upon sailors. At night, the birds rend ships' sails, and weigh down the folds of sailcloth, so the ships become unbalanced. Quails never fly on the south wind, for they fear the strength of this swollen breeze. They commonly commit themselves to the northern breezes, as they are stronger and drier. Thus they are better able to carry the quails' bodies, which are somewhat fat, and, because of this, slow. (**22**) The bird who leads the flock is called *ortygometra*. When he approaches the land, he is seized by a watching hawk; as a result, the work becomes universal. Having stirred up a leader of another kind, the quails escape the first danger. (**23**) Their favourite food is the seeds of poisonous plants. For this reason, the tables of wise men spurn them. This is the only animal except man to suffer from the falling sickness.

(24) So small a channel divides Euboea from the Boeotian continent that it is doubtful whether it ought to be numbered among the islands. For they say that this island is joined to the mainland by a bridge, and that through the ingenuity of this very short construction, it can be visited on foot.

Euboea extends to the north by way of the promontory Cenaeum, and by way of two others, it extends to the south. Of these, Geraestos watches Attica, and Caphereus juts out towards the Hellespont. (25) After the fall of Troy, either the wrath of Minerva or (as more certain memory avouches) the star of Arcturus caused grave loss to the Argive fleet here.

(26) Paros is famous for marble, which occurs most frequently in the town Abdelum.[258] Before it was called Paros it was known as Minoia, for it was conquered by Minos, and as long as it remained under Cretan law they called it Minoia. (27) Besides marble, Paros gives the stone sard, which is in fact superior to marble, but is regarded as being the most worthless among gems.

(28) Naxos is separated from Delos by 18 miles. The town Strongyle is situated there. Naxos was first called Dionysias, either because it played hostess to Father Liber, or because in the fertility of its vines it conquered all other places.

(29) There are many others of the Cyclades besides these, but the aforementioned are those which ought to especially be remembered.

(30) Icaros, which gives the Icarian Sea its name, is one of the Sporades. This isle, between Samos and Myconos, is rendered inhospitable by jutting rocks, and has no harbours. It is infamous for the inhumanity of its shores. Therefore, Varro wishes to believe that Icarus of Crete perished there by shipwreck, and that the name was assigned to the place because of his death.

(31) In Samos, there has been no citizen more famous than Pythagoras. Offended by the arrogance of the island's tyrannical regime, he abandoned his house and his country. He arrived in Italy in the time of Brutus the consul, who expelled the kings from the city.

(32) Melos, which Callimachus called Mellimada, is the roundest of all the islands. It is hard by Aeolia.

Carpathus is the reason we call thus the Carpathian gulf.

The sky is never so cloudy that Rhodes is not in the sun.

The Lemnians worship Vulcan. Thus, the Lemnian metropolis is called Hephaestia. **(33)** On Lemnos is also the town Myrina, into the forum of which the Macedonian Mount Athos throws a shadow. This is not vainly observed among marvels, since Athos is separated from Lemnos by 86 miles. Truly, Athos is elevated to such a degree that it is judged higher than the place where the rains come from. This belief draws credit from the following: the ashes are never washed way from the altars which stand on the peak, nor are the ash-heaps in any wise destroyed, but remain in the heaps in which they were left.

(34) The town Acroton was on this summit. The lives of the inhabitants were prolonged by half as much again as those of people living in other lands. For that reason, these men were called "Macrobians" in Greek, which is "long-lived" in our language.

CHAPTER XII

(**1**) The fourth gulf of Europe begins at the Hellespont, and ends at the mouth of Maeotis.[259] The entire expanse of this gulf, which divides Europe and Asia, is drawn together into a strait seven stadia wide. (**2**) This strait is the Hellespont, which Xerxes crossed after making a bridge of ships.[260] From here, a narrow channel extends to the Asian city Priapus. Alexander the Great, on his mission to become master of the world, crossed to this city and conquered it.

Thence, the gulf spreads out into open sea. Towards the end of the Propontis, it again draws together. Soon it narrows to half a mile, making the Thracian Bosphorus, over which Darius transported his armies.

(**3**) This area harbours very many dolphins. These creatures provide multifarious causes for wonderment. First of all, the seas have nothing more speedy; many of them leap up and fly over the sails of ships.

Wherever they go, they go in couples. (**4**) They beget young; the unborn offspring mature in nine months. The babies are born in summertime, and the mothers nourish them with their teats. When the babies are very young, the mothers take them into their mouths. The mothers follow their babies for some time while they are still weak.

Dolphins live for thirty years, as has been investigated in an experiment, wherein some specimens' tails were chopped off.

Dolphins do not have their faces in the same place as other marine creatures do—they are almost in their stomachs. Unlike other aquatic animals, they can move their tongues. (**5**) They have sharp dorsal fins, which bristle up when they become angry, and are concealed, as in a sheath, when their minds are in repose. They say that dolphins do not breathe underwater, and they do not take in the breath of life except in the air above. For a voice, they have a moan similar to that of a human being. They are appropriately named "Snubnose". This name pleases them, and they follow those who call them by it.

(**6**) Dolphins hear men's voices more easily when in the breezes of the north wind; contrariwise, their hearing becomes blocked up when the wind is blowing from the south. They are delighted by music: they rejoice in the songs of the *tibia*. Wherever there is harmony, they arrive in throngs.

(**7**) In Campania, during the reign of the divine Augustus, a boy began to entice a dolphin with broken bread. The habit did so much prevail, that the dolphin trusted the boy enough to take food from his hand. Soon, when his boyish daring grew, the dolphin carried the boy on his back in the Lucrine Lake; after this the boy rode him from the Baian shore all the way to Puteoli. (**8**) This kept on happening for so long a time —for many years— that even while it was still occurring, it ceased to be miraculous. But when the boy died, the dolphin perished before the eyes of all, because of the grief of the loss. I would be disinclined to report this, if it were not included in the writings of Maecenas and of Fabianus and of many others besides. (**9**) Soon after, at Hippo Diarrhytus, on the African coast, a dolphin was fed by the people of Hippo, and offered himself to be handled; he was also wont to carry those who were set upon his back. This was not only done by the people of Hippo, for even the proconsul of Africa, Flavianus himself, touched this dolphin, and anointed him with oil. The dolphin was sent to sleep for some time by the oil's strange odour, and was thrown about as though dead; for many months after he defected from his usual observance. (**10**) At Iasus, a city of Babylon, a dolphin fell in love with a boy, and followed him over-eagerly when he left their accustomed playtime. He shot himself into the sand, and exhausted himself. Alexander the Great interpreted the dolphin's love to be sacred, and placed the boy in charge of the priesthood of Neptune.

(**11**) Hard by the same city, as the author Hegesidemus[261] affirms, another boy by the name of Hermias was similarly riding a dolphin in the sea when he was drowned by the turbulence of the waves. The dolphin carried him back to land, and as though confessing his guilt, showed his repentance by himself dying—he did not go back out to sea. (**12**) There are other examples, even if we pass over that of Arion, of whose departure the honesty of the annals has given proof.[262]

To these things we may add, that if ever new dolphin babies run riot, a more mature preceptor is given to them by the elder dolphins. The young ones learn from this teacher to baffle the attacks of raiding marine animals, although in those parts, except for seals, such animals are rare.

(**13**) There are many tuna in Pontus. They spawn the most there, for nowhere else do they grow to full size more quickly. This certainly is due to the sweet waters. The tuna come in spring time; they enter via the right-hand shore and leave by the left. It is believed this happens because the tuna see more acutely with their right eyes than with their left ones.

CHAPTER XIII

(1) The Ister rises from the German ranges, issuing from a mountain which faces the Rauraci of Gaul. It takes sixty rivers into itself, of which almost all are navigable. It has seven mouths, which flow into Pontus. Of these, the first is Peuce, the second Naracustoma, the third Calonstoma, and the fourth Pseudostoma. The fourth, Borionstoma, and the following mouth, Spilonstoma,[263] run more lazily than the preceding. As for the seventh, it is truly sluggish, and has a marshy appearance; it does not have a name because it does not resemble a river. The first four mouths are so great that for the distance of forty miles, their waters do not mix with the sea. They keep their sweet draught with an uncorrupted taste.

(2) Throughout the whole of Pontus are a great number of beavers, which they call by another name, *castores*. The beaver is similar to an otter, and is a very powerful animal by reason of its bite. When it attacks a man, it does not relax the gnash of its teeth until it senses the snap of breaking bones. Their testicles are sought after for their healing properties. Thus, when the beaver understands himself to be hemmed in, lest his capture be useful to someone, he devours his own "twins".[264]

(3) Pontus also yields gems of different kinds, which we call "Pontic". Some have golden stars in them, other blood-red stars. They are indeed considered sacred, for they are gathered more for reasons of display than for any purpose. Another kind is not stained with specks, but is overlaid with long lines of colour.

CHAPTER XIV

(1) The Hypanis rises among the Auchetae; it is the principal river of Scythia. It is clean and wholesome to drink all the way to the borders of the Callipides. Here the fountain Extampeus, infamous for its bitter waters, is located. Extampeus mixes its waters with those of the clear stream, and turns the river to its own defect, so Hypanis plunges into the sea dissimilar to itself. (2) Thus, tales about the Hypanis are at variance between different peoples. Those who are acquainted with the upper reaches of the river, praise it, while those who know the end of it have good cause to curse it.

CHAPTER XV

(1) The source of the river Borysthenes[265] is among the Neuri. In this river are fishes of excellent flavour, which have no bones except for a very tender cartilage.

(2) The Neuri, as we have heard, are transformed into wolves. They change back into their former shapes once the time to which this lot is attributed has expired. (3) Mars is the god of this people. Swords are worshipped instead of images. As their sacrificial victims they have humans. They feed their altar fires with the bones.

Adjacent to the Neuri are the Geloni. They make garments for themselves from the skins of their enemies as well as trappings for their horses.

The Agathyrsi border upon the Geloni; they paint themselves blue and dye their hair blue. This is not done indiscriminately, for the more eminent a man is, the more he is tinged with these distinguishing marks. It is an indicator of insignificance to be less coloured.

(4) Next are the Anthropophagi,[266] whose cursed food is human flesh. The gloomy solitude of the surrounding lands is what created this custom of this impious people. Because of their abominable custom, surrounding nations and fugitives avoid them in fear. For this reason, all the way to the sea they call Tabis, and throughout the length of its shore, which lies in the northeast, the land is without a human, and utterly deserted, until one comes to the land of the Serae.

(5) The Chalybes and the Dahae, who live in a part of Scythia which is in Asia, are just as cruel as the most brutal peoples.

The Albani, who inhabit the coast,[267] and wish themselves to be thought the posterity of Jason, are born with white hair. Their hair is white when it first begins to grow. Thus, the colour of their heads gives this people their name.[268] The pupils in their eyes are a bluish-grey, so they see more clearly by night than by day.

(6) Dogs which excel all other beasts are born among this people. They subdue bulls, overwhelm lions, and hinder whatever they are presented with. For these reasons, they too deserve to be spoken of in these chronicles. (7) We read that as Alexander the Great was making for India, two dogs of this kind were sent to him by the king of Albania. One of them scorned the swine and bulls offered to him, as he was offended by

such inferior and ignoble prey. He lay still for a long time, and Alexander, through ignorance, ordered him to be killed for a lazy animal. But the other, at the advice of those who had brought the present, despatched a lion sent to him. Soon, seeing an elephant, he rejoiced; first, he cunningly fatigued the beast, and then, to the great wonder of the spectators, threw him to the ground. This kind of dog grows to a very large size, and makes, with awe-inspiring barking, a noise beyond the roaring of lions.

(8) The above items were specifically about Albanian dogs; the rest concerns the features common to all dogs. All dogs alike esteem their masters, as is well-known from sundry examples. In Epirus a dog recognised his master's murderer in a crowd, and revealed him by barking. After Jason the Lycian was killed, his dog scorned food, and died from starvation. (9) When the funeral pyre of King Lysimachus was lit, his dog threw himself into the flames, and was consumed by the fire along with his master. The king of the Garamantes was brought back from exile by his two hundred dogs, who fought those who resisted them. The people of Colophon and Castabala lead their dogs to war, and in battle, build their front lines with them. (10) When Appius Iunius and Publius Sicinius were consuls, there was a dog which could not be driven away from his condemned master. The dog accompanied his master into prison; when the man was executed, the dog followed after, howling. When, from pity, the people gave him food, he carried the meat to the mouth of his dead master. Finally, when the body was thrown into the Tiber, the dog swam after it and tried to bear it up.

(11) Dogs recognise their own names, and remember their journeys.

The Indians relegate their female dogs to the forests when they are in season, so they mate with tigers. The offspring from the first conception are judged useless, owing to their excessive savagery; likewise the second. Those from the third conception are reared.

(12) Egyptian dogs lap swiftly from the Nile, as they are wary of being ambushed by crocodiles.

(13) The Essedones are numbered among the Anthropophagi in this part of Asia. They also, by way of their impious food, pollute themselves by murder. Among the Essedones it is a custom to follow the funeral processions of parents with singing. The bereaved children collect a gang of their nearest relatives, rend the very corpses with their teeth, and make a feast of the flesh, mixing it with the flesh of sheep. The parents' skulls are girded with gold, and are used as drinking-cups.

(14) The Scythotauri murder foreigners as enemies. The Nomades follow the grazing. The Georgi, situated in Europe, cultivate fields. The Asiatae, also situated in Europe, neither admire others' property, nor permit others to admire theirs. The Satarchae have condemned the use of gold and silver, and have banished avarice from their common weal forever.

(15) The customs of the Scythians who live further inland are even more savage. They inhabit caves. Their drinking-cups are not as those of the Essedones, but are made from the skulls of their enemies. They love battle, and drink the blood from the very wounds of those they kill. A man's honour is proportional to the number of murders he has committed. It is a disgrace among them to have committed none. They ratify treaties by a draught of each other's blood. This is not so much their own custom, but is usurped from that of the Medes. (16) Indeed, in the war which was waged between Alyattes the Lydian and Astyages, the king of Media, in the 49th Olympiad, the 604th year after the fall of Troy, the oaths of peace were confirmed in this manner.[269]

(17) Amphitus and Cercius, the charioteers of Castor and Pollux, from whom rose the clan of the Heniochi, established Dioscurias, the city of the Colchians.

(18) Above the Sauromatae (who are situated in Asia, who gave Mithridates sanctuary, and from whom the Medes had their origin), the Thali have a common boundary with those nations which touch the straits of the Caspian Sea in the east. These straits are miraculously reduced by rain, and increased by heat.

(19) The Araxes pours out from the Heniochi mountains, and the Phasis pours out from the Moschi mountains. The Araxes raises his head a small distance from the source of the Euphrates and is borne to the Caspian Sea.

(20) The Arimaspi, who are situated around Gesclithron,[270] are a one-eyed people. Above them and the Riphaean ridge is a country which is continually covered with snow. They call it Pterophoros, as the prolonged fall of hoar-frost there looks like feathers.[271] (21) It is a condemned part of the world. By the nature of things it is immersed in a cloud of eternal fog, and is utterly numbed by the very receptacle of the north wind. Alone of all the lands, it knows not the succession of the seasons; it receives from the heavens nothing other than perpetual winter.

(22) In Asiatic Scythia the lands are rich, but nevertheless uninhabitable.

While these lands abound in gold and gems, the gryphons hold universal sway over them. Gryphons are extremely ferocious birds, and have a rage worse than any madness. Owing to the necessity of facing the gryphons' cruelty, the approach of visitors is rare. Indeed, the gryphons mangle anyone they see, as though born to punish the rashness of greed. (**23**) The Arimaspi fight them in order to steal a kind of stone, the nature of which we will not scorn to examine. This place is the native land of the *smaragdi*[272] which Theophrastus placed third among stones. For although there are Egyptian, Chalchedonian, Median and Laconian *smaragdi*, those of principal esteem are Scythian. The eyes can see nothing more pleasing or more useful than these stones. (**24**) In the first place, they are greener than water-grass and river herbs. Secondly, they restore the tired gaze by the mildness of their colour; *smaragdi* revive eyes which the brightness of another gemstone has weakened. They do have a disadvantage: although they are difficult indeed to wound, you cannot carve them, lest their beauty be damaged by the pits of the images. (**25**) The worth of *smaragdi* is assessed in the following ways: if they are transparent; if, when they are spherical, they colour the things nearest them by the rebounding air; if, when they are concave, they reflect the faces of those looking at them; if they are not altered by shadows either in the light of oil-lamps or in the sunlight. Yet those for which a level surface has been laid facing upwards and smoothed acquire the optimum positions.[273]

(**26**) They are found when the Etesian winds are blowing, for then, when the soil blows away, they glitter. The Etesian winds move the sands greatly. Others, of less value, are to be seen in the seams of rocks or in copper mines. They call these cuprous *smaragdi*.[274] (**27**) The inferior sort of these have some description of dirt on the inside, similar to lead or hair, or even to salt. The plain ones are praised. But they are efficacious with undiluted green oil, although they are wet by nature.

(**28**) *Cyneus* is also from Scythia. The best glitters with a blue colour. Experienced persons divide these stones into males and females.[275] The brightness of the females is pure, and a fine dust, beautiful to behold, variegates the males with gold-coloured specks.

(**29**) Rock-crystal is also to be found in this place. Although the greater part of Europe, and a small part of Asia furnishes rock-crystal, that which Scythia gives is the most precious. Rock-crystal is much used for making drinking-cups, but the cups cannot suffer anything other than cold drinks.

(**30**) Rock-crystal is found in hexagonal shapes. Those selecting crystals aim for the clearest, lest some ingrained redness or cloudiness obscure the lucidity.

(**31**) It is thought that ice gathers and makes rock-crystal, but this argument is to no purpose, for if it were so, neither Alabanda in Asia, nor the island of Cyprus would produce this material, for the heat in these places is excessive.

Livia, wife of Augustus, dedicated a crystal of 150 pounds in size in the Capitoline treasure-chambers.

CHAPTER XVI

(1) If the stories which flow all the way from the Hyperboreans[276] to ourselves were rashly believed, we might consider tales of these people to be falsehoods and invalid rumours. But since the most trustworthy authors and those of sufficient credit make the same reports, nobody should fear fraud. On the subject of the Hyperboreans, I will thus mention the following.

They inhabit the land behind Pterophoros, which, I hear, lies above the North Wind. They are a most blessed people.

(2) Some think they reside in Asia rather than in Europe, and believe that they occupy the space midway between the setting of the Antipodean sun and the rising of our sun. Logic refutes this theory, as there is such a vast sea surging between the two worlds. The Hyperboreans, therefore, are to be placed in Europe.

(3) The hinges of the world[277] are said to be near their land, as well as the uttermost extent of the stars. It is believed that there is six-month-long light there, with the sun disappearing for one day only. However, some think that the sun does not rise daily there, as it does for us, but rises only at the spring equinox, to set again at the autumnal equinox, creating six months of endless day, and another six of continual night.

The climate is very mild; the breezes breathe wholesomely, and there are no harmful winds.

The homes of the Hyperboreans are forests or groves. The trees furnish them with nourishment from day to day.

(4) They are ignorant of discord, and are not troubled by disease. Every one of them has the common wish of living innocently.

They hasten the onset of death; by wilfully killing themselves, they prevent a slow demise. (5) When they have had enough of life, after feasting and anointing themselves, they leap headlong into the sea from a famous cliff. This kind of grave is judged to be the best.

It is also said that the Hyperboreans were accustomed to send their most esteemed virgins to take the first of their crops to Delian Apollo. (6) However, since, through the perfidy of their hosts, the virgins did not return unimpaired, the Hyperboreans soon took back the sacred dignity of the offerings, which they were wont to escort abroad, within their own borders.

CHAPTER XVII

(1) Another Asian people is situated towards the furthest north-east, where the ridges of the Riphaean Mountains end. Similar to the Hyperboreans, they are called the Arimphaei. They too take delight in the budding orchards, as they eat berries. The men and women alike are disgusted by hair, and both sexes shear their heads. They love quietude, and do not love violence. (2) They are thought to be sacred, and even the most ferocious nations account it a sin to lay hands on them. If someone fears danger from his own countrymen and flees to the Arimphaei, he is safe, just as though he were protected in a sanctuary.

(3) Above the Arimphaei, the Cimmerians and a race of Amazons extend towards the Caspian Sea, which runs into the Scythian ocean after flowing away through the back end of the Asiatic regions.

(4) A great space intercedes between the Arimphaei and the mouths of the river Oxus, which are held by the Hyrcanians. This people possesses wild forests, which are abundant in savage beasts, and teem with tigers. (5) Their remarkable speed and well-known spots[278] have rendered this kind of beast famous. They shine with a tawny colour. This tawniness in interspersed with strips of black, and on account of the contrast, the whole is most becoming. I do not know whether speed or endurance contributes more to the swiftness of their feet. No distance is so long that they will not traverse it in a short time; nothing can be so far ahead of them that they will not immediately overtake.

(6) The power of tigresses is especially shown when they are urged on by their maternal feelings, and they pursue those who steal their cubs. Although the thieves arrange to carry away the booty with infinite cunning, and organize a series of fresh horses for themselves, if the sea is not there for their succour, all their daring is in vain. (7) Tigresses are very often observed to dive from the shore in impotent madness if ever they see the plunderers of their cubs sailing back again, as though castigating their own tardiness with voluntary ruin. However, from all the young, one is scarcely ever carried off.

(8) Panthers are also considered to be in Hyrcania. On the tops of their bodies they are painted with small circles, and the ornaments of their backs may be thus decorated with eye-like circles of a yellow, dusky or white colour. It is reported that cattle are marvellously affected by the smell and sight of panthers. (9) Because of this, in order to safely lay waste the senseless herds which are lost in contemplation, the panthers

hide their heads and present the rest of their bodies to view. But the Hyrcanians, as man is ever full of devices, kill them with poison more often than with steel. (10) They smear flesh with aconite, and scatter it at the crossings of paths. This, when eaten, chokes the panthers. They therefore give the name of *pardialanches*[279] to the plant. But the panthers devour human excrement to guard against the poison, resisting destruction by their own clever device. Their will to live is strong to such a degree that they delay dying a long time after their bowels have been extracted.

(11) Pards, a second kind of panther, are also in these woods. They have been satisfactorily studied, so we need not extensively pursue them. The offspring of lionesses are degraded by adulterous unions with them. Lions are indeed thereby created, but are inferior.

CHAPTER XVIII

(1) Since we are investigating Pontic matters, it must not be omitted whence the Mediterranean Sea[280] raises its head. For indeed, it is thought that this gulf originates from the straits of Gades, and has no other beginning than the flow of the rushing Ocean. They say that the pervading gush of the Ocean causes the advances and retreats along many Mediterranean shores (for example, as in parts of Italy).

(2) Those who believe the opposite say that all the flow floods from the mouths of Pontus. This they support by a not unreasonable argument: the seething tide flowing forth from Pontus never goes back again.

CHAPTER XIX

(1) The island of the Apollonitae is 80 miles away from the Thracian Bosphorus. It is situated on this side of the Ister. From there, Marcus Lucullus carried off the Capitoline Apollo to us.

Before the Borysthenes is the island of Achilles with its sacred shrine, which no bird enters. If by chance one does fly in, it hurriedly makes its escape.

(2) Hecataeus names the Northern Ocean "Amalcium" from that part where the Scythian river Propanisus flows into it. In the language of the native people, the name signifies "frozen".

Philemon says that the Cimbri call the area up to the promontory Rubeae Morimarusa, that is, the Dead Sea. Whatever is above Rubeae is known as the Cronian Sea.

(3) The Caspian Sea, on the other side of Pontus, above the Massagetae and the Apalaei Scythians, was proved to be fresh water by Alexander the Great. Soon after, Pompey the Great discovered the same. As Varro, a comrade of his, tells, he himself wished to test the truth of the tale by drinking of it. **(4)** This is thought to come about through the number of the rivers. So great an abundance of these flow together there that they change the nature of the sea.

I will not omit that at the same time the selfsame Great[281] was permitted to come through to Bactria out of India in eight days, all the way to the river Alierus (which flows into the river Oxus), and thence to the Caspian. From the Caspian he proceeded to the river Cyrus, which flows between Armenia and Hiberia. **(5)** From the Cyrus he pressed on to the Channel of Phasis, in a terrestrial journey of not more than five days, with the ships following after him. Through this excursion, it was proved that it is possible to journey to Pontus all the way from India by water.[282]

(6) The author Xenophon of Lampsacus[283] states that one may sail from the shore of the Scythians to the island Abalcia in three days. This island is of immense size, and is almost the same as a continent. It is not far separated from the Oeonae islands, the inhabitants of which live on the eggs of sea birds and wild oats.

(7) Other nearby islands are likewise constituted. The indigenous Hippopodes have human shape down to their ankles — but their legs end in equine feet.

(8) Xenophon also speaks of the Phanesii, the ears of whom expand to great size, so that the rest of their bodies are covered with them. They need no other clothing.

(9) Before we depart from Scythia, it is an obligation to [not] neglect the singular wild beasts which are found here.

There are many deer in this land. We shall, therefore, pursue the subject of deer. When the male of this species is incited during mating time, he rages with a fury of desire. (10) Although they may mate with the females previously, the females do not conceive prior to the appearance of the star Arcturus. They do not educate their offspring at adventure. The mothers carefully stow their young, and when they are hidden in the depths of the thickets or foliage, they beat them with their feet so they lie concealed. (11) When their strength has matured enough for speed, the mothers teach them by training and running, and accustom their offspring to leap by traversing rough and dangerous paths.

When deer hear dogs barking, they choose ways down wind, so their scent retreats with them.

Deer marvel at the whistling of shepherd's pipes. They hear most acutely when their ears are standing straight; when their ears are stooping, they hear nothing. Everything astounds them: they therefore put themselves more easily in the way of being shot by arrows.

(12) If they swim across seas, they do not seek the shores by looking, but by smell. They place the weak in the last place, and by turns bear up the heads of the weary on their hindquarters.

(13) Of their antlers, the right one is more efficacious for healing. If you are eager to put serpents to flight, you can burn whichever antler you wish. In addition, the fumes of the burning uncover defects, and reveal whether anyone has the falling sickness. The branches of the antlers grow with age. This growth continues for six years; thereupon the branches do not grow more numerous, but they can become thicker. (14) After deer are castrated their antlers never grow; nor, however, do they fall off. (15) The teeth of deer show their age; in old age either few or none are found.

They swallow serpents: with the breath of their noses they drag them out from their burrow lairs.

They find dittany; when they have fed on it they cast off arrows which they have received. **(16)** They also eat the herb which they call *cinaris*, as an antidote for harmful plants.

The rennet of a fawn killed in the uterus of its mother is a marvellous remedy for poisons.

It is well known that deer are never febrile. For this reason, ointments made from their marrow settle the burnings of sick men.

(17) We read that many people who eat deer flesh in the early parts of the day are accustomed to be without fever and to live to great ages. This only happens, however, if the deer which they eat are killed by one wound.

(18) Alexander the Great tied collars to many deer in order to determine their life-span. After one hundred years they were captured, and did not then show a sign of old age.

(19) Those they call "goat-stags" are almost the same in appearance, only they have shaggy flanks and woolly chins with hanging beards. They are not to be seen anywhere except around the Phasis.

CHAPTER XX

(**1**) Mount Saevo, which is itself vast, and not less in size than the Riphaean hills, is the beginning of Germania. The Inguaeones hold it. From them, first after the Scythians, the name "Germania" rises.

(**2**) This land is rich in resources, and is frequented by numerous and savage peoples. It extends between the Hercynian forest and the cliffs of the Sarmatians. Where it begins, it is watered by the river Danuvius,[284] and where it ends, by the river Rhenus. From its inner parts, the very wide rivers Alba, Guthalus and Vistula flow out into Oceanus.

(**3**) The Hercynian forest produces birds whose wings, when night has prevailed and thickened the shadows, flash forth and shine through the darkness. Whence, the men who live there for the most part design their nocturnal excursions so they can use the birds for directing their journeys. The people cast them down in front on the dark paths, and the birds show the way by the guidance of their glittering feathers.

(**4**) In this tract and certainly in the whole northern region, bison are extremely common. These wild beasts are similar to cattle, with shaggy necks and bristly manes. They run more swiftly than bulls. When captured, they cannot be tamed. (**5**) There are also aurochs, whom the ignorant multitude call *bubali*, although *bubali*, which look almost the same as deer, are native to Africa.

Those creatures we formerly called aurochs grow bull-like horns, which extend to so great a size that they are cut off for reason of their conspicuous largeness, and are made into draught-carriers for royal tables.

(**6**) There is also a beast called the *alces* which must be compared to the mule, and which has such a long upper lip that it cannot eat unless retreating into its former footsteps.

(**7**) The island Gangavia, above the region of Germania, produces an animal like the *alces*. But, like the elephant, this creature is not able to bend its hocks, and does not, therefore, lie down when it must sleep. Trees hold up those who are drowsy. Men split these trees so that they are almost falling, so the beasts, supported by their accustomed props, fall. They are thus captured; it is otherwise difficult to seize them, for in that stiffness of knee they have an incomprehensible swiftness. (**8**) Of the Germanic islands, Gangavia is the greatest, but there is nothing great about it excepting itself.

(9) Glaesaria gives crystal and amber. The Germans call this amber *glaesum* in their language. The characteristics of this material were only vaguely known before Germanicus Caesar explored all of Germania's shores. There is a tree, of the pine type, which weeps amber from its middle in autumn.[285] We may in addition understand from the character of the name that amber is the sap of a tree;[286] if you burn it, the smell certainly will indicate pine, whence it is produced. Lest it is believed that the Padanian woods weep this stone, further investigation is worth the effort. The barbarians brought this splendour into Illyria, (10) and it passed to the Transpadani through Pannonian trade; because our people had first seen it there, they also thought it was made there.[287] (11) By a gift, all the trappings of the emperor Nero were adorned with amber. It was not difficult, for at the same time, the king of Germania sent him a gift of 13,000 pounds of it.

(12) When amber is first formed, it is rough and covered with a rind. After it has been boiled in the fat of a sucking pig, it is polished to produce the gloss which we see. (13) Amber has other names, which stem from its appearance: it is called *melleum* and *Falernum* from its similarity to honey and to wine.

It is well known that it snatches leaves and draws chaff to itself. The knowledge of doctors teaches us that it certainly cures many ailments of the vitals.

India also has amber, but Germania has the most and the best. In view of the fact that we had come to the island of Glaesaria, we tackled the subject of amber.

(14) *Gallaica* is to be found in the continent of Germania. It is to be placed before the Arabian variety, for this is conquered by the beauty of the German gem. The Arabians say that it is not found anywhere except in the nests of the birds which they call *melancoryphi*. This no-one accepts, since, although it is rare, it may be seen in stones among the German peoples. It is verdant with a pale green colour; in esteem and value it approaches the emerald. Nothing becomes gold more delightfully.

(15) There are many types of *ceraunium*.[288] The German variety is white, but it glitters with blue. If you have it in the open air, it draws to itself the brightness of stars.

CHAPTER XXI

(**1**) Between the Rhenus and the Pyrenees is Gaul. It extends between Oceanus and the Cebenna and Jura mountains. It has outstandingly rich earth, and is well-suited to fruit-bearing. Very much of it is sown with vines and orchards; it is most blessed with every crop useful to living beings. It is well-watered by rivers and springs. Sometimes the springs are sacred and hot.

It is infamous because of the rites of its inhabitants, who, it is said (for I do not ascribe this rash statement to myself), in their detestable rites of sacrifice make the offerings of religion by the offence of a human victim.

You may go out from here into whatever part of the world you wish: into Italy and Hispania by land or by sea, and into Africa by sea only. (**2**) If you seek Thrace, the best and fertile fields of Raetia greet you, famous for the Brigantine Lake. Then there is Noricum, cold and less fruitful, where the very fertile land is carried off by the ridges of the Alps. (**3**) Next is Pannonia, with strong men and fertile soil, flat and productive, surrounded by the famous rivers Dravus and Savus. Then comes Moesia, which our ancestors justly named the "barn of Ceres".

(**4**) In the part which is Pontic, a herb is seen, which dyes oil they say is medicinal. When this is set on fire, if you eagerly cover it with water, it blazes up all the more; it cannot be put out by anything other than by casting sand on it.

CHAPTER XXII

(1) The Gallic sea-coast used to be the border of the world. But the island of Britannia, from its size, almost merits the name of another world, for it is 800 miles and more in length, as we measure it all the way to the Calidonian angle. That Ulysses was driven into this Calidonian nook is proved by an altar inscribed with Greek letters.[289]

(2) Britain is surrounded by many islands which are not unheard of. Of these, Hibernia approaches Britain in magnitude. The uncouth customs of this island's inhabitants make it a savage land; otherwise, it is so rich in pasture that if the cattle are not now and then kept off the feeding grounds, the abundance endangers them.

(3) In this place there are no snakes, birds are rare and the people unwelcoming and warlike. When they are victorious in battle, they first drink the blood of the slain, then besmear their own faces with it. They consider that which is right and that which is wrong to be the same. {4} If a woman in labour brings forth a male child, she places his first food on her husband's sword. On its very point, she gently stuffs the beginning of nourishment into the infant's mouth, and makes barbaric prayers that he meet death not otherwise than under arms in war.

{5} Those who strive for style mark the hilts of their swords with teeth of sea-monsters. These have an ivory-white brightness. For the greatest glory for the men is in the splendour of their weapons.[290]

There is never a bee among them. If someone scatters dust or stones carried from that land among the hives, the swarms will abandon the honeycombs.

(4){6} The sea which flows between this island and Britain is wavy and unquiet, and is unnavigable except for a few days in the whole year. The Hibernians sail in boats of wickerwork, surrounded with a wrapping of cow hide. The sailors abstain from food for as long as they hold their course.

(5){7} Those who have calculated honestly and truthfully estimate this sea to be spread out to a width of 120 miles.

(7){9} This turbid strait also divides the island Silura from the shore which is held by the Dumnonii, a British tribe. The men of this island even now preserve an old custom: they do not use coins. They give and accept, obtaining the necessities of life by exchange rather than by money. They reverence gods, and the men and women equally declare knowledge of the future.

(8){10} The island Tanatus is blown upon by the Gallic strait, and is separated from the British mainland by a narrow channel.[291] It is blessed with fruitful plains and productive soil. It is not only healthful for its own inhabitants, but also for those of other places. Since Tanatus is crawled over by no snake, the earth transported from there and imported somewhere else kills snakes.

(9){11}[292] There are many other islands around Britain. Of these, Thule is the farthest away. There, when it is the summer solstice, and the sun is making its crossing down from the star of Cancer, there is no night. Similarly, at the winter solstice, there is almost no day. Above Thule we hear that the sea is sluggish and frozen.

{12} For those seeking Thule, the voyage from the Calidonian promontory to the Ebudes islands is two days long. These are five in number, and their inhabitants do not know grain, but live on fish and milk. {13} The islands are ruled by one king, as they are divided from one another by narrow straits. The king has nothing of his own; everything is held in common. {14} For fairness he is restricted by certain laws, and lest avarice divert him from truth, he learns justice in poverty, inasmuch as having no property, he is nourished by the state. {15} He is given no woman for his own, but in times of vicissitude, when troubled, he obtains one on loan. Whence, neither the wish for nor the hope of children is conceded to him.

{16} The Orchades provide the second outpost for those journeying. But the Orchades, three in number, are seven days and as many nights further on from the Ebudes. They are vacant of men, have no forests, and tremble with rushy herbs. Others of them are bare of sand and have cliffs. {17} From the Orchades all the way to Thule, the voyage is five days and nights. But Thule is fertile with plentiful, long-lasting fruits. At the beginning of the spring, those who dwell there live on fodder, among the herds, then on milk, and in winter on the fruits of the trees which they saved. They use the women in common: no-one is married.

(10){18} The circumference of Britain is 4875 miles. In this space are many great rivers, and hot springs refined with opulent splendour for the use of mortal men. Minerva is the patroness of these springs. In her shrine, the perpetual fires never whiten into ashes. When they dwindle away, they change into stony globules.[293]

(**11**){19} So I may pass over the plentiful and varied abundance of metals in which the soil of Britain is everywhere strong, I will describe the stone *gagates*. In Britain there is the most, and the best. If you are curious as to its beauty, it is a black jewel; if to its character, it is almost weightless; if to its nature, it burns in water and is quenched by oil. If you are curious as to its power, it detains things close to it when heated by rubbing, like amber.

(**12**){20} For the most part, Britain is held by barbarians. Even from childhood, they are marked by local artists with various figures and images of animals. When a man's body has been inscribed, the marks of the pigment increase with growth. The wild nations in this place consider nothing to be greater proof of patience than that through the unforgetful scars, their bodies may drink in the most dye.

CHAPTER XXIII

(1) When we turn back towards the continent, Hispanian subjects summon us.

Whether you are considering the wealth of the soil and the crops, or the fruit of the vines, the Hispanian tracts of land can be compared with the best, and are subordinate to none. (2) Hispania abounds in all materials—both in splendid riches and in life's necessities. If you seek silver or gold, Hispania has them; it also has many iron-mines. It yields to no-one as far as vines are concerned, and its olives conquer all.

(3) It is divided into three provinces, which were made ours by the Second Punic War.[294]

Nothing in this place is idle, and nothing is fruitless. Those parts which do not give harvests thrive with fodder, and even the barrenness of the arid areas supplies materials for seamen's ropes.[295]

(4) They do not cook salt there, but gouge it out. They purge cinnabar from the shining sand. They dye wool, in order that they may set down for its red colour the undiluted poison of the scarlet colour.[296]

(5) In Lusitania there is a promontory which some call Artabrum, and which others call it the Olisiponian. It divides the heaven, lands and seas. In the case of the lands, Hispania's flank ends. In this way, the promontory divides the climate and the seas, because the Gallic Ocean and the fore part of the North begin from its outer edge, while the Atlantic Ocean and the West terminate.

(6) The town of Olisipo was founded here by Ulysses. Here also is the river Tagus. Tagus is given preference above the other rivers because of its gold-bearing sands.

(7) In the area close to Olisipo the mares frisk with marvellous fecundity. They conceive after they have been infused by the blast of the west wind; thirsting for males, they are married by the breath of the breezes

(8) The river Hiberus gives its name to all of Hispania, and the river Baetis to the province. Both are well-known.

The Carthage among the Hiberians, which was made a colony, was founded by the Poeni. The Scipiones founded Tarraco, which is the capital of the province Tarraco.

(9) The Lusitanian shore blossoms with a great number of *ceraunium* gems. These are preferred to even the Indian variety. The colour of this *ceraunium* is like an alloy of gold and bronze. Its character is proved by fire. If the stone endures flames without damage, it is thought to be a help against lightning.

(10) The Cassiterides islands watch the side of Celtiberia, and are fertile in lead. There are also the three Fortunate Islands, of which the name alone is notable.

(11) Ebusus, which is 700 stadia from Dianium, has no serpents, inasmuch as its earth puts serpents to flight. Colubraria, which is in the direction of the Sucro, is full of snakes.

(12) The Baleares were the kingdom of Bocchus, and were at one time so plentiful in rabbits that the grain was destroyed.

At the beginning of Baetica, which is the outermost end of the known world, there is an island 700 feet from the mainland. The Tyrians, who came there from the Red Sea, named it "Erythrea". The Poeni named it "Gadir" in their own language, that is, "hedge". Many monuments prove that on this island Geryon pursued his old age, although certain people think that Hercules carried the cattle off from another island which is in sight of Lusitania.

(13) The Gadian strait, which is called after the town Gades, separates the regions, sending the Atlantic swell into our sea. For the Ocean, which the Greeks thus name because of its swiftness,[297] bursts in from the sinking of the sun and coasts by with Europe on the left and Africa on the right. He divides the mountains Calpe and Abinna, which they call the Pillars of Hercules, and pours between Mauretania and Hispania. (14) From this very strait, the length of which is 15 miles, and the width scarcely seven, the Ocean opens the entrance to the inner sea from a certain mouth. It mixes with the Mediterranean gulfs, and drives forward towards the Orient. Of these gulfs, that which bathes Hispania is called the Hiberican Sea or the Balearican. That which bathes the province of Narbonensis is called the Gallic Sea, and then the Ligustican Sea. From this point to Sicily is called the Tuscan Sea. The Greeks name it the Ionian or Tyrrhenian Sea, and the Italians the Lower. From Sicily all the way to Crete is the Sicilian Sea. (15) Thence is the Cretan Sea, which continues to Pamphylia and Egypt. The mass of water, after whirling into the northern side, and into the great curves next to Greece and Illyria, is constricted through the Hellespont and into the narrows of the Propontis. The Propontis

divides Europe and Asia, and goes through towards Maeotis.

(16) The reasons for the names of the seas are not uniform. The names of the Asiatic and Phoenician seas stem from the provinces; those of the Carpathian, Aegaean, Icarian, Balearican and Cyprian seas from islands. The names of the Ausonian, Dalmatian, Ligustican and Tuscan seas are from peoples; those of the Adriatic, Argolican, Corinthian and Tyrian seas are from towns and those of the Myrtoan sea and of the Hellespont from the falls of mortals.[298] The name of the Ionian sea comes from the memory of a king,[299] and that of the Bosphorus from the transit of a cow, or from the narrows or passage fordable by cows.[300] The name of the Euxine comes from the customs of the inhabitants.[301] Formerly, it was called "Axinos". The Propontis is named for the order of the streams.[302]

The Egyptian sea is given to Asia, the Gallic to Europe, and the African to Libya; as each of these seas are closest to these countries, they have come into the quarters of these regions.

(17) These are in the lands' embrace. However, the Ocean surrounds the farthest lands, and the seas there are named after their own shores: the Arabian, Persian, Indian, Eoian, Serican, Hyrcanian, Caspian, Scythian, German, Gallic, Atlantic, Libycan and Egyptian.

(18) Around the shores of India, the flowing tides of the Ocean both rush forward very vigorously and make great departures. This is either because the waters swell up, lifted on high by the force of the heat, or because in that part of the world there is a greater abundance of rivers and springs.

(19) Even now it is deliberated what should cause the ocean to swell up and to subside again into itself, since it is itself superfluous. It is not unobscure that many theories have been put forward which are rather to show off the genius of their proposers than to seek the truth. But, omitting the doubtful arguments on the question, I have found these opinions the most trustworthy.

(20) The natural philosophers say that the world is an animal which was pressed together from various elemental bodies, and that it is moved by a ruling spirit. Diffused through every limb, it drives the strength of its eternal mass of waves. (21) Therefore, just as in our own bodies there is movement of air, the nostrils of the world are located in the depths of the Ocean. Through them, breath is sent out or drawn in, both breathing out the seas and calling them back.

(22) But those who follow the teachings of the stars contend that the movements themselves are provoked by the orbits of the moon, to such a degree that the changes of the waters, between meagreness and plenitude, are in respect of the moon's growth and reduction. The time is not always the same; just as the moon sinks and rises, the wavering retreats fluctuate.

CHAPTER XXIV

(1) From Spain we shall sally forth to Libya. For when one leaves the Baetican town Baelon, Tingi comes next, beyond the intervening thirty-three mile strait. Antaeus was Tingi's first founder; now it is a colony of Mauretania. (2) Hereafter, because the Egyptian Sea finishes in this circuit and the Libyan begins, it seems good to me to call Africa "Libya". Yet certain people have accepted instead that Libya was named thus after Libya, the daughter of Epaphus, and that Africa was named after Afrus, the son of Hercules the Libyan.

(3) Lix, also a colony, was established in the same region, in the place where Antaeus' palace was. Antaeus knew very well how to interweave and disentangle knots on the ground, as though born from Mother Earth. He was vanquished by Hercules in this very spot.[303]

(4) Lest rumour's immoderation wound the truth, I will here give an account of the gardens of the Hesperides and the ever-watchful dragon. Out of the sea here is borne an estuary which has a winding channel; its sinuous sides are tortuous to such a degree that to those looking at it from afar, owing to its broken turnings, it resembles the gliding of a snake. (5) Thus it encircles what they call "the gardens". People, understanding the channel to be the guardian of the apples, paved the way for the fabrication of lies. The island is perforated by the bays of the returning channel, and is situated within the coils of the water. Except for trees similar to wild olive, and an altar sacred to Hercules, nothing other offers by which it might prolong the memory of antiquity. (6) In truth, it is a greater wonder— more amazing than golden shrubs and leafy —that although the ground here is lower than the level of the sea, the depression is never overflowed by the approach of the strait. The waves stick to the very edges because of some natural door-bar, and the advancing billows are resisted by the inmost eyebrows of the shores. Without doubt, the level ground remains dry owing to the admirable nature of the place, despite the advent of the downward-flowing waters.

(7) The town Sala overhangs the river Sala. From here, though the territory of the Autoli people, is the way to the Atlas wilderness. (8) Mount Atlas rises from the middle of sandy desolation. When it rears up, its head plunges above the clouds, into the vicinity of the lunar orbit. Where the mountain stretches towards the ocean (to which it gave its own name), it flows with springs, bristles with groves and is rugged with cliffs. It is a barren waste, and the land is bare and without grass. Where the mountain turns towards Africa, it is blessed with fruits which grow

of themselves. It is shaded with tall trees which have an oppressive odour and foliage similar to cypress. The foliage is clothed with a down which is no cheaper than silken fleece. (**9**) On this side, a herb called euphorbia also grows abundantly, the sap of which makes the vision clear and overcomes the power of poison to no small degree. (**10**) The summit of the range is always snow-covered. Elephants, quadrupeds, serpents and wild beasts have together overtaken the passes. All is silent and concealed throughout the day, which is not without dread. But in the night the mountain shines with fires, and choirs of Aegipans ring on all sides. Songs of *tibiae*, and the jangling of cymbals are also heard along the sea-coast.[304] (**11**) Mt Atlas is 205 miles away from Lix; Lix is 112 miles away from the Gadian strait. Mount Atlas was previously inhabited; the appearance of the place indicates former cultivation. All the way to our time the traces of vines and date-palms are extant. (**12**) The top was traversable for Perseus and Hercules, but is inaccessible to everyone else. Thus the inscription of the altars makes the truth plain. From where Atlas watches the west, woods notorious for wild beasts blockade it for 496 miles between the river Anatis.

(**13**) The rivers around Mount Atlas are not to be passed over in silence. Although they are separated by rather wide distances, they nevertheless do certain service to Atlas' name. (**14**) Asana has brackish water. Bambotum is crammed with crocodiles and hippopotami. Further on is yet another river which flows with a black colour through the most secret inmost scorched deserts. The deserts never claim this river with their perpetual burning and excessive sun, which is more than fiery heat.

(**15**) Both the books of the Carthaginian Hanno and our annals assert these things about Atlas, which the Mauri name Addiris. Juba, the son of Ptolemy, who became master of both kingdoms of Mauretania, also mentions them.[305] Suetonius Paulinus also,[306] who carried the Roman banners above Atlas first and almost alone, reliably established this knowledge.

CHAPTER XXV

(1) Tingitana, one of the Mauretanian provinces, meets the solstitial region.[307] Where it stretches towards the inner sea, seven mountains rise, which, because of their similarity to one another, are called the Brothers. They border upon the strait. (2) Elephants are very numerous in these mountains. This admonishes me to here speak of this type of animal. Elephants have an understanding close to the intelligence of humans. They have memories and keep the discipline of the stars. When the moon begins to shine they seek the rivers in herds. Next, drenched with liquid, they salute the rising of the sun with what movements they can. Then they return to the forests.

(3) There are two breeds of elephant. The more noble breed is indicated by its larger size. They call the smaller breed "bastards". An elephant is understood to be young if its tusks are white. Of these tusks, one is always in use. The other is spared, lest, blunted by continual abrasion, it is less effective for fighting. (4) When elephants are pursued by hunters, they break both tusks together, so, having damaged the ivory, they are not sought after. For they understand that this is the cause of their danger.

They wander in herds. The eldest by birth leads the herd; the nearest in age collects the followers. (5) When they are about to cross a river, they put the smallest in front, lest the elders wear away the river bed by their ingress, and make deep ruts in the low fords.

The females do not mate before they are ten years old, and the males before they are five. In a period of two years, elephants do not mate on more than five days in a year. They do not return to the main herd until they have cleansed themselves with fresh water. (6) Because elephants never fight over females, they know no adultery.

The virtue of compassion is in them. If they by chance see a man wandering through the desert, they lead him all the way to known paths. Or if they meet with thronging cattle, they make passage for themselves with their trunks gently and placidly, lest they kill any animal in the way by an accidental collision.

(7) If ever battle is fought, elephants have a not mediocre care for the injured. They receive the weary and wounded into the middle of the herd.

When elephants come into captivity at the hands of men, they are tamed by draughts of barley.

(8) When they are about to pass over the seas, they will not climb into the ships before an oath is sworn to them about their return.

Mauretanian elephants fear Indian elephants, and, as though conscious of their own smallness, scorn to be seen by them.

The wombs of elephants do not grow heavy over a period of ten years, as the common people think, but in two, as Aristotle specifies. They do not bring forth more than once, nor more than singly.

(9) Elephants live for 300 years. They are most intolerant of cold. They eat tree-trunks and swallow stones. They consider dates the most pleasing of foods. They actually flee the odour of a mouse most of all; they even refuse fodder which has been touched by a little mouse. (10) If by chance any of them devour a chamaeleon, a worm which is poisonous to elephants, the elephant heals itself of the pest by eating wild olive.

Elephants' skin is very hard on their backs, and softer on their bellies. They have no bristles or hair.

Between elephants and snakes is continual enmity. (11) Indeed, traps are prepared by the following craftiness. The serpents lurk on paths along which the elephants are accustomed to wander. After the leading elephants have passed, the serpents assail the hindmost elephants, so those who preceded them cannot aid them. The serpents first bind the elephants' feet with knots so their legs are ensnared, and their means of advancing is impeded. (12) For the elephants, unless prevented by this coily hindrance, bring themselves into contact with either trees or rocks, so they may kill the brazen serpents by means of their oppressive weight. (13) The especial cause of this combat, they say, is this. Elephants have rather cold blood, and for this reason, in the scorching heat snakes long for it most avidly. Wherefore, snakes never attack elephants unless they are burdened with water, as when the elephants' veins are inundated, the serpents may take greater satiety from those they overwhelm. (14) The serpents seek the elephants' eyes above all, because they know that these alone are vulnerable. They also seek the inner parts of the elephants' ears, as this place cannot be defended by the trunk. When they drink the blood, and the beasts fall, the snakes are crushed. (15) Thus on both sides the poured blood soaks the land, and whatever tints the earth becomes a pigment which they call cinnabar.

Italy first saw elephants in the 472nd year after the founding of Rome, in the Epirote war in Lucania. Because of this, they were called "Lucanian cows".[308]

(16) The colony Caesarea is in Caesarensis. It was founded by the divine Claudius, and was formerly the residence of Bocchus. After a while it was kindly given to Juba as a gift.

Caesarensis also has the town Siga, which was inhabited by Syphax.

(17) We should not depart from Icosium in silence. When Hercules was passing over the spot, twenty men who deserted from his company selected a place and built walls. Lest somebody boast in private that the place was named after himself, the name of the city was given from the number of the builders.[309]

CHAPTER XXVI

(1) The waters of the river Amsiga are given to Numidia. When they led wandering peoples in search of pasturage, the inhabitants of this land were called "Nomads".

Numidia has many noble cities, but Cirta is pre-eminent. Next in importance is Chulli: its purple-dyed fleeces are regarded as equal to the Tyrian.

(2) This whole region borders on Zeugitana. Where it is wooded, Numidia rears wild beasts; where it is steep and mountainous, it nourishes horses. It is also praised for the excellence of its marble.

(3) Numidian bears excel others in fierceness, and have longer hair; their reproductive power is equal to those born in any other place. I will speak on this subject without delay.

(4) Bears do not mate in the same way as do other four-footed beasts. Suited to mutual embraces, they copulate just as human couples. Winter kindles desire in them. The males treat the pregnant mothers with respect and keep to themselves; they sleep in the same dens, but in partitioned private sleeping quarters, divided by trenches.

Pregnancy is quite speedy; in fact, the womb gives forth by the 30th day. This precipitate fertility produces unformed offspring. (5) The mother bears bring forth very small lumps of flesh, which are white in colour and have no eyes. Because of the haste and immaturity, the cubs, excepting the outlines of the claws, are nothing but undeveloped bloody matter. The mothers gradually shape the cubs by licking and cherishing them. Sometimes they hold them clasped to the breast, so they might be warmed by continual incubation and draw in the breath of life. (6) Meanwhile, the mothers take no food. Indeed, for the first fourteen days they fall into sleep, and cannot be woken even if wounded. When they have given birth, they lie hidden for four months. When they go forth into the open day, they suffer so from the unaccustomed light, you would think them overcome by blindness.

(7) The head of the bear is feeble; their greatest strength is in their arms and loins. Whence, they sometimes stand on their hind feet. They ambush beehives, as they greatly desire honeycombs; and they do not pursue anything more avidly than honey.

(8) When they have tasted the fruits of the mandrake, they die, but if

they fight against the destructive power of the poison, they devour ants to recover their health.

(9) If bears ever prey on bulls, they know the body parts against which they should above all direct their attacks: they seek the bulls' horns and noses the most. They seek the horns so that they may exhaust the bulls by their weight, and the nostrils so that they may inflict sharper pains in a tender place.

(10) When Marcus Messala was consul, Lucius Domitius Ahenobarbus was curule aedile, and he exhibited 100 Numidian bears and as many Aethiopian hunters in the circus at Rome. This spectacle was recorded amongst his memorable titles.

CHAPTER XXVII

(1) All Africa begins from the foot of Zeugitanus, from the Promontory of Apollo, which is opposite to Sardinia. Advancing to the Promontory of Mercury, which faces the forepart of Sicily, it extends to two projections. One of these is called the Candidan Promontory, and the other, which is in the territory of Cyrenaica, they call Phycus. (2) This last stretches through the Cretan gulf, opposite the island of Crete, which faces Laconian Taenarum.

(3) The sands of the Catabathmus insinuate into Egypt, to which the Cyrenenses are neighbours. The Catabathmi extend between the two Syrtes, and the shallow and ebbing sea make the place inaccessible. The reason for the diminution and advancement of the salt water is by no means easy to discover, as its movements are so uncertain; now it resides in hilly shallows, now it floods with unquiet tides. (4) As the author Varro affirms, the ground there is susceptible to penetrating winds; the sudden force of the gusts very quickly either removes or swallows down the obstacles.

(5) All this region is divided from Aethiopia and the ends of Asia by the Nigris river, which gives birth to the Nile, and from Hispania by the strait. On the side which lies towards the south, it is destitute of springs and notorious for thirst; on the other side, which faces north, it has plentiful sources of water.

(6) In the Byzacene tract, which extends for 200 miles or more, the soil is so exceptionally rich that seed sown there is renewed with its growth of fruit 100 times.

(7) That many strangers have come together in this place, I give this argument about the cities and places. The promontory Borion, which is smote upon by the north wind, was so named by immigrant Greeks. Hippo, afterwards called Regius, and likewise the other Hippo (called Diarrhytus from the straits flowing between), most noble towns both, were founded by Greek knights.

(8) The Siculi built the town Clypea, and first named it Aspis, and also Veneria, into which they carried across the rites of Venus Erycina.

The Achaeans so designated Tripolis in their own language from the number of the cities; that is, Oea, Sabrata, and Leptis Magna.[310]

(9) The people of Tyre were the founders of Hadrumetum and Carthage.

What the veracious books record about Carthage I shall here record. (**10**) Cato asserts in his senatorial oration that this city was built by the lady Elissa, of the Phoenician house, when King Iapon was master in Libya. She called it *Carthada*, because this meant "new city" in the Phoenician tongue. Soon, their speech was changed to Punic, and both the former and the latter were respectively called "Elisa" and "Carthage". Carthage was razed 737 years after it was established. (**11**) Next, it was given to Italian colonists by Gaius Gracchus, and called by him Iunonia. For some time it was ignoble and had powerless status; at length, 102 years interposing, when Marcus Antonius and Publius Dolabella were consuls, it came to the renown of the second Carthage, the other beauty of the earth after the city of Rome.

(**12**) Verily, as I return towards Africa, it is itself surrounded by its own sea.

(**13**) Many beasts, indeed, are in Africa's interior, but it is principally held by lions, which, as Aristotle holds, alone of that type they call "toothed", can see as soon as they are born. These may be broken into three sorts: the smaller, which have curly manes, are generally cowardly and unwarlike; the larger, which have smooth hair, are more fierce. But those which are produced by leopards lack manes and remain undistinguished. All equally refrain from gorging. They do so because they drink and catch food on alternate days; oftentimes, if they do not enjoy good digestion, they postpone their usual repast another day. (**14**) If the consumed flesh is greater than what is right, and they are weighed down, they put their claws into their mouths and voluntarily bring it to light. (**15**) They also do the same when fleeing in a state of satiety. Weakness of the teeth indicates old age. Indications of mildness are many: they spare those who prostrate themselves, and they rage against men rather than women. They do not kill children except in great hunger. Neither are they without mercy: in fact, it is well known from many examples that they can be lenient; when many captives were exposed to several lions, they were repatriated untouched. Also the name of a woman of Gaetula is recorded in the books of Juba, who implored obstructing wild beasts and returned unharmed.

(**16**) They mate behind, as do lynxes, camels, elephants, rhinoceros and tigers. (**17**) At the first birth, lionesses bring forth five cubs, then they melt away the number by one with the years passing, and at last the maternal fecundity recedes to one. Then they become barren for eternity.

(**18**) The tail and the forehead indicate the courage of a lion, just as the mettle of a horse is to be understood by its ears: Nature gave these marks to each noblest beast.

Lions' greatest strength is in their breasts, and they have especial firmness in the head. When pressed by dogs, they scornfully withdraw and sometimes halt in doubtful retreat, and feign fear. (19) They do this if hemmed in in naked and open plains, but if in woody places, as though not shrinking from witness of their cowardliness, they take themselves away in flight as fast as they can.

When they give chase, they aid their pursuits by leaping. When they flee, they cannot leap. When they walk, they enclose the sharp points of their claws in the sheaths of their paws, lest their sharpness be blunted by the abrasion. In this they are scrupulous to such a degree that they do not run without withdrawing their little curved blades.

(20) Surrounded by hunters, they gaze at the ground in contemplation, so they might be the less terrified by the sight of the hunting spears. They never look aslant and wish least that they should themselves be observed.

They fear the songs of domestic poultry, and the noise of wheels, but fear fire more.

(21) I have heard of little creatures called *leontophoni*, which are caught and incinerated. Flesh polluted with a dusting of their ashes, and planted at crossroads may kill lions, if they take never so small a piece thereof. (22) Therefore, lions oppress the *leontophoni* with a natural hatred. When given opportunity, they kill them; they abstain from biting them, but tear them to pieces with the strength of their paws. Scaevola, son of Publius, first made exhibition of these beasts when he was curule aedile.

(23) Africa also gives forth hyenas. The necks of these creatures are stiffened with a spine which is one continual unit, and they cannot turn except by an entire revolution of the body. Hyenas possess many marvellous features. First, they range around shepherds' huts and learn, by assiduous listening, to mimic the human voice, so they may savage men called out in the night by their cunning. (24) They also imitate the sound of people vomiting, and thus devour the dogs attracted by their false retching. If by change dogs out hunting touch the shadow of a hyena while pursuing him, they lose their voices and cannot bark. Hyenas, by way of spying out buried bodies, dig up tombs. It is an easier matter to capture a male hyena, for in the females a more crafty cunning is instilled at birth. Their eyes change colour and have a complex variety. (25) In the pupils of hyenas a stone is found which they call *hyaenia*. It possesses this power: when placed under the tongue of any man whatever, he prophesies the future.

Any animal which the hyena walks around three times cannot move. For this reason, they proclaim that the hyena has magical knowledge.

(26) In a part of Aethiopia, the hyena mates with lionesses. From these unions, monsters named *corocottae* are born. This creature also feigns the voices of men. It never moves the pupils of its orbs, but stares, gazing without blinking. In its mouth it has no gums, and one continual tooth. In order that this is never blunted, it is by nature closed up in a sort of casket.

(27) Among those which they call "grazers", Africa has wild asses. Individual male asses rule over herds of females. The males stand in fear of lustful rivals. So it is that they watch over their pregnant females, and if opportunity arises, they bite off the testicles of the new-born colts. The females are thus wary and secrete their offspring in secluded places.

(28) Africa is so abundant in serpents that it may be deservedly given the palm award for that evil.

Cerastae carry four-fold little horns; they display them as bait, and destroy the birds they attract. They diligently hide the rest of their bodies in the sand, so that no sign of them is visible saving that part aforementioned. By this trick they ambush and kill birds, who have been lured by the hope of food.

(29) The *amphisbaena* grows twin heads, one in the proper place, and the other where the tail should be. For this reason the snake glides in a circular shape, as the heads, contrary to what is right, strain from both ends.

(30) *Iaculi* climb trees, down from which they whirl with great force, and pierce any animal which happens to be exposed to them.

The back of the *scytale* shines outstandingly, and the beauty of its spots gives pause to anything which beholds it. The *scytale* crawls rather slowly, but through its own marvellousness it seizes those astounded creatures which it is not otherwise able to overtake. (31) Nevertheless, as bright as its scales may be, it is the first to slough its winter coat.

The species of asps are many and varied, and indeed, they have disparate manners of harming. The *dipsas* destroys by thirst; the *hypnale* kills with sleep. This last is even—as Cleopatra may bear witness—purchased for death. The poisons of other serpents, since they are treatable, merit less of fame.

(**32**) The *haemorrhois* brings forth blood with its bites, and, having destroyed the circulation, it lures out whatever is left of life through a stream of blood.

Whomever the *prester* pierces becomes distended, and dies swollen to immense corpulence.

(**33**) The sting of the *seps* is followed by putrefaction.

There are also *ammodytae*, *chenchres*, *elephantiae*, *chersydri* and *chamaedracontes*. There have been as many deaths as there are names.

Scorpions, skinks and lizards are reckoned worms, not serpents. (**34**) If these monsters hiss, they strike more slowly.[311] They have feelings; they do not rashly stray except in couples. If one is captured or killed, the other, left behind, is maddened.

The heads of females are more slender, their bellies more swollen and their venom more harmful. The male is equally smooth, higher, and also meeker.

(**35**) The vision of all serpents is dull. They seldom look directly ahead, and not without cause, as they do not have eyes in front, but on their temples, so far back that they hear more readily than they see.

(**36**) There was dispute between Aethiopia, Africa and Cyprus as to which yielded the best type of the gem heliotrope. Heliotrope is green in colour, not so vivid, but rather cloudy and restrained, spotted above with crimson stars. (**37**) The reason for the name is from the effect and power of the stone.[312] When dropped into a copper bowl, it changes the rays of the sun with bloody reflections and casts its splendour outside the water and steals it. This also is able to be said: that the herb of the same name, mixed and consecrated with the right prayers, takes he by whom it is swallowed away from the sight of men.

(**38**) If one intends to journey between the Syrtes by land, one must order the route by the stars; otherwise the course will be unclear. For the wind alters the appearance of the crumbling soil; the smallest breeze effects so great a difference that the locales are changed, and no landmarks remain to be recognised, since not only high hills subside into valleys, but valleys are piled over with sand.

(**39**) Thus the continent suffers from the nature of its own sea. It does not matter where the storms are, since the elements act together towards the destruction of travellers. The winds rage on land, and the land on the sea.

(40) The two Syrtes are separated by 250 miles. The smaller is considerably more peaceful. I have heard that when Gnaeus Servilius and Gaius Sempronius were consuls, the Roman fleet finally sailed over the shallows between them without coming to harm.[313]

In this bay, on the island of Menis, Gaius Marius had a hiding place after the Minturnine Swamps.[314]

(41) Above the Garamantes used to live the Psylli. They were fortified against harmful venoms by incredible strength of body, and they alone did not perish from the bites of serpents, and although assailed by lethal fangs, endured in unimpaired health. They even offered their newly-born to the serpents. (42) If the child was the fruit of unlawful love, the crimes of the mother were punished by the destruction of the little one; if the mother was chaste, the right of paternal blood protected the child of honourable ancestry from death. Thus they proved the truth of origin by a judging poison. But this people were overrun by the Nasamones and perished. Nothing other than the reputation arising from the vestige of their name remains of the Psylli.

(43) The Nasamones yield a stone called nassamonite, which is bloody all over and shadowed with black veinlets.

We learn that within the inmost recess of Syrtis Major, around the altars of the Philaeni,[315] lived the Lotus-Eaters, and it is no uncertain claim.

From the altars of the Philaeni, it is not far to the swamp into which the river Triton flows. It is here they believe the goddess of the arts herself was descried.[316]

(44) Syrtis Major displays a town they call Cyrene, which Battius the Lacedaemonian founded in the 45th Olympiad, when King Marcius held sway over Rome, in the 586th year after the fall of Troy. This place was the homeland and dwelling-place of Callimachus the poet.

(45) Between Cyrene and the temple of Hammon is a distance of 400 miles. A spring sacred to Sol is near to this temple, which draws the soil into knots of water, and also solidifies ash into clods. In which earth, miraculously, a lake spurts forth, surrounded on every side, contrary to what is expected, with dry fields.

(46) In this place one collects a stone called the Horn of Hammon, for it is so twisted and bent that it resembles a ram's horn. It has a golden radiance, and it is said that it engenders prophetic dreams if placed under the head of somebody who is sleeping.

(47) There is also a tree by the name *melopos*, from which moisture flows sluggishly forth. It is called *hammoniacum* after the place.

(48) In addition, *sirpe*[317] grows among the Cyrenaics. It has odiferous roots, more like those of a brushwood herb than of a fruit-tree. In the summer time, its stem exudes a dewy grease which sticks to the little beards of feeding billy-goats. When dried, it turns into icicle-like specks, and it is collected for the use of the table, or rather of healing. (49) It was first called "sirpic milk", since it pours like milk does. Finally, deriving from custom, it was named *laser*. The seeds have been almost completely rooted up, first by an invasion of barbarians, who laid the fields waste, and later by the inhabitants themselves, by reason of an intolerable excess of tax.

(50) Africa is on the left of Cyrene, and Aegypt is on the right. In front is the cruel and harbourless sea, and behind, divers nations of barbarians and inaccessible wildernesses, which bear the basilisk, an evil unique in all the lands. (51) It is a serpent, almost half a foot in length; its head is lined, as though with a little white head-band. It is given to the destruction not only of men and other living things, but also of the land itself. Wherever it chooses to make its toxic den is polluted and burned. It devastates vegetation and kills trees, and also contaminates the very breezes. So it is that no bird can fly unharmed over air infected by its unwholesome breath. (52) When it is agitated, it crawls along with one half of its body, and rears the other half up high. Even serpents recoil in terror from its hissing, and when they hear it, they all hurry to flee in any possible direction. (53) Anything that dies from its bite is not devoured by wild beasts or touched by birds. Nevertheless, the basilisk is defeated by weasels, which men in those parts stuff into the caverns in which it takes shelter. Yet it does not lack power even when dead. Indeed, the men of Pergamum acquired, for a pretty penny, the remains of a basilisk, so spiders would not spin on their shrine, famous for the workmanship of Apelles, nor birds fly into it. The corpse was placed there suspended in a golden net.

(54) Around the farthest end of the Syrtes, the river Lethon flows to the town Berenice. They believe this river rushes forth from an underground source, and it is remembered by the old poets for its waters, which induce forgetfulness. Berenice, who was married to the third Ptolemy, built this town in Syrtis Major.

(55) All the country spread out between Aegypt, Aethiopia and Libya—as far as it is wooded—is filled with various types of apes. I hope that anyone offended by the name does not take the following knowledge amiss. (56) For indeed, the value of toil lies in omitting nothing in which the providence of nature is to be seen. Among these apes is a common sort which is seen everywhere. They have the talent of mimicry, by which they come more easily to the hand. They eagerly imitate the gestures of hunters, who purposely leave behind an ointment-box of bird-lime. Because the apes saw the hunters feign the deed, they smear their eyes with it, and thus, with their vision obscured, it is easy to seize them. (57) They exult at the new moon, and are sad when a planet is horned and hollow. They love their young immoderately; indeed, they may more easily lose the cubs they hold dearer and carry in front of themselves, since the neglected ones always stick behind the mothers.

(58) *Cercopitheci* have tails: this is the only distinction between them and the apes.

The *cynocephali* are themselves of the number of the apes. They are very frequent in parts of Aethiopia. They leap violently, bite savagely and are thus never tamed.

(59) Sphinxes are also considered among the apes. They have shaggy heads, rather deep and prominent breasts, and are amenable to the forgetfulness of the wild state.

(60) And there are those they call satyrs, which are exceedingly pleasing in appearance, and restless with gesticulations and movements.

Callitriches differ from the others in almost all respects. They have bearded faces and broad tails. It is not hard to catch them, but it is rare to carry them away in captivity, for they will not live otherwise than in Aethiopia, their own clime.

CHAPTER XXVIII

(1) Between the Nasamones and the Trogodytae live the Amantes people. They construct buildings from salt. They raise these like crags from the mountains, secure them with piles of quarried stone and use them as temples. There is such great abundance of this ore there that they may make their houses from salt. (2) These are the Amantes who trade precious stones (carbuncles) with the Trogodytae.

On this side of the Amantes, nearer to the Nasamones, the Asbytae subsist on *laser* (plant-juice). This nourishes them; for them, it is edible.

CHAPTER XXIX

(1) There is a town of the Garamantes called Debris, which has a marvellous spring. Why so? It is alternately cold during the day and hot during the night. Now it rages with fiery steam, now it trembles with icy coldness, through the same channels. (2) It is incredible to note that nature should manufacture such dissonant variety in so short a course. He who wished to investigate in the shadows of night would believe that there was eternal heat in the stream; he who examined it by day would judge the wintry spring to be nothing other than perpetually freezing. (3) For this reason, Debris is not undeservedly celebrated among the nations. The quality of its waters changes according to celestial movements, although contrary to the discipline of the stars. When evening tempers the heat of the world at sunset, the spring begins to heat, and it may be harmful to touch it if you cannot abstain from doing so. (4) With the rising of the sun, when everything is warmed and heated up with its rays, the spring vomits out wintry water, so it cannot be drunk even by people who are thirsty. Who would not wonder at a spring which becomes cold through heat, and becomes heated through cold?

(5) The chief city of the region of the Garamantes is Garama. The way to it was for a long time tortuous and impassable, for robbers buried the wells in sand, so that, having removed the water by transitory deceit, the way might become notorious for thirst, and debar the arrival of travellers. (6) But during the war in Vespasian's principate, which was waged against the Oenses, this difficulty was overcome by the convenient discovery of a shorter passage.[318] (7) Cornelius Balbus subdued the Garamantes, and with this victory was the first to triumph over them. Indeed, he was the first foreigner (inasmuch as he was born at Gades) who attained the glory of a triumph. The cattle of the Garamantes graze with bent necks, for if they direct their faces to the pasture straight on, their horns impede their passage to the ground.

We hear that in the neighbourhood of Cercina is an island called Gauloe, where serpents are neither born nor live if brought there. In addition, the dust from there wards off snakes if strewn anywhere in the world. Thrown over scorpions, it kills them immediately.

CHAPTER XXX

(1) The Aethiopians and the people of Mount Atlas are separated by the Nigris river, which is thought to be part of the Nile.[319] It is similarly green with papyrus and fringed with reeds; it brings forth the same animals and floods at the same seasons. It also returns within its banks at the time when the Nile is content with its own channel.

(2) The Garamantic Aethiopians do not have private marriage, but permit everyone to have sexual relations in common. Thence it is that only mothers recognise their sons; there is no deference for the paternal name. (3) For who could truly know his father in this extravagance of uncleanliness run riot? The Garamantic Aethiopians are thus counted as degenerate among all peoples. This is not undeserved, seeing that they have overthrown chastity and have destroyed knowledge of descent through their wicked custom.

(4) The name of the Aethiopians extends widely. In the part of Africa where Libya sees Meröe, there are many and varied nations of them. Of their number are the Nomades, who live on the milk of the *cynocephali.*[320] The Serbotae are twelve feet tall. (5) The Azachaei devour elephants they capture by hunting. The Psambarae have no eared quadrupeds, not even elephants, in their territory. Their nearest neighbours hand over their highest royal power to a dog. They divine his commands by his movements.

(6) They say that the maritime Aethiopians have four eyes, but the truth is otherwise. In fact, they say this because they see excellently well and aim their arrows very accurately.

The Agriophagi[321] hold the ground towards the west, and eat only the flesh of panthers and lions. They have a king who has one eye in his forehead.

(7) There are also the Pamphagi,[322] who eat everything which is chewable, and anything which happens to be born. There are also the Anthropophagi, whose name expresses their customs.[323]

(8) They say that the Cynomolgi[324] have canine jaws and prominent snouts. The Artabatitae go prone like four-footed beasts, and rove abroad without abode, like wild animals.

The people bordering on Mauretania gather land locusts at a fixed season, and harden them in brine; then they have them as their lone preserver of life. But of these, none exceed forty years of age.

(9) From this Ocean to Meröe, which the Nile makes with his first embrace,[325] is 620 miles. Beyond Meröe, above the rising of the sun, the Macrobian Aethiopians are said to dwell. Their lives are longer than ours by half. (10) These Macrobii maintain justice, love equality, are healthy and vigorous, and are graced with particular beauty. They ornament themselves with copper and make gold fetters for their criminals. There is a place among them called Heliustrapeza, which is loaded with sumptuous dishes, of which anyone may eat indiscriminately. They consider that they are thus divinely exalted.

(11) Also in that place is a lake, in which people's bodies, if bathed, shine as if with olive oil. The water of this lake is extremely health-giving. It is so limpid that fallen fronds do not float on it; immediately the leaves fall, they sink to the bottom because of the thinness of the water.

(12) Above this are deserted and savage wildernesses all the way to the Arabian gulf.

Next, in the farthest Orient,[326] are races of monstrous appearance. Some have hideous visages without noses, and their faces are of a uniform flatness.

(13) Others have closed up mouths, and can only swallow sustenance into the small holes by way of oaten stalks. Not a few of them lack tongues, and use nods and gestures instead of speech. (14) Certain of these nations, before the time of the Egyptian king Ptolemy Lathyrus, were ignorant of the uses of fire.

Aethiopia holds everything from the south-east to the south-west. Whatever of it is under the southern axis blooms with groves, which are at their most verdant in winter.[327] From the middle part, a high mountain overhangs the sea, and quietly flaming on it summits, glows eternally with gentle fire. (15) Among these fires of continual heat there is a great abundance of dragons. True dragons have small mouths, which do not gape open to bite. They have a narrow tube, through which they drag breath and thrust out their tongues. Of course, they do not have their strength in their teeth, but in their tails, and they cause harm by lashing these rather than with their jaws.

(16) A stone called *dracontia* is excised from the brains of dragons. But it cannot be pulled out unless the dragon is alive. For if the serpent dies first, the hardness dissolves and vanishes with its life. The kings of the Orient especially glory in its use, although, by reason of its hardness, it permits no flattery of artifice. Whatever is noble in it is not made by the

hand of man, and it shines with no other colour than with its natural white. (**17**) The author Sotacus writes that he has even seen this gem, and teaches by what methods it may be stolen. The bravest men search out the pits and retreats of the serpents. Then they stand ready for them when they come out to feed. They run past them as fast as they can and cast before them plants steeped in things which are most powerful for provoking sleep. (**18**) The dragons are then rendered insensible by sleep, and the men sever their heads. From their daring booty they then carry back the rewards of their rashness.

(**19**) The areas held by the Aethiopians are full of wild beasts, one of which they call the *nabun*. We call it the giraffe. It has a neck like a horse, feet like cattle's and a head like a camel. It shines with a reddish colour, and is sprinkled on top with white spots. (**20**) This animal was first shown at Rome at the games of Caesar the Dictator.

At almost the same time, monsters called *cephi* were exhibited there. Their hind feet, from the ankle to sole, resembled human limbs, and their fore feet recalled men's hands. But they were not seen by us more than once.

(**21**) Before the games of Gnaeus Pompey, the shows of the Romans were ignorant of the rhinoceros. This colour of this beast is like box-wood. On its nose is a single backwards-facing horn, which it sharpens to a point by repeated grinding on stones. It uses it to fight elephants, to which it is equal in length, but shorter in the leg. The rhinoceros instinctively seeks out the elephant's belly, which it knows is the only part penetrable to its blows.

(**22**) The *catoblepas* is produced close to the river Nigris. It is a sluggish beast of medium size, and bears its burdensome head with difficulty. It has a destructive glance, for whoever encounters its eyes dies immediately.

(**23**) The ants here are shaped like huge dogs, and dig up the golden sand with their feet, which are like lions'. They guard it lest someone steal it, enticing and pursuing them to the death.

(**24**) Aethiopia engenders the *lycaon*. It is a wolf with a mane on its neck, of so many colours that they say no colour is absent from it. (**25**) Aethiopia also engenders the *parandrus*, which is the size of an ox. It has cloven footprints, branching horns, and a deer-like head. It is the colour of a bear, and has equally shaggy hair. This *parandrus*, it is asserted, changes its shape when alarmed; when it takes cover, it becomes similar to whatever is near to it, be it white like a stone, green like a thicket, or whatever else it prefers. (**26**) Cuttle-fish do the same in the sea, and chamaeleons on land. But both the cuttle-fish and the chamaeleon are hairless; it is easier for them, from the slipperiness of their skin, to imitate what is near. It is, then, an extraordinary and remarkable thing that the *parandrus'* rough hair should give rise to changes in colour. Because of this, *parandri* are difficult to catch.

(**27**) It is characteristic of Aethiopian wolves that they have the upward thrust of a bird when springing; they are less proficient at running than at leaping. Nevertheless, they never attack men. They are long-haired in winter, and bald in summer; they are called *thoae.*

(**28**) The porcupine is also very common in this place; it is similar to the hedgehog. Its back is bristly with spines, which it frequently shoots out with a voluntary heave, so it might wound attacking dogs with unremitting showers of barbs.

(**29**) The *pegasus* is bird of these skies, but this *pegasus* has nothing equine about it excepting its ears. The *tragopan* is another bird, larger than an eagle. Its head is armed, and carries ram-like horns.

(**30**) The Aethiopians gather cinnamon. This shrub grows from a short stalk, with small and stunted branches, and is never above two cubits in height. Those which grow more thinly are considered the more select, while those which grow more thickly are scorned. (**31**) It is collected by priests, who slaughter sacrificial victims beforehand. When favourable omens are given, they are careful that their harvest neither anticipates sunrise nor continues past sunset. Whoever holds first place among the priests divides the heaps of twigs with a spear which has been consecrated for that purpose. A portion of 1/3 is dedicated to the sun, and if it has been divided correctly, it ignites spontaneously.

(**32**) Among the things we have spoken of, the *hyacinthus* stone, which has a shining sky blue colour, is to be found. It is a valuable stone if discovered without blemish, for it is not a little subject to flaws. It is frequently either tempered with a violet colour, or covered with cloudiness, or softened to a white wateriness. The best type is not blunted by too solid a colour, nor over-clear with an eager transparency, but sweetly draws its bloom from both, dyed with the right proportions of light and purple. (**33**) This stone perceives the winds and changes with the sky: it is not equally bright when the day is cloudy as when it is clear. In addition, the stone is colder when put into the mouth. It is certainly not suitable for carving, as it defies all grinding. Yet it is not utterly invincible; it can be scratched and inscribed by a diamond.

(34) *Chrysoprase* is also to be seen in the places *hyacinthus* is. Light conceals this stone, and shadows reveal it, for this divergence is in it: it glows by night and is pale by day.

Out of this same soil we take *haematite*, which has a bloody redness, and for this reason is called *haematite*.

CHAPTER XXXI

(1) The area which is spread out from the Atlas all the way to the Mouth of Canopus, which is the end of Libya and the threshold of Egypt (it was named after Canopus, the helmsman of Menelaus, who was buried on the island which makes the mouth of the Nile), is held by different peoples. These have withdrawn into the secrets of the trackless wilderness. (2) The Atlanteans exist utterly removed from the customs of humans. None have individual appellations, and none have special names. They receive the rising of the sun with curses, and pursue his setting with curses. They are scorched by the burning sky of this region, and hate the god of light. It is affirmed that they do not dream, and that they keep away from all living creatures. (3) The Trogodytae dig pits, and hide themselves in them. They have no love of possessions: they have renounced riches for a voluntary poverty. They boast only one precious stone, which we call *hexecontalithos*.[328] It is spotted with such diverse markings that the colours of sixty gems can be discerned within its little compass. These men live on the flesh of serpents. They are ignorant of speech, and shriek rather than talk.

(4) The Augilae only worship the dead. On the first nights of marriage, they force their wives to lay themselves open to adultery. Soon after, they bind them to perpetual chastity with the strictest laws.

(5) The Gamphasantes abstain from fighting, and shun commerce. None of them permits himself to mingle with foreigners.

It is believed that the Blemmyae (not those who live in the vicinity of the Red Sea) are born headless, and have their mouths and eyes in their chests.

Satyrs resemble men in nothing other than shape.

(6) The Aegipans are those which we see to be painted.

The Himantopodes, rather than walking, crawl about with weak pushes of their legs, proceeding by sliding more than by stepping.

The Pharusi, who were companions of Hercules when he went to the Hesperides, became weary of the journey and settled here. To this place Libya.

CHAPTER XXXII

(1) Egypt withdraws inwards towards the south, until it meets the Aethiopians at its rear. The Nile flows around its lower regions.[329] The Nile divides at a place called the Delta, and encircles areas between its rivers, like islands. As we shall declare, it is asserted that the spring the Nile rushes from is almost unknown. (2) Its source is on a mountain of Lower Mauretania which is near to the ocean. This is affirmed by the Punic Books; we have learnt this from what King Juba has handed down. Straightway the Nile makes a lake called Nilides. (3) It is inferred that the Nile begins thence, as the lake produces the same plants, fishes and animals as does the river. And if ever Mauretania, where the source is, is inundated with thick snow or plentiful rains, the flood in Egypt is increased. (4) But when the Nile is discharged from this lake, it is absorbed by the sands, and is hidden in secret underground tunnels. (5) Next, it rushes forth into the sight of Caesariensis, displaying the same characteristics as we noted of its source. Then it sinks down again, and does not rise up before it reaches the Aethiopians after an extended journey. Here it makes the river Nigris, which, as we said above,[330] is the border of Africa. Thence, people call it the Astapus, as the water flows out from the shadows.[331] (6) The Nile embraces many great islands. Of these, the majority are so wide, and so vast in size, that someone could scarcely travel past them in the course of five days, even if he proceeded rapidly. (7) The most well-known of these is Meröe. Having been divided around it, the right channel of the river is called Astosapes, and the left Astabores. Then, having traversed great expanses, it becomes violent with obstructing rocks; it is carried by streams of such a size through opposing crags that it falls rather than flows. At length, from the final cataract (for thus the Egyptians call certain of the Nile's straits), it is safe. (8) Then the river leaves the name Giris behind, and travels along uninterrupted. It is made into seven mouths; turned to the south, it is received into the Egyptian Sea.

(9) Those ignorant of astronomy and geography have given a variety of reasons for the floods of the Nile. Some affirm that the Etesian winds force an abundance of clouds to the place where the river begins, and that the spring itself, swelled by the moisture above, has as much magnitude of flood as of fuel the clouds have furnished to the waters. (10) Others say that because the river is struck against by blowing winds, and cannot move forward with its accustomed speed, it becomes swollen, its waters wrestling in the narrows. The more strongly, they say, the contrary winds resist, the higher is the swift river beaten back and elevated into vertices of height. The weight of the torrent presses on, and it is compressed into its original fissure, its violent force rushing together in this way, from one

side the elements insistent, from the other the resistant waves springing up, so that a barrier is formed, which causes the departure.

(11) Not a few affirm that the river's spring, which is called Phialus, is raised by the motions of the heavenly bodies; dragged forth by the shining sunbeams, it is suspended by the heavenly fire. This is not, however, without a certain discipline—that is, the new moon.

(12) The origin of the Nile's flooding is completely drawn from the sun. The first swelling is made when the sun passes through Cancer. Afterwards, when Cancer's thirty parts have been played out, and when the sun enters Leo, and the star Sirius rises, all the waves are discharged, and the entire fluctuation erupts. (13) The priests judge this time to be the world's birthday: that is, between the 20th and the 22nd of July.[332] When the sun passes into Virgo, all the inundation is recalled, and when the sun enters Libra, the river is captured deep inside its own banks. (14) This also they add—that the flood harms equally whether it rages abundantly or sparingly, since scarceness brings a bare minimum of fertility, and the more eager plenty delays the tillage because of its long-lasting moisture. (15) They say that in its greatest excess the Nile rises to 18 cubits, and at its most equable, it is tempered at 16. If it rises to 15, there is no lack of successful harvest, but anything below this causes famine. (16) They also give the Nile this distinction: that it foretells the future. At the battle of Pharsalus, it did not exceed five arm-spans. It is plain that it alone of all rivers breathes forth no breezes. The river begins to belong to the realm of Egypt from Syene, where the borders of Aethiopia are. Thence, until it falls into the sea, it holds the name of "Nile". (17) Among all the things possessed by Egypt which are worthy of mention, the ox they call Apis is especially to be wondered at. They worship him as a god. He is distinguished by a white spot which grows naturally on his right side, recalling the appearance of the horned moon. (18) The length of his life is pre-determined. When the time has elapsed, he is killed by being drowned in the sacred spring, so he does not live longer than is permitted. Soon, not without public mourning, another is sought. When he is discovered, 100 priests follow him to Memphis, so when he has been initiated by way of rites, he may begin to become sacred. (19) The temples which he enters or sleeps in they mystically call "bride-chambers". Apis gives revealing omens about the future, especially if he takes food from the hands of those seeking counsel. He rejected the right hand of Germanicus Caesar, and thus revealed the danger he was in. Not long after, Caesar was killed. (20) Boys follow Apis in flocks, and suddenly, as though frenzied, tell of things to come. Once a year a female ox is shown to Apis. She herself is not without certain marks. She is found, presented and killed on the same

day. **(21)** The Memphites celebrate the birthday of Apis by a casting of golden bowls. They throw them into an appointed spot in the Nile. The solemnity is carried out over seven days. During this time the crocodiles maintain an armistice with the priests and do not touch anyone washing in the river. But on the eighth day, when the ceremonies are finished, they resume their accustomed atrocities.

(22) The crocodile is an evil four-footed beast. It thrives equally well both on land and in the river. It does not have a tongue. It moves its upper jaw. Its jaws meet with a horrible tenacity, and its chains of teeth press together like combs. The majority of these creatures grow up to 20 fathoms in size.

They bring forth eggs like geese's eggs. **(23)** The crocodile marks out a place for its nest with a natural foreknowledge, concealing its young in a place beyond the reach of the Nile's flood. The male and female take turns at looking after the brood.

Except for a gap on its face, the crocodile is armoured. It also has brutal claws.

(24) During the nights it passes its time in the water, and in the day it rests on the land. Its skin is of great strength, so much so that its back deflects missiles hurled by catapults. **(25)** The *strophilos* is a small bird. Aiming at hanging bits of meat, it scratches slowly at the mouths of the crocodiles, and bit by bit, coaxing and tickling, it goes all the way in to the beasts' jaws. When an *enhydrus*, a kind of ichneumon, notices this, it infiltrates the crocodile and plunders its guts. Then it leaves, having eaten away the beast's stomach.

(26) There is also a kind of dolphin in the Nile, whose backs have serrated crests. These dolphins zealously entice the crocodiles into swimming. Submerged, the dolphin swim underneath the crocodiles with fraudulent cunning, and sever their tender bellies, killing them.

(27) On an island in the Nile live men very small in stature, but with a boldness which extends all the way to offering themselves to opposing crocodiles. For these monsters pursue those who flee, and fear those who make a stand. Therefore, when captured, they become subjugated and enslaved between their own waters. Thoroughly tamed by dread, they are so accommodating and forgetful of their wildness, they carry their conquerors as riders on their backs. **(28)** Whenever, therefore, the crocodiles detect the smell of this island or this people, they flee far away.

Crocodiles have rather dull vision in water. On land it is most acute. They catch no food in the winter; they undergo four months of starvation from the beginning of the cold weather.

(**29**) Skinks are also very frequent around the Nile. Indeed, they are similar to crocodiles, but smaller and narrower in shape. They are an indispensable aid to health: physicians infuse drinks with them, thereby destroying the power of poison.

(**30**) The hippopotamus is nurtured by this same land and river. It has a horse-like back, mane and neigh, a turned-up nose, cloven hooves, tusks like a wild boar's and a twisty tail. In the night, it lays waste the grain-fields. With crafty cunning, it proceeds towards these backwards, so that when it goes to return, its deceptive footmarks ensure no ambush is prepared for it. (**31**) When overfull with excessive feasting, it seeks newly cut reeds, and walks to and fro through them for so long a time, that the sharp ends of the plants wound its feet, and its satiety is lightened by the flow of blood. Then it plasters the area with mud, until the wounds heal into scars. Marcus Scaurus was the first to bring hippopotami and crocodiles to Rome.

(**32**) The ibis bird frequents the same banks. It plunders serpents' eggs, and carries off the choicest of them as food to their own nests. Thus the success of noxious broods is prevented. (**33**) These birds are not useful only within the Egyptian borders. The swamps of Arabia send forth swarms of winged serpents, whose venom is so quick-acting, that, after a bite, death follows more quickly than pain. The ibis, from an innate wisdom, go out aroused and in readiness for battle and devastates this foreign evil before it reaches the borders of their land. Mobbing the pestilential horde in the air, they devour all of it. For which reason, ibis are deservedly held to be holy, and no-one may injure them. They lay eggs with their mouths. Only Pelusium produces black ibis; all other places breed white ones.

(**34**) Concerning the trees which grow only in Egypt, the Egyptian fig is particularly worthy of mention. It has leaves like the mulberry, and grows fruit not only on its branches, but on its trunk as well. It is narrow right up to the point of its productiveness. In one year, it bears fruit seven times. Where you pluck a fruit, another bulges out without delay. (**35**) When its wood is thrown into water, it sinks. When it has sat in the liquid for some time, it is made lighter and rises up. It is dried by moisture, something against the nature of other woods.

(**36**) The Egyptian palm must also be spoken of. It is specifically called *adipsos*, and so it ought to be, as the fruit, once tasted, wards off thirst.[333] Its aroma is the same as that of the apple. But the fruit only allays thirst if it is plucked before it is ripe, for if it is taken when mature, it steals the senses, hinders the feet, and retards the tongue: taking possession of the faculties of the mind and body, it manufactures the vice of drunkenness.

(**37**) Peoples who live where the borders of Egypt stretch towards Diacecaumen discern the moment in which they say the world recommences its yearly motion by the following method.[334] A sacred grove is chosen, where animals of the most diverse kinds are fenced in. These, when the heavens arrive at the appointed configuration, give vent to their feelings with what outward signs they can.

(**38**) Some howl, some bellow, some shriek and some bray. Some flee together to wallowing-holes. This evidence is as a teacher to them for discerning the beginning of the year. (**39**) The same peoples say that it was handed down to them by the first ancestors of their tribe that where the sun now sets, it formerly rose. (**40**) Thebes is famous among Egyptian cities for the number of its gates, to which Arabians and Indians convey cargoes. The region Thebaica is named after this city. (**41**) Abydos is also famous, formerly for the palace of Memnon, now for the temple of Osiris.

The magnitude of its works and its Macedonian founder ennoble Alexandria. The architect Dinocrates, when he had laid it out, held another place in his memory through the agency of its founder. (**42**) Alexandria was founded in the 112th Olympiad, when Lucius Papirius, son of Spurius, and Gaius Poetelius, son of Gaius, were the Roman consuls. It was established not far from the mouth of the Nile, which is called Heracleoticos by some, and Canopos by others. (**43**) There is also Pharos, a colony settled by Caesar the dictator. Nocturnal navigation is steered from it by burning lights. For Alexandria is approached by a treacherous harbour, with deceptive shallows and uncertain seas. It admits sailors through three channels only—Poseidon, Teganus and Taurus. Because of this, machines devised for the office of lighting harbours are called *phari*.

(**44**) The pyramids are pointed towers, above the height of everything which can be manufactured by the hand of man. Having surpassed shadows, they have none.

Now let us turn our pen away from Egypt.

CHAPTER XXXIII

(**1**) Above the mouth of Pelusium is Arabia, which extends to the Red Sea. Varro says this sea was named the "Erythraean" not for the colour alone, but after king Erythra, son of Perseus and Andromeda. The same author affirms that on the shores of this sea is a spring; if sheep drink of it, the colour of their fleeces change. Formerly white, they lose the colour they had until drinking, and afterwards, darken to black.[335] (**2**) The town Arsinoe is also on the Red Sea.

Arabia extends all the way to the rich, spice-bearing land held by the Catibanian and Scaenitan Arabs, also famous for the mountain Cassius. (**3**) The reason for the name of the Scaenitae is thought to be that they live in tents, and do not have other homes.[336] The tents themselves are goat blankets; they say that the covers are woven from the hair of goats. (**4**) In addition, they abstain entirely from eating pigs' meat. This kind of animal, if brought here, immediately dies. The Greeks named Arabia "Eudaemon", which is "Blessed" in our tongue. It is inhabited on a hill made by the hands of men, which is between the rivers Tigris and Eulaeus. This last is so famous for the purity of its flow, that all the kings there drink its waters and no other.

(**5**) You may hereby understand that Eudaemon was not vainly named: besides spices, of which it produces a great number, it alone yields frankincense. The whole country does not produce it: in its midst are the Astramitae, in a district of the Sabaei, which is separated from the incense-bearing region by eight days' journey. It is called Arabia, that is, "sacred", for so it is understood to signify. (**6**) The brushwoods are not public property, but, which is a novelty among barbarian nations, are passed by right of inheritance to family successors. (**7**) Whoever holds mastery over the grove, the Arabians call "sacred". These same men, when they either chop down or cut open the grove, neither take part in funerals nor pollute themselves with the company of women. (**8**) Before the truth was well-known, some used to equate the frankincense tree with the mastic-tree, and others with the terebinth. Then the books which King Juba dedicated to Caesar, son of Augustus, made it plain that it was a tree with twisted twigs and branches like a maple's, which poured forth juice as does the almond-tree, and that it is cut at the beginning of the dog-days, when the sun is at its hottest.

(**9**) Myrrh grows in the same forests. Its roots rejoice when the soil around them is loosened, which produces the same effect as raking grape-vines. When laid bare, the roots flow with thickish tears. The juice which comes forth spontaneously is the more valuable; that elicited by wounds in the bark is judged less so. (10) Its rough bark is twisted into whorls and spikes, and its leaves are similar to those of an olive, though more wrinkled. It grows to a maximum height of five cubits. The Arabians maintain fires with its twigs, the fumes of which are so harmful, that if they did not counteract them with the scent of burned styrax, they would frequently contract incurable diseases.

The same Arabians gather cinnamon.[337] This shrub is grown from a short stalk, with small and stunted branches, and is never above two cubits in height. Those which grow more thinly are considered the more select, while those which grow more thickly are thought less useful. It is collected by priests, who slaughter sacrificial victims beforehand. When favourable omens are given, they are careful that their harvest neither anticipates sunrise nor continues past sunset. Whichever of the priests holds first place divides the piles of twigs with a spear which has been consecrated for this service. A portion of 1/3 is dedicated to the sun, and if it has been divided correctly, it is burned by the sunbeams, and taken up by fire.

(11) Among the same people the phoenix bird is born. It is the size of an eagle, and has plumes projecting from an imposing head into a cone shape. It has tufted cheeks and its neck is a brilliant gold. Its hinder parts are purple, except for the tail, which is of roseate feathers, interspersed with shining sky-blue. (12) It has been proven that the phoenix lives for 540 years. It builds its funeral pyre with cinnamon; it puts it together near Panchaea, and places the heap above the altar in the city of the Sun. (13) Authorities are convinced that its life coincides with the cycle of the Great Year, although many of them say a Great Year lasts not 540 years, but 12,954.[338] (14) When Quintus Plautius and Sextus Papinius were consuls, a phoenix flew into Egypt. It was captured in the 800th year since the founding of the City, by order of the emperor Claudius. It was displayed in the *comitium*. This occasion, contrary to enduring censure, is preserved in the city's records.

(15) The *cinnamolgus* is likewise a bird of Arabia. It weaves its nest from cinnamon fruits in the highest trees. Since the nests are inaccessible, owing to the height and fragility of the branches, the inhabitants aim at the heaps with leaden darts. They sell what they pull down for high prices, because merchants esteem this cinnamon more than others.

(16) The Arabians live far and wide, spread out, with different manners and customs. They have a great deal of hair, wear a headdress on their heads; a part with equal binding around, the beard shaved to their skin.

They busy themselves with trade, not buying foreign wares, but selling their own, as they obviously have both rich forests and rich seas.

(**17**) Shadows which are on the right for us are on the left for them. Some of them live like savages, and eat snakes; they care neither for the soul nor for the body, and therefore are called "snake-eaters".

(**18**) From this sea-coast king Polycrates carried the first sardonyx gem into our world, where it aroused the firebrand of luxury. But the sardonyx is so well-known by everyone, that I think not much need be said about it. Its surface is esteemed if it is an undiluted red; it is rejected if full of sediment. (**19**) Its middle is encircled by a white border. The best type neither scatters its colour into the next section, nor itself borrows from the other. The rest ends in black. If transparent, it is judged faulty: if it wards off clearness, it makes for beauty.

(**20**) The Arabian also finds the *molochite*, which is a richer green than the *smaragdus*. It has a natural power which wards off danger from infants.

The Arabian also finds *iris* in the Red Sea, which is a six-cornered hexagonal quartz-like crystal. When struck by the rays of the sun, it gives a reddish reflection of the air out of itself, like a rainbow.

(**21**) The same Arabians collect *androdamas*, which has a silvery brightness and equal square sides. You might think it borrows somewhat of the diamond. It is supposed it was named for this reason: it assuages the fury of heated minds, and checks swelling anger.

(**22**) We also obtain *paederos* and *arabica* from here. *Arabica* is like ivory: it refuses to be engraved. To those holding it, it is useful against muscle pain. In the *paederos*, all that is excellent is united: it shines like a crystal vessel, and blushes like purple cloth. It has a golden halo on its outermost edge, which looks as though it were underwater. It affects the eyes with this beauty, and draws the vision, holding the gaze of those who regard it. Due to its agreeableness, it is also pleasing to the Indians.

(**23**) I have said enough about Arabia. Let us return to Pelusium.

CHAPTER XXXIV

(1) From Pelusium, Mount Cassius is also the shrine of Jupiter Cassius. Ostracine is the place renowned for the tomb of Pompey the Great. Idumaea, rich in date-palms, begins from here. Next is Ioppe, which is the oldest town in the entire world, in as much as it was founded before the inundation of the lands. (2) This town displays a rock which to this day retains traces of the chains used to bind Andromeda. Rumour set it about (and not in vain) that she was exposed here to the sea-creature. Marcus Scaurus exhibited the bones of this monster at Rome, among other marvels, during his aedileship. (3) The occurrence was noted in the chronicles, and measurements were preserved in trustworthy books: the length of the ribs exceeded 40 feet, and the monster was loftier than the elephants of India. Furthermore, the vertebrae of its spine were more than half a foot wide.

CHAPTER XXXV

(**1**) Judaea is famous for its waters, but the nature of all these waters is not the same. The river Jordan is exceptionally sweet; it is discharged from the spring Paneas, and flows past the most beautiful regions. Soon it is plunged into Lake Asphaltites, and is tainted by its waters. (**2**) Asphaltites brings forth bitumen;[339] it is not inhabited by any animals. Nothing can drown in it. Even bulls and camels have swum there without coming to harm.

(**3**) There is also Lake Sara, which extends for 16 miles, surrounded by very many celebrated cities, itself equal to the best of them in merit. But Lake Tiberias is set before all: it is salubrious with natural heat, and the use of its waters is efficacious in promoting health.

(**4**) The capital of Judaea was Jerusalem, but it was destroyed.[340] Jericho succeeded it, but was also abandoned, conquered in the war with Artaxerxes.[341]

The spring Callirrhoe is next to Jerusalem, and is greatly commended for its curative heat. It is called thus for praise of its waters.

(**5**) Balsam is produced in this land. Until our victory, the crop was confined within the borders of 20 *iugera* of land. But when we got possession of Judaea, the groves were so increased that now we are yielded balsam by very extensive hills.

The balsam-tree has stocks similar to the grape-vine. It is planted with a mallet-shoot,[342] and flourishes with drag-hoes. It rejoices in water, and loves to be pruned. Its leaves are tenacious, and the tree is perpetually covered. (**6**) The wood in the trunk dies without delay if it is touched with iron. Because of this, they are wounded (but only in the bark) with a cunning slit, made either with glass or little knives made of bone. Out of this slit pours gum of excellent sweetness. After the sap, the fruit holds the second place in value, the bark the third, and the final honour is given to the wood.

(**7**) Far from Jerusalem lies a sorrowful bay. It was stricken by heaven, as the black soil, which scatters like ashes, testifies. (**8**) Here there were two towns, one named Sodom, and the other Gomorrah; near to them grows a kind of apple, which, although it may appear ripe, cannot be eaten. For the outer skin contains only ashy soot, which, when lightly touched, puffs out like smoke and crumbles into airborne dust.[343]

(**9**) The inner west of Judaea is held by the Esseni, who, gifted with a remarkable discipline, have withdrawn from the customs of all other peoples, fastened to their tradition, as I believe, by the providence of divine majesty. There are no women there: they have utterly divorced themselves from sexual appetite. They do not know money. They live on dates. (10) Nobody is born there, but they do not lack a multitude of men. The place is devoted to modesty: although very many men from peoples all about hurry there, nobody is admitted unless he is worthy, accompanied by true faith and integrity. (11) He who is guilty of even a minor crime, however much he wishes to gain entry with the highest influence, is debarred by divine influence. Thus, incredible to say, this people is perpetual through an immense space of time, though free of child-birth.

(12) The town Engada was among the Esseni, but it was destroyed. Nevertheless, the beauty of its celebrated and noteworthy forests, with their groves and date-palms, endures, diminished by neither time nor war.

At the border of Judaea is the fortress Massada.

CHAPTER XXXVI

(1) I will pass over Damascus, Philadelphia and Raphana, but I will tell of the first inhabitants and founder of Scythopolis. When Father Liber had given his nurse to the earth, he founded this town in order to increase the distinction of her grave with the walls of a town. (2) As inhabitants were wanting, he chose Scythians from among his companions. In order to strengthen their resolve towards ready resistance against invaders, he gave their name to the place as a reward. (3) In Seleucia, near Antioch, there is another Mount Cassius.[344] From its summit, the sun's globe is visible from the fourth watch, and by a small rotation of the body (the rays dissipating the heat), day can be discerned on one side, and night on the other. The view from Cassius is so great that you may see the light earlier than the day begins.

CHAPTER XXXVII

(1) The Euphrates river flows out of Greater Armenia. It rises above Zima, below the roots of a mountain next to Scythia, which the local people name Catotes. Here it receives several other rivers into itself, and grows strong. Filled full with the converging waters, it struggles against the obstruction of Mount Taurus, which it splits at Elegea, although the mountain resists it with a width of twelve miles. After running a long time, it leaves Commagene on the right and Arabia on the left. (2) Flowing past many peoples, it divides Babylon, once the capital of the Chaldaeans. It enriches Mesopotamia with yearly floods, which cover the land like the river of the Egyptians does. It brings fertility to the soil at almost the same time as does the Nile, when the sun is located in the 20th part of Cancer. The flood is lessened when the sun has passed through Leo and is making its journey towards the uttermost reaches of Virgo. (3) The gnomonicists[345] contend that the sun falls in similar parallels, which the right-angled symmetry of the line makes equal in position in the lands. (4) Whence, it appears that these two rivers, although they flow out of different regions, are located to the measure of the same plumbline, and have the same cause of increase.

(5) It seems reasonable to speak now of the river Tigris. It raises its head in a region of Armenia. It flows marvellously clear, from a famous spring in a high place which is named Elegos. It is not large right at its beginning. At first it flows slowly, and not under its own name, but when it reaches the frontiers of the Medes, it is called "Tigris", for this is the Medes' word for "arrow". (6) It flows into Lake Aretisa, which supports all weights.[346] Aretisa's fish never enter the channel of the Tigris, nor do the river's fish go across into the lake. The river passes through the lake swiftly, and is a different colour. Soon the Tigris comes up against Taurus, and is drowned in a deep cave. It flows underneath, and shoots out the other side at Zomada, dragging sedges and much other rubbish along with itself. Then, it repeatedly sinks down and resurges. It flows past the Adiabeni and the Arabians. It embraces Mesopotamia and receives the most noble river Choaspes; it carries the Euphrates into the Persian Gulf.

(7) As many countries as drink from the Euphrates glitter with a different stone. *Zmilanthis* is gathered in the channel of the river itself. It is a gem with the appearance of Proconnesian marble, except that the middle of the greyish stone shines forth like the pupil of an eye.

(8) *Sagda* has come to us all the way from the Chaldaeans. It would be by no means easy to find, if it did not, as they say, give itself up to be seized.

For its inborn spirit seeks ships which pass over it in the depths, and it joins itself tenaciously to their keels. It is difficult to take *sagda* off except by shaving away some of the timber. **(9)** This *sagda*, because of its known properties, is held in highest esteem among the Chaldaeans. It is green, and because of this charm, it is liked more than other stones.

(10) A myrrh-stone is common among the Parthians. If you judge this stone by eye, it is not impressive, being the colour of myrrh. But if you happen to investigate it more thoroughly, and arouse it by chafing it until it is hot, it breathes out the sweetness of nard.

(11) In Persia, there is so great an abundance and diversity of stones that it would be a lengthy matter merely to recall their names. **(12)** *Mithridax*, when struck by the sun, flashes with many colours.

Tecolithos is spurned when looked upon, as it is similar in appearance to an olive-stone. But its medicinal virtue conquers the beauty of other stones. When it is dissolved and drunk it gets rid of kidney stones and relieves bladder pain.

(13) The *hammochrysos*, in sands mingled with gold, has little squares now of gold-leaf, now of dust.

(14) *Aëtites* is yellow and smooth. It holds another stone inside it, and resounds with its rattling when moved. However, they say that the little stone inside does not make the clanging, but the spirit of the most knowledgeable. **(15)** Zoroaster gives preference to this stone above all others and assigns the greatest power to it. It is found either in the nests of eagles or on the shores of the sea, most of all in Persia. Bound under the hope of the womb, it protects a woman from miscarriage.

(16) *Pyrites* is black, and does not permit itself to be strongly held. If ever it is tightly pressed in the hand, it burns the fingers.

(17) *Chalazias* has the shape and whiteness of a hailstone, with the most durable and invincible hardness.

Echites has spots like those of a viper.

(18) *Dionysias* is dusky and sprinkled with red spots. This same, if ground up and mixed with water, is redolent of wine, and (what is a wonder with that scent) resists drunkenness.

(19) *Glossopetra* falls from the sky when the moon is waning. It is similar in appearance to the human tongue. The Magi hold it to be of considerable power, and think that it causes the lunar movements.

(20) The Jewel of the Sun is very white, and looks like a glittering star; it throws golden-red rays out of itself.

The Hair of Venus has a dark shine, showing inside it the likeness of red hair.

(21) *Selenites* is transparent, with a white and honey-coloured radiance. It contains an image of the moon; they say that it diminishes or increases from day to day, according to the course of the planet itself.

(22) *Meconites* resembles poppies.

Myrmectites is inscribed with the likeness of crawling ants.

Chalcophthongos resounds like beaten bronze. Kept virtuously, it preserves clearness of voice.

(23) *Siderites* looks the same as iron. It is truly noxious: wherever it is brought, it arouses discord.

Phlogites shows within itself the likeness of billowing flames.

Anthracias glitters with sparkling stars.

(24) *Enhydros* sweats, so you might think a gushing spring was enclosed in it.

CHAPTER XXXVIII

(1) If we speak of Cilicia (which is now to be done) as it is now, we shall seem to detract from the credit of antiquity, but if we describe the borders which it once had, it would be inconsistent with present circumstances. Therefore, the best we can do between each fault is to report the situation of the country in both eras.

(2) Formerly, Cilicia extended all the way to Pelusium in Egypt. The Lydians, Medes, Armenians, Pamphylia and Cappadocia were under the rule of the Cilicians.[347] Soon it was subdued by the Assyrians, and smaller bounds were decreed for it.

Most of Cilicia lies in the plain. It receives the Issican sea into a wide bay, and is closed in behind by the mountain ridges of Taurus and Amanus.

(3) The name of the country derives from Cilix, concealed from us by an ancient age, almost beyond the reach of memory. It is said Cilix was the son of Phoenix (who is older than Jupiter), one of the first nurslings of the Earth.

Cilicia has Tarsus, mother of cities, founded by Perseus, the famous son of Danae. (4) The city is intersected by the river Cydnus. Some record that this Cydnus is cast down from Taurus, others that it is diverted from the channel of the Choaspes. The river Choaspes is so sweet that the Persian kings, as long as it flows between banks of Persian soil, claim draughts of it for themselves only. When they go abroad they carry its waters along with them. (5) From this parent, Cydnus draws its wondrous sweetness. Whatever is white, the Syrians call "cydnus" in their native tongue, whence the name was given to this river. In the spring, when the snows are melting, it swells; during the rest of the year, it is quiet and feeble.

(6) Around Corycus in Cilicia the saffron is most plentiful and the best. Although Sicily, Cyrene and Lycia produce saffron, the Corycian variety is supreme. It is the more fragrant, and more golden in colour; its juices are more effective for medicines. (7) There is also a town Corycos, and a cave, which carves out the mountain on the edge of the sea from the highest summit. It gapes in a very wide chasm. Its sides drop down into the depths of the earth, surrounding the middle emptiness with a wooded circle. Inside, it is verdant with hanging greenery. (8) The descent into it is 2½ miles long, lit with plentiful sunlight, and constantly gushing with springs. When you come to the bottom of the first gulf, another cave is spread out. This cavern is at first open with wide passages; after a while it

is darkened by progress into narrow places. In this cave is a sacred shrine of Jupiter. Those who so wish believe that the bed of the giant Typhon was placed in its innermost recess.

(**9**) Heliopolis was the ancient capital of Cilicia. It was the hometown of Chrysippus, most potent in Stoic wisdom. It was conquered by Tigranes the Armenian, and for a long time bore the name Soli. Gnaeus Pompey the Great, after defeating the Cilicians, surnamed it "Pompeiopolis".

(**10**) Mount Taurus first rises from the Indian Sea. Having cast itself towards the north on the right side, and towards the southern region on the left, and turned its front full towards the west, it goes between the Egyptian and Pamphylian Seas at the Rocks of Chelidon. It is clear that it wishes to extend the lands and penetrate the sea; but the resistance of the deep forbids it to extend its roots further. (**11**) Indeed, those who treat the natures of places show that it has attempted all passages with its promontories. Wherever it is bathed by the sea, it goes forth into projections, but it is hindered, now by the Phoenician gulf, now by the Pontic, sometimes by the Caspian or Hyrcanian. Thereupon, broken by these struggles, it writhes towards Lake Maeotis. Wearied by its many troubles, it joins itself to the ridges of the Ripaean mountains. (**12**) It is diversely named for the variety of nations and tongues it passes. Among the Indians it is Imaeus and Propansius; among the Parthians Choatras, after Niphates. Thence, it is Taurus, and where it rises to the highest altitudes, Caucasus. It also draws names from peoples. On the right side it is called Caspius or Hyrcanus; on the left, Amazonicus, Mosichus, and Scythicus. Besides these names, it has many others. (**13**) Where it splits open into gaping ridges, it makes gates, the first of which are the Armenian, then Caspian, and finally Cilician.

Taurus stretches forth a peak into Greece, which is known as Ceraunius. From the frontiers of Cilicia, it forms the border of Asia. As much of it as faces the south is scorched by the sun; whatever is opposite the north is beaten by winds and snow. Where it is wooded, it is wild, with many beasts and monstrous lions.

CHAPTER XXXIX

(**1**) While in Campania there is Vesuvius, and in Sicily, Etna, in Lycia there is Mount Chimaera. This mountain breathes out smoke during nocturnal seethings, whence the fable of a three-formed monster was brought about amongst the common people. They thought this animal was the Chimaera.[348] Seeing that the same fiery nature was beneath, the Lycians dedicated their nearest city to Vulcan, and called it Hephaestia, after his original name.

(**2**) Olympus was also, among others there, a famous town, but it was destroyed. Now it is a fortress. Within it are waters called "royal", for reason of the notable spectacle the flow presents to visitors.

CHAPTER XL

(1) Asia comes next, but I do not mean to speak of the Asia which, in the third separation of the world, has rivers as its borders: the Nile from the Egyptian Sea and the Tanais from Lake Maeotis. I will speak of Asia as beginning from Telmessus in Lycia, whence the Carpathian gulf also has its genesis. Lycia and Phrygia enclose this part of Asia from the east, the shores of the Aegean in the west, the Egyptian Sea in the south, and Paphlagonia in the north.[349]

(2) Ephesus is the most famous city in this region. The glory of Ephesus is the temple of Diana, work of the Amazons. It was so magnificent that Xerxes, when he had burned down all the other temples in Asia, spared it. (3) But Xerxes' clemency did not long protect these sacred shrines from evil. For Herostratus, in order to immortalise his name by committing a crime, set fire to the noble building with his own hands, from a desire to achieve wider fame, as he himself confessed. (4) It is recorded that the temple of Ephesus was burned down on the same day as Alexander the Great was born at Pella. He arose, as Nepos says, when Marcus Fabius Ambustus and Titus Quintius Capitolinus were consuls, in the 385th year since the founding of the City. (5) When afterwards the Ephesians restored it to an even more imposing grandeur, the craftsman Dinocrates was in charge of the work. This Dinocrates, as we explained above, designed Alexandria in Egypt by order of Alexander.[350]

The disasters in Asia have made it clear that nowhere else in the world are there such incessant earthquakes and frequent devastations of cities. In the reign of Tiberius, twelve cities fell simultaneously in one ruin.

(6) The talent of Asia is celebrated throughout the world. For poetry, there was Anacreon, Mimnermus, Antimachus, Hipponax and Alcaeus. Among them was also a woman, Sappho. The historians were Xanthus, Hecataeus, Herodotus, Ephorus and Theopompus. Of the Seven gifted with wisdom, there were Bias, Thales, and Pittacus.[351] Cleanthes was the most eminent of the Stoics; Anaxagoras was a revealer of Nature. Heraclitus devoted his time to the secrets of more subtle learning.

(7) Phrygia succeeds Asia. The town of Celaenae was there; this prior name was rejected and changed to Apamea, a town afterwards established by King Seleucus.

There Marsyas was born, and there he was buried, whence a nearby stream is called "Marsyas". (8) For not far off is a valley which testifies to his deed of sacrilegious rivalry and the audacious *tibiae* against the god, and shows the outcome of the affair.[352] It is ten miles from Apamea, and is called Aulocrene to this day. The river Maeander rises from the citadel of this town. It is sinuous, and its banks wind between Caria and Ionia. It discharges into the bay which divides Miletus and Priene.

(9) Phrygia itself is behind Troas. Its northern parts border on Galatia, and the southern on Lycaonia, Pisidia and Mygdonia. On the eastern side it is neighbour to Lydia, in the north to Moesia, and to Caria on the side which faces midday. The Lydian mountain Tmolus blooms with saffron. (10) The river Pactolus, which rushes with a golden flow, others call the Chrysorrhoa.

In these parts an animal called the *bonacus* is produced. Its head and the body which follows is like that of an ox, except that it has a mane like a horse's. Its horns run back on themselves with such multitudinous winding that if someone bumps against them, he is not wounded. (11) The protection the forehead denies to this monster is provided by its belly. When it turns to flee, it discharges dung with a quick evacuation of its stomach, for a length of three *iugera*. The heat of the dung burns whatever it touches. Thus it wards off pursuers with its noxious secretions.

(12) Miletus is the capital of Ionia. It was formerly the residence of Cadmus, who first founded the discipline of prose composition.

(13) Not far from Ephesus is the community of Colophon, which is famous for the oracle of Clarian Apollo. Mount Mimas rises near here. Its summits show the nature of oncoming weather by the clouds flying above.

(14) The capital of Maeonia is Sipylus, formerly called Tantalis. The bereavements of Niobe preserve the memory of the name.[353]

(15) The river Meles flows around Smyrna. Among the streams of Asia, it is easily the principal river.

The river Hermus severs the plains of Smyrna; it rises in Dorylaeum in Phrygia, and divides Phrygia from Caria. The ancients also believed that the Hermus foamed with waves of gold.

(16) Smyrna is especially famous as the homeland of the poet Homer, who died in the 272nd year after the fall of Troy, when Agrippa Silvius, son of Tiberinus, was king at Alba, in the 160th year before the foundation of the city. (17) 138 years intercede between Homer and Hesiod, who died at the beginning of the 1st Olympiad.

On the Rhoetian shore, the Athenians and Mytileneans established the town Achillion, at the tomb of the Thessalian leader. It is pretty well ruined.

(18) Next, almost 40 stadia away, in another nook of the same shore, is a town which was built by the Rhodians in honour of Aias of Salamis, to which they gave the name Aeantium.

(19) Hard by Ilium stands the tomb of Memnon. Birds from Aethiopia continually fly to it in flocks. The people of Ilium call them the *Memnoniae*. The author Cremutius records that these same birds gather in Aethiopia from every side in flocks every fifth year, from wherever in the world they might be, and come together at the palace of Memnon.

(20) The inland areas which are above a part of Troas are the region of Teuthrania, which was the native land of the Moesi. Teuthrania is watered by the river Caicus.

(21) There are many chameleons in Asia. The chameleon is a four-footed creature which looks like a lizard, except it has longer, straight legs which are joined to its belly. It has a long twisty tail, and hooked claws with a subtle inward curvature. It moves slowly, having almost the same gait as a tortoise. The skin of its body is rough, as I have indicated is the case with crocodiles. (22) Its eyes are withdrawn into sunken recesses, and it never obscures them by blinking. It sees not by moving its pupils around, but by directing the gaze of its rigid orbs. It gapes eternally, and without any reason, since it neither captures food nor is sustained by drink. It lives by no other nourishment than by draughts of the air. (23) Its colour is variable, and changes in a moment. It becomes the same colour as whatever it joins itself to. There are two colours which it is not powerful enough to create: white and red. The rest it can easily imitate. Its body is almost without flesh, and the vitals without a spleen. It has little blood, except in its heart. It lies hidden during winter, and comes forth in the spring. (24) It is poisonous to ravens. If it is killed by a raven, it destroys the very conqueror which has killed it, for if the bird consumes even a little of it, it immediately perishes. But the raven has a defence, as Nature has stretched forth its hand with a cure. When the raven understands itself to be afflicted, it eats a laurel leaf, and is restored to health.

(25) There is a place in Asia in the open plains called Pythonos Come,[354] where all the storks fly at the time of their first arrival. They tear to pieces the one who gets there last. These birds, they say, have no tongues, and the rattling sound they make is produced by their mouths rather than by their voices. (26) Storks possess extraordinary *pietas*: the same length

COLLECTION OF MARVELLOUS THINGS

of time as they spend educating their young, they themselves are in turn nourished by their own chicks. They cherish their nests so immoderately, that they lose their feathers from the constant sitting. **(27)** It is regarded an impious act in all places to harm storks, but in Thessaly most of all. Here there is an abundance of frightful serpents, which the storks pursue and eat, thus removing much evil from the Thessalian region.

CHAPTER XLI

(1) Galatia was captured in early times by the Tolosboci, the Veturi and the Ambituuti, ancient nations of the Gauls whose names survive to this day. Why Galatia was called so is expressed by the name itself.

CHAPTER XLII

(**1**) Bithynia is at the entrance of Pontus, facing towards the region of the eastern sun and opposite Thrace. It is wealthy, and rich in cities. It begins at the springs of the river Sagaris. Formerly it was called Bebrycia, then Mygdonia, then Bithynia, after King Bithynus.

(**2**) The river Hylas flows into this country and into the city of Prusias. Lake Hylas also waters the country; it is believed that the boy Hylas, the delight of Hercules, who was raped by the Nymphs, rests there. In his memory, the people to this day perform a ceremonial run around the lake and shout out "Hylas!"[355]

(**3**) In Bithynia, hard by Nicomedia, is a place called Libyssa, famous for the tomb of Hannibal. After his judgment at Carthage, he fled to King Antiochus; after Antiochus' unfortunate battle at Thermopylae, the king being discomfited by the vagaries of fortune, he resorted to the hospitality of Prusias. Lest he be handed over to Titus Quintius, who was sent into Bithynia for this reason, and come to Rome as a captive, he poisoned himself, and defended himself against Roman chains by death.

CHAPTER XLIII

(1) On the coast of Pontus, after the straits of Bosporus, the river Rhesus and the port of Calpae, is the river Sagaris, which rises in Phrygia; it is called "Sagarius" by many. It makes the beginning of the Mariandynian gulf, on which is the town Heraclea, on the river Lycus, and the port Acone. Acone is famous for the prospering of wicked weeds; we name noxious herbs "aconite" after this place. (2) Nearby is the Acherusian cave, which, they say, is a dark fissure opening to deep places extending all the way to Hell.

CHAPTER XLIV

(**1**) Paphlagonia is surrounded in the rear by the marches of Galatia. Paphlagonia faces Taurica from the promontory of Carambis, and rises to Mount Cytorus, which extends for 36 miles. It is famous for the place called Enetus, from which, as Cornelius Nepos holds, the Paphlagonians, soon to be known as the Veneti, crossed over into Italy.

(**2**) The Milesians founded many cities in this region. Mithridates founded Eupatoria, which was subdued by Pompey and named Pompeiopolis.

CHAPTER XLV

(1) Of all the realms which neighbour on the Black Sea, Cappadocia withdraws the furthest distance inland. On the left side, it passes both the Armenias and Commagene; on the right, it is surrounded by many Asian peoples. It goes on to the ridges of Taurus and the rising of the sun. It passes by Lycaonia, Pisidia and Cilicia. (2) It goes above the tracts of Syrian Antioch, and continues into Scythia at another point. It is divided from Greater Armenia by the river Euphrates. Greater Armenia begins where the mountains of Panedrus are.

(3) There are many famous cities in Cappadocia. In order to turn my feet from the others, I will mention the colony Archelais, which was settled by Claudius Caesar. The river Halys flows next to it. (4) The Lycus bathes Neocaesarea; Semiramis founded Melita. The Cappadocians reckon Mazaca, which is situated below Argaeus, to be the mother of cities. Argaeus is high among the snowy ridges. Indeed, it does not lack hoar-frost even in the burning summer. The local people believe that a god lives there.

(5) This land, before all others, nourishes horses, and is most accommodating to equine success. I suppose, therefore, that the nature of horses must be here investigated. (6) Many examples have revealed that horses possess discernment, since several have been found which would recognise only their first masters. If ever they changed their accustomed master, they became forgetful of their tameness. So well do horses know those inimical to their side that in battle they attack and bite their enemies. (7) But this is a greater thing: when horses have lost riders whom they held dear, they bring death upon themselves by starvation. These characteristics are to be found in the most outstanding type of horse, for those who are of inferior breeding have given no accounts of themselves. (8) Lest we appear to make over-free claims against the truth, we will give a few examples.

Bucephalus, the horse of Alexander the Great, was called so either because of his wild appearance, or because of the mark, shaped like a bull's head, which he had branded on his shoulder, or because of certain little horns which protruded from his forehead when he was angry. He would calmly allow his groom to ride him, but when he bore the royal saddle he would deign to carry no-one but his master. (9) There are more than enough proofs of him in battle, when, by his own efforts, he carried Alexander out safely from the harshest conflicts. For this service, when he died in India, the king led his funeral procession, gave him a tomb, and even founded a city which he called Bucephala, in memory of his name. (10) The horse of Gaius Caesar[356] would not permit anyone to ride him except Caesar. They say that his front hooves had the appearance of human feet, just as on the statue placed before the shrine of Caesar's ancestress Venus. (11) When a victorious antagonist wished to despoil a king of Scythia whom he had killed in single combat, he was mangled by the heels and teeth of the king's horse.

Tombs of horses are common in the region of Agrigentum. This observance, we believe, was given for services of the highest honour.

(12) Spectacles in the circus have shown that horses take pleasure in such things. Some horses are provoked into running by the songs of *tibiae*, some by dancing, some by the different colours, and not a few by the lighted torches.

(13) Tears prove equine affection. When King Nicomedes died, his horse rejected life by way of starvation. When Antiochus had conquered the Galatians in battle, he was set to rejoice, and mounted the horse of the leader Cintaretus, who had been killed in the fight. The horse scorned the sharp-toothed curb to such a degree that he fell, and threw down both himself and his rider into equal ruin.

(14) The games in the Circus also showed the talents of Claudius Caesar's horses. When the driver of the four-horse chariot fell, they outstripped their opponents not less by cunning than by speed. After the correct distance had been run, they stopped at the place of the palm, demanding as it were, the reward for victory. (15) Some other horses also threw off their charioteer (who was named Rutumanna), took the chariot from the contest, and sprang forth to the Capitoline, not halting before traversing Jupiter Tarpeius three times on the right. (16) The male of this type of animal lives longer. Indeed, we have read of a horse which lived to 70 years of age. It is unambiguous that they can engender offspring in the 33rd year, inasmuch as they are sent to stud after their 20th year. A horse called Opus is also noted, who continued to serve the herd until his 40th year. (17) The lust of mares is extinguished by clipping their manes. A love-poison is produced in the foreheads of newly-born foals. It is dark in colour, like a fig, and is called *hippomanes*. If it is immediately snatched away, the mother will never offer the youngster her teats to suck.

(18) The fiercer and braver a horse is, the deeper he will plunge his nostrils into water when drinking.

Male horses are never taken to the wars by the Scythians, because the females can empty their bladders in flight.

Mares bring forth offspring sired by the wind, but they never live longer than three years.

CHAPTER XLVI

(1) Assyria begins at Adiabene, where the region of Arbela is. The victory of Alexander the Great does not allow this place to be passed over. For here he routed Darius' forces, and overcame the man himself. When his camp was plundered, a box crammed with unguents was found among the remaining possessions of the king, whence Roman excess first made contact with foreign perfumes.[357] (2) Nevertheless, for some time we were defended from the allurements of these vices by the men of old, even in the time of the Censors Publius Licinius Crassus and Gaius Julius Caesar. These men, in the 565th year since the foundation of the City, forbade the importation of foreign unguents. (3) Afterwards, our vices triumphed, and the delights of perfumes became pleasing even to the Senate. They were even a feature in punishments, as in the case of Lucius Plotius, brother of Plancus, who was twice consul. Proscribed by the Triumvirs, the perfume of his unguents betrayed his hiding-place in Salernum.[358]

(4) Media follows these lands. A tree of this country became famous because of the Mantuan poems.[359] The tree itself is huge, and its leaves are like those of a strawberry tree, only differing in one respect: they are prickly, with pointed spines. It bears a fruit which is inimical to poisons. It has a harsh taste, as of the bitterness of unmixed wine. Its fragrance is more than pleasant, and is discernible from far off. (5) Its fruitfulness is such that it is always weighed down with the burden of its produce, for immediately the fruit ripens and falls, others grow. The abundance has only this delay: the fruit must fall before others can be grown.

(6) Other nations have wished to grow these trees themselves, through the industry of transported shoots, but Nature resists, and other lands are not able to borrow the bounty given to Median soil.

CHAPTER XLVII

(1) The Caspian Gates extend for eight miles through a man-made passage. Their width is scarcely enough to admit a wagon. In these narrow places is also this difficulty: the rocks of the precipitous sides, owing to veins of melting salt, sweat out copious moisture, which is congealed by the force of the heat, as it were, into summer ice. Thus the way becomes impassable.

(2) In addition, the whole region, for 28 miles, in whichever direction one proceeds, has arid soil, and there is thirst without respite.

Serpents from surrounding lands come together here immediately upon the arrival of spring. Thus, the concurrence of danger and difficulty denies access to the Caspian except during winter.

CHAPTER XLVIII

(1) Eastwards from the Caspian is a place called Direum. Nothing can be compared to its fruitfulness. The Lapyri, Narici and Hyrcani live around about this place. (2) The region of Margiana is close by. It is famous for the commodiousness of its weather and its soil. This is true to such a degree that in all this land, Margiana alone rejoices in vines. It is enclosed by mountains, like a theatre, for the extent of 1500 stadia. It is almost inaccessible by reason of the dangerous sandy wilderness which surrounds it for 120 miles on every side. (3) Alexander the Great so admired the amenity of this region that he founded the first Alexandria there. Soon destroyed by the barbarians, it was restored by Antiochus, son of Seleucus, and called Seleucia, after the name of his house. The circumference of the city is 75 stadia. Into this city Orodes brought the Romans captured at the defeat of Crassus. (4) Alexander established another town on the Caspian, which was called Heraclea while it lasted. But it also was ruined by the same peoples, and then rebuilt by Antiochus. He preferred that it should afterwards be named Achais.

CHAPTER XLIX

(**1**) The river Oxus[360] rises from Lake Oaxus. The Bateni and the Oxistacae peoples dwell on the shores of this river, but the Bactrians hold the principal part of it. The Bactrians also have a river of their own, the Bactros, after which they named the town they inhabit, Bactrus.

(**2**) Those of these people which are behind,[361] are encircled by the ridges of the Propanisus mountains. Those opposite are restricted by the springs of the Indus. The rest are enclosed by the river Ochus.

(**3**) Above these peoples is Panda, the town of the Sogdiani, on whose borders Alexander the Great founded the third Alexandria, to commemorate the limits of his journey. (**4**) For here is the place where first Father Liber, then Hercules, then Semiramis and finally Cyrus set up altars. All considered this the most glorious—that his journey extended all the way to this place.

(**5**) The river Jaxartes[362] divides the borders of this whole generalship from the adjoining lands. The Bactrians alone call it the Jaxartes, for the other Scythians name it the Silis. The army of Alexander the Great believed this river to be the Tanais. Demodamas,[363] a captain of Seleucus and Antiochus, a sufficiently able author, crossed this river, going beyond the monuments of all, and discovered it to be different from the Tanais. (**6**) In order to advance his name, for the sake of commemoration of his glory, he built a high altar to Apollo Didymaeus.

It is here that the borders of the Persians and the Scythians come together. The Persians call the Scythians *Sacae* in their language; in turn, the Scythians name the Persians *Chorsaci*, and the Caucasus mountains *Croucasis*, that is, "white with snow".

(**7**) A great number of peoples here have observed the same law as the Parthians, with uncorrupted discipline, from the beginning of the agreed custom. The most famous of these are the Massagetae, the Essedones, the Satarchae and the Apalaei. (**8**) After these, as the most savage barbarians intercede, we shall direct our attention—almost inconstantly—to the well-known facts concerning the customs of other nations.

(**9**) Bactria produces the most powerful camels. Although Arabia also breeds many camels, they are different. The Arabian type has a double hump on its back, and the Bactrian a single hump. They never wear away their feet, for their feet are fleshy with certain backwards-facing excrescences of a lung-like quality. Thence, there is an antithetical problem when they walk: there is no supporting protection for the pressure of standing.[364] They are used for two purposes. Some are suitable for bearing burdens, while others are swifter. They will not accept a more than reasonable load, and neither will they wish to go beyond an accustomed distance. (10) At mating time they are enraged by lust to such a degree that they are cruel when they seek their pleasure. They hate horses. They endure thirst for four days. When an opportunity of drinking arises, they take enough to satisfy themselves for their past privation, and to serve them for a long time in the future. (11) They desire muddy water, and refuse clear. Unless the liquid is already rather filthy, they stir up the silt by continuous trampling so it becomes turbid.

They live for 100 years, unless by chance they are carried across into a foreign country, and contract diseases from the changed air.

The females are prepared for the wars. It was found that their desire to mate is removed by a certain operation. For it is thought that camels become stronger if they are prevented from mating.

CHAPTER L

(1) Where our course is turned to the Eastern Ocean, from the Scythian Ocean and the Caspian Sea, there are at first deep snows. Soon there are huge wastes, then the Anthropophagi, the most savage of races, then regions overrun with wild beasts. Almost half the distance is rendered impassable. (2) A mountain overhanging the sea, which the barbarians call Tabis, signals the end of these difficulties. After, there are still extensive wildernesses. Along the expanse of this shore, which faces the summer east, the first men we are aware of after the wild places are the Seres people. They flood leaves with sprinklings of water, and comb out the fleeces of the trees by means of the liquid; they subdue the delicate fineness of the down to subservience by moisture. (3) This is the silk permitted for common use to the detriment of strictness. Because of it, lust for luxury persuaded in the first place women, and now even men, to exhibit rather than to clothe their bodies.

The Seres are gentle and very peaceful among themselves. They otherwise shun the society of the rest of mankind, to such a degree that they reject the trade of other nations. (4) The merchants go across their land on the principal river. On the banks, with no verbal exchange between the parties, the Seres judge the value of the things put down with their eyes, and hand over their own wares, but do not buy ours.

CHAPTER LI

(1) The Attacene gulf, and the race of the Attacori follow. To them prerogative furnishes marvellous clemency and temperance of air. Indeed, the hills ward off noxious breezes. The hills are cast out on all sides, and the healthful sunniness is shut off; the hills prevent unhealthy airs. For that reason, as Amometus[365] affirms, the lifestyle of the Attacori is similar to that of the Hyperboreans. Between this people and India, the most knowledgeable writers locate the Ciconae.

CHAPTER LII

(1) India begins from the Median mountains, and extends from the southern to the eastern sea. It is most salubrious, owing to the breezes of the west wind. It has summer twice in a year, and collects the harvest twice in a year.

(2) Posidonius thinks that it stands opposite Gaul. Surely there can be no doubt in the matter, for India was discovered by Alexander the Great, and afterwards scoured by the diligence of other kings, and it has wholly yielded to our knowledge. (3) Indeed, Megasthenes[366] stayed for some time with the kings of India, and wrote on things Indian, in order that he might give the truth, which he had seen with his own eyes, to posterity. Dionysus[367] also, who was sent by King Philadelphus as a witness, for the sake of testing the truth, wrote the same. (4) They report that there are 5,000 large towns in India, and 9,000 peoples. India was also for a long time believed to comprise a third of the world. This abundance of men and cities is not remarkable, since the Indians alone have never moved away from their native soil.

(5) Father Liber was the first to enter India, inasmuch as he was the first to hold a triumph. 6,451 years and three months are numbered between him and Alexander the Great. The reckoning is calculated via the kings, 153 of whom were discovered to have reigned in this time.

(6) The greatest rivers in the land are the Ganges and the Indus. Some hold that the Ganges rises from unknown springs and floods in the manner of the Nile; others prefer to believe it begins in the mountains of Scythia. (7) The Hypanis is also a very notable river. It was the end of the march of Alexander the Great, as the altars set up on the banks testify. The minimum width of the Ganges is eight miles, and the maximum twenty. The depth, where it is shallowest, is 100 feet.

(8) The Gangaridae are the most distant of India's people. Their king has 1,000 knights, 700 elephants and 60,000 foot-soldiers in his army.

(9) Certain of the Indians cultivate the fields; most of them serve in the military. Others deal in merchandise. The best and wealthiest attend to public affairs: they administer justice and sit alongside the kings.

There is there a quiet class, of very distinguished wisdom. When they have had their fill of life, they bring death on themselves by throwing themselves on lighted funeral pyres.

(10) Those who abandon themselves to a more savage lifestyle, and pursue existence in the forest, hunt elephants. When the elephants have been tamed, they either plough fields or bear burdens.

(11) There is an island in the Ganges which is occupied by a very populous nation. The king has 50,000 foot-soldiers and 4,000 knights in his armies. Whoever is gifted with royal power does not go to war without a great number of elephants, knights and foot-soldiers.

(12) The Prasians are a very puissant people. They inhabit a city called Palibothra, whence some have named the people themselves the Palibothri. Their king calls 600,000 foot-soldiers, 30,000 knights and 8,000 elephants daily for military service.

(13) Above Palibothra is Mount Malleus. For half the year, in winter, its shadow falls on the northern side, and in summer it falls on the southern side. The Great Bear is visible once a year in this region, for not more than fifteen days. The author Baeton[368] holds that this happens in most parts of India.

(14) The people adjoining the river Indus in the southern regions are, beyond the others, scorched by the heat. The colour of the people reveals the strength of the sun.

(15) The Pygmies hold the mountains. The people who live next to the Ocean live without a king.

The Pandaean people are ruled by women. They deem their first queen to have been a daughter of Hercules.

(16) The city of Nysa is also in this region, and a mountain sacred to Jupiter, by name Meros. Meros has a cave in which the old people among the Indians assert Father Liber to have been reared. From the evidence of the name (the story running riot), it is believed that Liber was born from Jupiter's thigh.[369]

(17) Beyond the mouth of the Indus are two islands, Chryse and Argyre. They are so rich in metals that a great many people have recorded that their soils are composed purely of gold and silver.

(18) All Indians have long flowing hair, dyed a blue or saffron colour. Their chief adornments are precious stones.

(19) Their funerals are without trappings. In addition, as is set forth in the books of the kings Juba and Archelaus, the attires of the peoples are as discrepant as their customs. (20) Some clothe themselves in robes of linen, others in robes of wool. Some go naked, and others cover only their private parts. A great many even dress in flexible tree-bark.

Some peoples are so tall that they can vault over elephants, as though they were horses, with a very easy leap.

(21) Many of them do not deem it good to kill animals, or to eat flesh. The majority are nourished by fish alone, and are sustained by the sea.

(22) There are those who slaughter their kinsfolk and parents before they are diminished by either age or sickness, as though it were a sacrifice. Then they feast on the flesh of those killed. In those parts this is not accounted criminal, but righteous.

(23) There are also those, who, when diseases lie upon them, go far away from others to a secret place, calmly awaiting death.

(24) The territory of the Astacani is green with woods of laurel and groves of box. Indeed, it has very copious harvests of vines and of all the trees which the Greeks delight in.

(25) The Indians have philosophers (they call them "gymnosophists"), who, from the rising to the setting of the sun, fix their eyes on its bright orb, searching the fiery globe for secrets, standing all day on burning sand on alternate feet.

(26) At the mountain called Nulo there live some people who have backwards feet, with eight toes on each.

(27) Megasthenes writes that in the mountains of India there are some people who have heads like dogs, are armed with talons, dress themselves in clothes of hide, and have no human speech, but make barking noises with mouths agape.

(28) In the works of Ctesias,[370] it is said that certain women in India give birth only once, and that the children immediately become grey-haired. It is said in turn that there is another people whose hair is white in youth, and blackens with old age, and that they live many years beyond the limit of our life-spans.

(**29**) We also read of the Monocoli, born with one leg, which is of singular swiftness. When they wish to defend themselves against the heat, they lie on their backs and are shadowed by the great size of their feet.

(**30**) Those who live near the source of the Ganges need no food, and live by the scent of the woodland fruit. When they go on journeys, they carry some in order that they might be nourished by the smell. But if by chance they draw in foetid air, it is certain that they will die.

(**31**) It is also held that there is a type of women who conceive aged five years, but do not live beyond eight years.

(**32**) There are some who are without heads, and have eyes in their shoulders.

There are some who live in the forests, with hairy bodies and teeth like dogs, who make terrifying snarling.

However, among those who take more especial care to live according to reason, many wives are married to the same man; when the husband dies, each speaks of her merits before the most solemn judges. The one who, by the opinion of the judges, was more dutiful and excelled the others, receives this reward: that by her own will she might ascend the pyre of her husband and give herself as an offering at his funeral rites. The rest live in ill-repute.

(**33**) The serpents are of such immensity that they swallow deer and other animals of like size whole. Moreover, as great as the Indian ocean is, they penetrate the islands separated from the mainland by a great distance to seek food. And that this very thing happens is not common knowledge through any great size, so that they may make their way across to the places determined through such a great breadth of sea.

(**34**) There are many wonderful beasts in India. We will examine a few of their great number.

The *leucrocota* excels all beasts in speed. It is the size of a wild ass, and has the haunches of a deer. It has the breast and legs of a lion, the head of a badger, and cloven hooves. Its mouth gapes from ear to ear, and it has continual bone in place of teeth. This is its shape: in voice it imitates the sound of men speaking.

(**35**) There is also the *eale*. Otherwise like the horse, it has a tail like an elephant, is black in colour, and has jaws like a boar. In front it carries horns over a cubit long. These are serviceable for use in what movement it wishes, for they are not rigid, but can be moved, as need requires, for fighting. When it fights, it extends one horn; the other it folds back, so, if the sharpened point of one is spoiled by some blow, the prong of the other succeeds it. It has been compared to the hippopotamus, and indeed, it rejoices in the water of streams.

(36) Indian bulls are tawny in colour, and exceedingly fleet. Their hair is turned backwards, and their heads are all mouth. The hardness of their hides rejects all spears, and they are of such inexorable wildness that when captured they kill themselves from madness.

(37) Amongst these the *mantichore* also is born. It has three ranks of teeth, joined in alternate lots. It has the face of a man, grey eyes, and is the colour of blood. It has the body of a lion, and a tail sharpened like the sting of a scorpion. Its voice is so sibilant that it imitates the songs of pipes and the shouting of trumpets. (38) It avidly desires human flesh. It is so active on its feet, and has such power in its leap, that neither the most extensive spaces nor the widest obstructions can check it.

There are in addition one- and three-horned cattle with solid, not cloven, hooves.

(39) But the cruellest of all is the *monoceros*, a monster which roars horridly, has the body of a horse, the feet of an elephant, the tail of a pig, and the head of a deer. (40) A horn of wonderful lustre sticks out of its forehead, to a length of four feet. It is so sharp that whatever it attacks is easily pierced by its blows. It does not come alive into the power of men. It may, indeed, be killed, but not captured.

(41) The waters bring forth no lesser wonders. The Ganges rears eels 30 feet long. Statius Sebosus[371] says, among especial marvels, that this same river abounds in worms, blue in both name and colour. They have two arms, not less than six cubits in length, of such great strength that they drag elephants who come to drink into the depths, seizing their trunks by biting.

(42) Indian seas have whales bigger than four *iugera* in size. They are called *physeterae*, and are huge beyond the bulk of mighty pillars. They lift themselves above the yard-arms of ships, and discharge such a tide (which they have sucked up) from their water-pipes that they often sink the mariners' ships with their rainy floods.

(43) India alone breeds the parrot, which is green in colour with a crimson neck. Its beak is so hard that when it casts itself down from on high, it saves itself by the strength of its bill, using it as though it were a foundation of extraordinary firmness. (44) Its head is so strong that if ever it stands in need of a blow of correction (for it strives to speak like a man), it must be beaten with a little iron rod. While it is a chick, and in its second year of age, it learns more quickly what is shown to it, and retains it more tenaciously. When it is a little older, it is forgetful and unteachable. (45) The number of toes distinguishes between the better and worse types of parrot. Those who have five toes are pre-eminent; the rest have three toes. The parrot's tongue is broad, broader by far than those of other birds, whence it happens that it utters words distinctly. This talent was so marvelled at by Roman voluptuaries that barbarians made a trade in parrots.

(46) The trees of the Indians are raised to such a lofty height that they cannot shoot arrows over them. (47) They have orchards of figs. The trunks measure 60 paces around, and the shadows of the branches consume two stadia in every direction. The size of their leaves is comparable to that of Amazonian shields. Their fruit is of an excellent sweetness.

(48) There are marshes which grow reeds of such thickness, that cloven in half, they can serve sailors as boats. From their roots a pleasant liquid is expressed, as sweet as honey.

(49) Tylos is an Indian island. It bears date-palms, produces oil, and abounds in vines. It conquers all lands with this sole marvel: whatsoever tree grows there is never without leaves.

(50) Here are the Caucasus mountains, whose perpetual ridges penetrate the greater part of the world. On the side which faces the sun, pepper trees grow. They declare that this tree is like the juniper, but bears different fruit. {51} The first to sprout, like a fringe of hazel, is called "long pepper". The type which falls off and is dried by the hot sun takes its name from its colour. The type stripped from the tree itself, as is, is called "white pepper".

{52} As India alone produces pepper, it also alone produces ebony. By no means all of India brings forth this type of tree; only a very small part does so. The tree is for the most part finely made, and frequently has few twigs. It swells to the thickness of a stock, and has cracked, very net-like bark with gaping veins, to such a degree that for all the protection it has, its innermost part is scarcely hidden by a thin covering. {53} All the wood is medicinal; it is almost the same in appearance and brilliance as the stone jet. The Indian kings have their sceptres made from it, and the images of their gods are of nothing other than ebony. They say that harmful liquid is rendered safe by this material, and that whatever injury it holds is averted by the ebony's touch. {54} Owing to this advantage, they have cups made of ebony. It is thus no wonder if it is of high value, because it is honoured where it grows.

(52){55} Pompey the Great was the first to exhibit ebony from India at Rome, in his triumph over Mithridates. India also produces scented reeds, powerful against the inconveniences of internal afflictions, and many other perfumes with marvellously sweet breath.

(53){56} The first place among Indian stones is given to the diamond, inasmuch as it drives away madness, resists poisons, and expels empty fears of the mind. (54){57} It is fitting to mention these things about the diamond first, as we consider them to be practical uses. Now we shall return to the appearance and colour of diamonds. An excellent sort is to be found in a certain type of crystal. Its unclouded radiance is similar to that of the substance in which it is formed. It is smoothed into a hexagonal point on both sides, so as to be cone-shaped, and it is never found above the bigness of a hazelnut kernel. (55){58} Closest to this in distinction is the type found in gold. It is paler, and shines rather with the colour of silver. The third kind occurs in veins of copper, and is nearer to the appearance of brass. The fourth is gathered from iron. It excels the others in weight, but not in strength. (56){59} For both this kind and the kind found in copper can be broken, and for the most part can also be pierced by other diamonds. But the kind which we first mentioned are not conquered by iron, nor subdued by fire. Nevertheless, if they are soaked for a long time in goat's blood, after several hammers and anvils are broken and wasted, they finally yield and split into shards. These fragments are in demand among engravers, who use them for inscribing gems. (57){60} Between the diamond and the lode-stone there is a certain hidden dissension. If the diamond is placed near, it does not allow the lode-stone to snatch iron. Or if the lode-stone has already drawn iron to itself, the diamond snatches it away and steals it, as though it were booty.

(58){61} India likewise bears *lychnites*. The blaze of oil-lamps stirs up the vigour of its light, for which reason the Greeks called it *lychnites*. (59){62} It has two manifestations. Either it shines out with purple brightness, or it is filled more undilutedly with a blush of scarlet. If it is pure, it lets in an uninterrupted clearness throughout itself, and if it flares up in the rays of the sun and becomes enraged, or made hot by rubbing with the fingers, it draws chaff husks and filaments of papyrus to itself. **(60){63}** It stubbornly resists engraving, and if at any time it is carved, when the seal presses down, it restrains a part of the wax as though a creature with a bite.

(61){64} The Indians grind beryls into hexagonal shapes, in order that the dull and mild colour is made stronger by the reflection of the angles. There are manifold types of beryl. The exceptional are grey and blue, with green in the middle, showing the grace of the pure sea. **(62){65}** Below these are the *chrysoberyls*, which sparkle more dully, and are draped around with golden clouds.

There are also *chrysoprases*, drawing a mingled light of gold and leek, adjudged equal with the class of beryls. **(63){66}** The hyacinthine sort, which certainly recall *hyacinthus*, are also approved. But those which are like crystals, darkened with running fibres (for this is the name of the fault) the wisest count among the common stones. **(64){67}** The kings of India love to fashion this type of gem into very long cylinders. When pierced, they hang them on the bristles of elephants, and use them as collars, or often, they enhance them to a richer brightness with gold bosses, and place them on both sides of their heads, so that through the industry of the metal, the stones might show a more brilliant light.

CHAPTER LIII

(1) Before the rashness of man (after the sea had been thoroughly explored) had revealed the truth, it was thought that the island of Taprobane[372] was another world. Indeed, it was believed that it was inhabited by the Antichthones. But the bravery of Alexander the Great did not suffer the ignorance of this common error to longer remain; he extended the glory of his name all the way to this remote place. (2) Consequently, Onesicritus, commander of the Macedonian fleet, was sent to explore this land. He increased our knowledge by learning how big it is, what it produces, and in what manner it is held. It is 7,000 stadia in length, and 5,000 in width.

(3) Tabrobane is divided by a river flowing through it. One part is full of wild beasts and elephants, bigger by far than those produced by India. The other part is held by men.

It abounds with pearls and all other gems.

It is situated between the East and the West.

(4) The island begins at the eastern sea and stretches to India. The voyage to Tabrobane from the Prasian territory in India was at first twenty days, but this was when it was accomplished by way of reed ships like those from the Nile. Soon the journey was made by our ships in a voyage of seven days. (5) A shallow sea lies between, not more than six fathoms deep, yet excavated to such a degree by certain channels that no anchors can arrive at the bottoms of the chasms. (6) The stars are not used to navigate, for the Great Bear is not seen there, and the Pleiades are never observed. They only see the moon above the land from the 8th day to the 16th. (7) The star Canopos, bright and very large, shines there. They have the rising sun on the right, and the setting sun on the left. As no physical observations may be used to navigate, in order that those proceeding towards a goal find the right place, they carry birds. To direct their voyages, they have as pilots the passages of birds seeking land. The way is not sailed above four months in a year.

(8) In the principate of Claudius, we knew only the above about Taprobane. Then Fortune opened up a wider way to knowledge. For a freedman of Annius Plocamus (who then managed the revenue of the Red Sea), was seeking Arabia when he was caught by the north wind in front of Carmania. On the fifteenth day, he finally landed on this shore, arriving at the port which is named Hippuros. (9) Then, he learned the language in six months and was sent to meetings with the king. What he learned, he reported. (10)

The king was astounded at the money which had been captured with the freedman, because it was marked with different faces, but was of the same weight. Contemplating this uniformity, the king desired the friendship of Rome all the more eagerly. He sent ambassadors, the chief of whom was called Rachia, and from them everything became known.

(11) The men of Taprobane are taller than all others. They soak their hair in dye, have blue eyes, are fierce of countenance, and the sound of their voices is terrifying. (12) Such of them who die untimely live for 100 years; all the others have a longer lifetime, almost above the extent of human frailty. (13) Nobody sleeps either before daybreak or throughout the day; they dedicate part of the night to quiet, and wakefulness precedes the rising of the light. Their buildings are raised to a modest height above the ground. The price of grain is always constant. They are ignorant of vines; they have an abundance of fruits. (14) They worship Hercules.

In the election of the king, the nobility does not prevail, but the vote of everybody. The people choose someone of tested character and long-standing mildness, who is advanced in years. (15) But this is sought in him: that he has no children. He who is a father, even if his life has been under scrutiny, is not allowed to rule. If by chance when reigning he begets a child, he is stripped of power. This is most guarded, lest the kingdom become hereditary. (16) Even if the king displays the greatest fairness, they prefer not to give him complete control. He takes thirty advisers, lest he alone judge in capital cases. Also, if the judgement is displeasing, the people appeal it; the verdict is then decided by 70 chosen judges, and to this everyone must acquiesce. (17) The king, with a different custom to everyone else, dresses in a *syrma* robe, as this is the garment in which we see Father Liber is clothed.

(18) If the king is convicted of some sin, he is punished with death, but not at the hands of the common people. By the public consensus of the whole state, supplies are forbidden to him. Even the power of speech is denied him.

(19) They strive to cultivate everything. They indulge in hunting; they do not pursue common prey, but seek only tigers and elephants. (20) They also ransack the seas for fish, and rejoice to catch sea turtles. These are of such size that their shells make houses which shelter numerous families without artifice.

(21) The greater part of this island was burned up in the heat, and lapsed into vast wildernesses. The sea which bathes its shore is bushy with bright

green (plants), so that the crests of the trees are frequently chafed by the steering-oars of ships.

From the tops of their mountains, the islands can see the shores of Serica.

(**22**) They admire gold, and they use its splendour to make beautiful jewelled drinking cups.

They quarry marble with tortoiseshell patterns.

(**23**) They gather a great number of very large pearls. This type of stone is found in molluscs. At a fixed time of year, these molluscs run riot because of conception. They thirst after dew as after their mates. For desire of it they gape. When the shower of the moon melts away the most, they drink in the desired moisture by gaping. Thus they conceive and become pregnant.

(**24**) The condition of the pearls depends on the quality of what the molluscs drink in. For if they accept something pure, the little orbs are white; if it is something murky, they either are tired and pale, or stained with red. (**25**) Thus, the molluscs' offspring are more from the sky than from the sea. As often as the molluscs receive the mist of the morning air, the brighter the pearls become; as often as they receive the evening mist, the darker the pearls become. The more the molluscs drink, the more the stones grow. If a gleam flashes unexpectedly, the molluscs squeeze shut in untimely dread. Blocked up from sudden terror, they draw in abortive defects: the stones either become very small, or non-existent. (**26**) The molluscs have senses. They fear that their offspring will become tainted, and when the day burns with more fiery rays, they sink down into the deep, lest their stones become stained by the rage of the sun. Subsiding into the depths, they protect themselves from the heat. Age brings relief to this providence. For radiance is destroyed by it, and the pearls in the growing molluscs turn yellow. The pearl is soft in water, and hardens when removed. (**27**) Two the same are never found: thence the name *uniones*[373] was given. It is thought they are never found above a *semuncia* in size. Molluscs fear the ambushes of fishermen. Thence it is that most of them hide either between the rocks or amongst the sea-dogs.[374]

The molluscs swim in flocks. A swarm has a designated leader; if he is captured, then even those who escaped turn back into the nets.

(**28**) India gives pearls; so do the shores of Britannia. The divine Julius wished it to be understood by an adjacent inscription that the breastplate he dedicated in the temple of his ancestress Venus was made from British pearls.

(29) It is commonly known that Lollia Paulina, wife of the emperor Gaius, had a tunic of pearls then valued at 40,000,000 sesterces. Her father Manilius despoiled parts of the Orient in his greed to obtain it, and offended Gaius Caesar, son of Augustus. Forbidden the friendship of the emperor, Manilius poisoned himself.

(30) This also the diligence of old records: that pearls were first brought into Rome during the time of Sulla.

CHAPTER LIV

(1) From its island, the mainland follows: therefore, from Taprobane, we shall return to India. But if I should continue [and treat all] the Indian cities and peoples, I would go against my promised method of abridgement.

(2) Near to the river Indus there was a city, Caphisa, which was demolished by Cyrus.

Semiramis founded Arachosia, which is positioned on the river Erymanthus.

The town of Cadrusium was set up near the Caucasus by Alexander the Great. There also is Alexandria, which spreads out to a width of 30 stadia. There are many other cities, but these are the most eminent.

(3) After the Indians, the Ichthyophagi hold the mountainous areas. Alexander the Great subdued them, and forbade them to eat fish.[375] Beforehand, they were nourished thereby.

(4) Above these are the wastes of Carmania and Persia, then a voyage, in the course of which is the Island of the Sun, red, and inaccessible to all kinds of living things. Any animal brought to it is destroyed.

(5) Those returning from India first see the Great Bear at Hyane, a river of Carmania. (6) The dwellings of the Achaemenids were in this area.

Between the promontory of Carmania and Arabia lie 50 miles. Then there are three islands, around which come forth sea-snakes twenty cubits in length.

(7) The way from Alexandria in Egypt to India must here be explained. The course is the Nile, which carries one all the way to Coptos by way of the blowing Etesian winds. Then, one goes by land as far as Hydreum. After several days' journey have been accomplished, one arrives at Berenice, the port of the Red Sea. (8) Thence, one strikes Oceli, a port in Arabia. Zmirim follows, which is the nearest market town of India, infamous for pirates. Next, after going through scattered ports, one arrives at Cottonare, to which pepper is conveyed in boats made of single pieces of wood.

(9) Those seeking India set sail in midsummer, either before the beginning of the Dog Days, or immediately after, and those returning sail back in

the month of December. **(10)** Propitious winds out of India are south-easterly, but when one sails into the Red Sea, the winds are either south-westerly or southerly.

The length of India is reported as being 1,750 miles. That of Carmania is 100 miles. A part of Carmania is not without vines. **(11)** In addition, there is a race of men there who live on nothing other than the flesh of tortoises. They are hairy all over, up to the face, which is itself ugly. They dress in fish skins, and are called the Chelonophagi.[376]

(12) The Red Sea bursts forth onto these shores, and is broken into two gulfs. The eastern one is called the Persian, since the Persian people inhabited the coast; it is 6200 miles about. On the opposite side, where Arabia is, the other gulf is called the Arabian Gulf. They named the ocean which flows in there the "Azanian".

(13) Persis is joined to Carmania, and begins from the island Aphrodisia. It is rich in a variety of resources. Having been translated to the Parthian name, it lies opposite the west on the shore which stretches out for 1550 miles. **(14)** Its most famous town is Susa, in which is the temple of Susan Diana. 135 miles distant from Susa (or Carbyle), is the town of Barbitace. Here all humans, because of their hatred of gold, buy up this kind of metal and cast it into the depths of the earth, lest they be polluted by its use, and corrupt equality with avarice.

(15) Hereabouts the measures of the lands are most inconstant, and not without reason, since some nations around Persis use *schoini*, and others *parasangi*.[377] The inconsistent methods make the truth of the measurements uncertain.

CHAPTER LV

(1) Parthia is so great in size that it encloses the Red Sea in the south, and the Hyrcanian Ocean in the north. In it there are eighteen kingdoms, divided into two groups. The eleven which are called the "upper" begin from the Armenian frontier and the shores of the Caspian, and stretch to the lands of the Scythians, with whom the Parthians exist amicably. (2) The remaining seven "lower" kingdoms, for thus they are called, have the Arii to their east, Carmania and the Ariani to the south, the Medes in the western region and the Hyrcanians to the north.

Media itself, flanking Parthia in the west, embraces both the Parthian kingdoms. Armenia is enveloped in the north; from the west it sees the Caspian people, and from the south, Persia. This tract of land then proceeds all the way to the fortress occupied by the Magi, Fidasarcida by name.[378] The tomb of Cyrus is there.

CHAPTER LVI

(1) Babylon, founded by Semiramis, is the capital of the Chaldaean nation. It is so famous that both the Assyrians and the Mesopotamians took its name.

(2) The city is 60 miles around, surrounded by walls 200 feet high and 50 feet thick, each foot being larger than our measure by three fingers. (3) The Euphrates flows through it. The temple of Iuppiter Belus is there, whom even the religion which accepts God reports as the founder of the heavenly discipline. In rivalry of this city, the Parthians founded Ctesiphon.

(4) Now it is time to return to the shores of the Ocean, and to pull my pen back to Aethiopia. For, as we formerly explained that the Atlantic swell began in the west and Spain, it is equally to be set down where, in these parts of the world, it first assumes the name "Atlantic".[379]

(5) The Azanian Sea advances all the way to the shores of Aethiopia, and the Aethiopian Sea to the Massylican promontory, whence it is again the Atlantic Ocean.

(6) A great many people have denied this whole region to be traversable, for reason of the heat of the sun. Juba, however, gives us to understand that all this sea is navigable, from India to Gades, and makes argument for the confirmation of this truth by mentioning peoples and islands. The north-west breezes can carry any fleet to Arabia, Egypt and Mauretania, provided that the course is steered from the Indian promontory which some name Lepte Acra and others Depranum. (7) He also adds the locations of outposts and the distances. From the Indian projection to the island Malichu he affirms that it is 1500 miles, and from Malichu to Scaeneos 225 miles. Thence, it is 150 miles to the island Adanu; thus, 1875 miles are traversed to the open sea.

(8) Juba struggles against the opinion of the many who hold that the greater part of this region is inaccessible to the human race because of the scorching heat of the sun. He says that the crossing of the traders out of the Arabian islands is harassed by those the Arabians call the Ascitans. The name is given for this reason: they man wicker boats covered with cattle hides, and from this manner of craft harass passers-by with poisoned arrows.[380]

(9) He also adds that the Aethiopian deserts are inhabited by the Trogodytae and Ichthophagi tribes. The Trogodytae are so swift that they overtake on foot the wild beasts they chase. The Ichthophagi are

powerful ocean swimmers, not less than marine beasts.

(10) Having investigated the Atlantic Sea all the way to the West, Juba also pays heed to the Gorgon Islands. The Gorgon Islands, as we understand, are opposite the promontory which we call the Horn of the West. (11) Gorgon monsters inhabit them, and truly this monstrous clan lives there still. (12) Finally, Xenophon of Lampsacus asserts that Hanno, the Punic general, passed through these islands. They found women swift as birds; out of all those they saw, two were captured, so hairy and rough of body that Hanno, in remembrance of the occurrence, hung up their skins in the temple of Juno, where they remained until the time of the destruction of Carthage.

(13) Above the Gorgons are the Islands of the Hesperides, which are, as Sebosus affirms, 40 days' sail into the inmost gulf of the sea.

(14) We accept that the Fortunate Islands lie, without doubt, over against the left side of Mauretania; Juba says they are situated under the South, but next to the West.

(15) I do not wonder that something great should be anticipated on account of the name, but the truth is not equal to the fame of the appellation. On the first island, which is called Embrios, there are no buildings, nor has there been. Reeds there grow to the size of trees. Black ones of these, when squeezed, give forth the most bitter liquid; white ones spew out water suitable for drinking.

(16) They say that there is another island called Iunonia, on which there is a little temple, with a low pointed roof. The third is close by, and has the same name; all of it is bare. The fourth is called Capraria, and is crowded beyond all measure with huge lizards.

(17) Nivaria follows. It has thick, cloudy air; therefore, it is always snowy. Then there is Canaria, replete with dogs of most distinguished form. Two of these were even presented to King Juba.

(18) On this island, traces of buildings remain. There are great numbers of birds here, fruit-bearing forests, palm-groves bearing dates, many pine-nuts, plentiful honey, and rivers abundant in *siluri* fish.

(19) It is also held that the wavy sea spits out sea monsters on to the shores of this island. When the monsters are decomposing into putrefaction, everything there is imbued with a foul reek: for this reason, the nature of the islands does not wholly agree with their nomination.

Endnotes

1   Letter I.3–4.

2   Aeolian Islands: VI §§1–3; Nilotic floods: XXXII §§9–15; dogs: XV §§6–12; the mantichore: LII §37; quails: XI §§20–23; partridges: VII §§28–32; gryphons: XV §§22–23; the Psylli: XXXVII §§31–32; one-legged Indians: LII §29; four-eyed Aethiopian hunters: XXX §6; tidal fluctuation: XXIII §§18–22.

3   See the opening lines of Letter II (p. 35).

4   For lists of citations, see Theodor Mommsen, *C. Iulii Solini: Collectanea Rerum Memorabilium* (Berlin, 1895), p. 243. Mommsen in fact believed the seeming Plinian and Solinean allusions in Ammianus to stem from a hypothetical intermediary work he entitled the *Chorographia Pliniana* (see also *Collectanea*, pp. XIX–XXIII and pp. 18-19 below).

5   *"C. Iulius Solinus", Catalogus translationum et commentariorum: Mediaeval and Renaissance Latin translations and commentaries: annotated lists and guides* (1960–) vol. VI, p. 74.

6   George Kish, in his introduction to the 1955 facsimile reprint of Arthur Golding's 1587 translation of the *Polyhistor*, theorises that Golding's work reflected the use of Solinus as a school text. On this, see also Willene Clark, *A Medieval Book of Beasts: The Second-Family Bestiary* (Woodbridge, 2006), p. 26. Félix Racine argues that the structure of Solinus' book (i.e., a list of places in roughly geographical order, interspersed with tales and extra information related to particular locales) echoed modes of geographical school instruction in later antiquity, which led to teachers such as Martianus Capella and Priscian using it to construct their geographical textbooks ("Teaching with Solinus: Martianus and Priscian", in *Solinus: New Studies*, ed. K. Brodersen [Heidelberg, 2014], pp. 157–71).

7   For the use of the *Polyhistor* in the Middle Ages, see, e.g., R. Wittkover, "Marvels of the East: A Study of the History of Monsters", *Journal of the Warburg and Courtald Institutes* 5 (1942), pp. 159–97. Paul Dover provides a useful overview in "Reading 'Pliny's Ape' in the Renaissance", in *Enyclopaedism from Antiquity to the Renaissance*, ed. J. König and G. Woolf (Cambridge, 2013), pp. 419–421.

8   Illustrative features deriving from the *Polyhistor* (especially pertaining to Africa) in fact continued to grace European world maps until the eighteenth century. Witness, for example, the famous de Mornes map of 1761. Dean Swift must have had something of the sort in mind when he penned his famous lines: "Geographers, in Afric-Maps/With savage creatures fill their gaps, and o'er uninhabitable downs/ Place elephants for want of towns" (*On Poetry: A Rhapsody*, 1733).

9   See, e.g., the remarks of Miles Davidson (*Columbus Then and Now: A Life Re-examined* [Oklahoma, 1997], pp. 71, 93).

10   For lists of editions, translations and commentaries, see M. E. Milham, "C. Iulius Solinus", pp. 73–85.

11   "Reading 'Pliny's Ape' in the Renaissance", pp. 440–1.

12 See the series of articles by Paul Dover surveying the marginalia added to editions
    of Solinus by the 15th-century Neapolitans Boffile de Giudice ("Of camels,
    crocodiles and human sacrifice: the North Carolina MS of Solinus' *De situ orbis
    terrarum* and readings of classical geography in the Renaissance", *International
    Journal of the Classical Tradition* 18 [2011], pp. 167–200) and Julio Pomponio
    Leto ("Reading 'Pliny's Ape' in the Renaissance") and the 16th-century Heinrich
    Bullinger ("How Heinrich Bullinger read his Solinus: reading ancient geography in
    16th-century Switzerland", in *Solinus: New Studies*, ed. K. Brodersen [Heidelberg,
    2014], pp. 171–195).

13 See pp. 26-9. below. This appellation dates back to at least the late 15th century;
    the annotation "Simia Plinii Maioris" appears in Julio Pomponio Leto's 1480
    edition. (See Dover, "Reading 'Pliny's Ape' in the Renaissance", p. 415.) The
    name was evidently popularised by the time Golding published his translation
    in 1587. Golding writes in his preface: "There are some that terme Solinus by
    the name of Plinie's Ape, in like manner as Iulius Capitolinus, Plinius Caecilius
    and Sidonius Apollinaris reporte, that Titian was called the Ape of the Orators".
    Whatever its exact origin, the name stuck, being repeated by the Dutch classical
    scholar Gerardus Vossius in 1627 (*De historicis Latinis libri* III, p. 720 in the Leiden
    edition) and in numerous reference works (e.g., Ciaconius and Kappens' *Bibliotheca
    Libros et Scriptores* [Paris, 1729], p. 479; John Watkins' *Historical, Biographical and
    Chronological Dictionary* [London, 1807], *s.v*; Robert Watt's *Bibliotheca Britannica*
    [Edinburgh, 1827] vol. II, p. 868). Kai Brodersen (*Mapping Pliny's World: The
    Achievement of Solinus, Bulletin of the Institute of Classical Studies* 54 [2011], p. 70)
    notices that Richard Burton, in his translation of the Arabian Nights, went so far as
    to regard "Plinii Simia" as Solinus' alternative name! (See *The Book of the Thousand
    Nights and a Night*, [Burton Club, 1885-8] vol. VI, p. 6 n.1.).

14 In his *Prolegomena*, he condemns anyone disagreeing with this hypothesis as
    "blind", thus castigating an acquaintance of his who was otherwise "clean-nosed"
    (i.e., perceptive).

15 A second edition was published in 1895 (see n.4 above).

16 Both quotations are to be found on p. VIII.

17 *Collectanea*, p. CV.

18 *Collectanea*, p. IX (*talis auctoris insectationem et ex tali hoste triumphum iis relinquimus,
    qui muscas venantur quosque nullius unquam victoriae puduit*).

19 Hermann Walter, *Die Collectanea Rerum Memorabilium Des C. Iulius Solinus:
    Ihre Entstehung und die Echtheit ihrer Zweitfassung*, Hermes Einzelschriften 22
    (Weisbaden, 1969), p. 30.

20 W. S. Teuffel, *History of Roman Literature* (*Geschichte der römischen Litteratur*
    [1870]), trans. G. C. Winter Warr (London, 1900), p. 292; C. Weymann, "Review
    of Mommsen 1895" *Berliner Philologische Wochenschrift* 16 (1896), p. 911; E. H.
    Bunbury, *History of Ancient Geography among the Greeks and Romans* (New York:
    1879), p. 676; W. H. Stahl, *Roman Science* (Madison, 1962), pp. 122, 137.

21 "Healthy Terror", *The Atlantic Monthly* 273.3 (1994), p. 19.

22 Ira David Hyskell, who published a study on Solinus' language (*A Study of the Latinity of Solinus,* [Chicago, 1925]) concluded Solinus' vocabulary amounted to 4,550 words, a very large number in view of (a) the length of the book and (b) that it did not lie in different fields of thought. The number of "new" and rare words used by Solinus is also considerable, though the total differs depending on the epoch chosen for the *Polyhistor's* genesis. Hyskell opts for Mommsen's date of the mid-third century. Hyskell's neologisms are noted in the appended *Index Verborum.*

23 Raymond Beazley, *Dawn of Modern Geography* (London, 1897–1906), vol. I, p. 249.

24 Critics have been hardly less scathing of Pliny. Frank Goodyear labels him an "aspirant to style who can hardly frame a sentence", and advances his work as a prime example of "the contortions and obscurities, the odd combinations of preciosity and baldness, and the pure vacuity to which rhetorical prose, handled by any but the most talented, could precipitously descend" (*Cambridge History of Classical Literature,* vol. II [Cambridge, 1982], p. 670).

25 Von Martels, "Between Pliny the Elder", pp. 390, 398.

26 In his *On Animals,* Albertus complains that Solinus was much given to falsification (XXII.101, XXIII.23).

27 See Mommsen's exhaustive list of citations (*Collectanea,* pp. 243–248), which runs into the hundreds.

28 "Zweder Von Martels, "Turning the tables on Solinus' critics", in Solinus: New Studies, ed. K. Bodersen [Heidelberg, 2014], p. 21.

29 *The Jeweled Style: Poetry and Poetics in Late Antiquity* (Ithaca, 1989), pp. 1–5.

30 "Between Pliny the Elder", p. 394.

31 Raymond Beazley, *Dawn of Modern Geography* (London, 1897–1906), vol. I, p. 248.

32 L. A. Brown, *The Story of Maps* (New York, 1949), p. 87.

33 J. N. Wilford, *The Mapmakers* (London, 1981), p. 34.

34 *New Worlds, Ancient Texts: The Power of Tradition and the Shock of Discovery* (Cambridge, MA, 1992), p. 37. Othello's famous speech describing the telling of tales to Desdemona contains the lines: "the Cannibals that each other eat,/The Anthropophagi and men whose heads/Do grow beneath their shoulders"; we are instantly put in mind of Solinus' descriptions of monstrous races in Chapter XXX. For further on Solinus and Shakespeare, see n. 36 below.

35 Brodersen ("Mapping Pliny's World", pp. 84–5) gives a comprehensive survey of Solinus' usage of these terms.

36 Through the Italian translation of Brunetto Latino, Solinus was an influence on Dante (see P. Toynbee, "Brunetto Latino's Observations on Solinus", *Romania* 23

(1894), pp. 62–77; also H. Tozer, *History of Ancient Geography*, [Cambridge, 1935] p. 365). Solinus was probably read by Shakespeare (though we cannot be certain; the fact that he calls his Duke from *The Comedy of Errors* "Solinus" suggests that he did: see Randall Martin, "Rediscovering Artemis in the *Comedy of Errors*", in *Shakespeare and the Mediterranean*, ed. Brock and Clayton, [Newark, 2004] p. 367).

37   As termed by Zweder von Martels ("Turning the tables on Solinus' critics", in *Solinus: New Studies*, ed. K. Bodersen [Heidelberg, 2014], p. 10).

38   Zweder von Martels, "Between Pliny the Elder and "Altertumswissenschaft": the style, contents and meaning of Solinus", in *Literatur Geschichte Literaturgeschichte: Beitraege zur mediaevistischen Literaturwissenschaft* (Leuven, 2003), pp. 384, 401.

39   It should here be pointed out that there are now signs of a renascent academic interest in Solinus. See, e.g., the above-cited work of Brodersen and von Martels, and the collection of papers contained in *Solinus: New Studies*, ed. K. Bodersen (Heidelberg, 2014).

40   Mommsen's *classis tertia*. See Mommsen, *Collectanea*, p. V. See also pp. 18-19 below.

41   Mommsen's *classis prima*. See pp. 18-19 below.

42   Four inscriptions have been found in Britain, one in Spain (Hispania Citerior), three in Italy, seven in the Gauls, three in Germany, and one in Dalmatia. These inscriptions are readily available via the Epigraphik- Datenbank Clauss-Slaby.

43   *Corpus Inscriptionum Latinarum* III (1873), 9601.

44   B. Cunliffe, *The temple of Sulis Minerva at Bath* II (Oxford, 1988), p. 151.

45   *L'Année Epigraphique* (1975), 599.

46   Mommsen, *Collectanea*, p. V.

47   See I §§ 117–123; Solinus relates with some relish the high respect in which even the great Pompey held the philosopher Poseidonius.

48   See J. Marincola, *Authority and Tradition in Ancient Historiography* (Cambridge, 1997), Appendix V, pp. 287–288.

49   This was the opinion of Mommsen (*Collectanea*, p. VI), on the strength that none of the other provinces mentioned are specifically noted. On the contrary, H. Walter ("C. Iulius Solinus und seine Vorlagen", *Classica et Mediaevalia* 24 [1963] pp. 149–154) argues that Solinus was not resident in Rome, nor even in Italy, but somewhere on the Empire's periphery. He adduces anachronisms and errors in Solinus' description of Rome which, he believes, would not otherwise have been present.

50   See I §§2, 8, 13, 21.

51 See William Ramsay, "Solinus", in *Dictionary of Greek and Roman Biography and Mythology*, ed. W. Smith (1844–9), vol. III, p. 855.

52 XI §34: *homines macrobios Graeci, nostri appellavere longaevos* ("these men were called "Macrobians" in Greek, which is "long-lived" in our language"); XXXIII §4: *hanc Arabiam Graeci Eudaemonem, nostri Beatam nominaverunt* ("the Greeks named Arabia 'Eudaemon', our people 'Blessed'").

53 XI §8: *Britomartem gentiliter nominantes, quod sermone nostro sonat virginem dulcem* ("they name her in their own tongue 'Britomartis' which in our language [i.e., Greek] sounds like 'sweet maiden'").

54 A survey of instances of words such as *nunc, nostri temporibus, adhuc* etc. is, with one exception (L §3), fruitless.

55 Mommsen, *Collectanea*, pp. VI–VIII.

56 *indicia nec dubia nec pauca* (*Collectanea*, p. VII).

57 *Historia Augusta, Elagabalus* 26; the Emperor's fondness for silk is also mentioned by Herodian (V.5.4). *Elagabalus* also reportedly gave presents of this sort (see Elagabalus 29).

58 Tacitus, *Annals*, II.33; Suetonius, *Caligula* 52.

59 *Historia Augusta, Tacitus* 10.

60 *Dawn of Modern Geography*, vol. I, p. 248.

61 Peter Lebrecht Schmidt,, "Solins Polyhistor in Wissenschaftgeschichte und Geschichte" *Philologus* 139 (1995), p. 33; Zweder Von Martels, "Between Tertullian and Vincentius Lirinensis: on the concept *constantia veritatis* and other "Christian" influences on Solinus", in *Learned Antiquity: Scholarship and Society in the Near East*, ed. MacDonald & Twomey (Leuven, 2003), pp. 66–7.

62 Brodersen points out ("Mapping Pliny's World", p. 66 n. 20) that both names are probably a *lectio facilior* (i.e., "easier reading", an amendment by a copyist) in order to avoid duplication. Brodersen additionally notes that Schmidt and von Martels fail to explain (a) why the dedicatee should be identified with Constantius II rather than Constantius I, and (b) why Solinus should then have neglected to mention Constantinople.

63 Schmidt, "Solins Polyhistor", p. 31; von Martels, "Between Tertullian and Vincentius Lirinensis", pp. 74–9.

64 XXI §1.

65 XXI §§9-11.

66 Walter, *Die Collectanea*, p. 74.

67 "Between Tertullian and Vincentius Lirinensis", p. 76 n. 41.

68 *Theodosian Code*, 10.20.21. The luxury was to be the exclusive reserve of the Imperial family.

69 While human sacrifice maintained a vestigial presence in Rome as a mythological motif, and through cultic traditions, the practice early became regarded as a symbol of barbarism, and had in any case been banned by senatorial decree since 97 B.C. Pliny (*NH* 30.13), as Solinus, labels the Gaulish rites as monstrous. On cannibalism, horror of such practices was by no means a peculiarly Christian characteristic. To pagan Greco-Romans also, cannibalism, particularly endocannibalism, was clearly intolerable, marking down its proponents as the antithesis of civilized. See also Appian's *Mithridatic War* 38, material which possibly relies ultimately on the *commentarii* of Sulla, and relates the rumours of (and the alleged evidence for) cannibalism in Athens in 86 B.C. as a chilling example of the extremities to which its inhabitants had been reduced.

70 This was disputed by Mommsen (as per n. 4), who believed Ammianus instead made use of the putative *Chorographia Pliniana*. See Mommsen (*Collectanea*, p. 243) for a list of "citations".

71 It is eagerly suggested by G. M. Columba ("La questione soliniana e la letteratura geografica dei Romani", Ricerche Storiche [Palermo, 1935], p. 179) that a copy was made by the hand of the emperor himself.

72 For Mommsen's lists of citations in Augustine and Priscian, see Collectanea, pp. 243–4).

73 *Die Collectanea*, pp. 72–4. Mommsen regarded this as an interpolation.

74 Letter I.7.

75 II §§2, 4.

76 Sibyls: II §§ 16–18; wolves: II §§ 35–6; Birds of Diomedes: II §§ 45–50.

77 Cannibals: XV §§4, 13; one-eyed hunters: XV §20; Pterophoros: XV §§20–21.

78 Flying serpents: XXXII §33; frankincense and myrrh: XXXIII §§5–10.

79 LVI §4.

80 Brodersen, "Mapping Pliny's World", pp. 72–86. Brodersen adds that perhaps it is no coincidence that the first undisputed reference to a map on display dates to A.D. 297, and that the probable date for the original of the Peutinger Table is A.D. 300 (pp. 87).

81 Letter I.7.

82   XX §§3, 6.

83   IX §17.

84   XV §§6–12.

85   Beazley, *Dawn of Modern Geography*, vol. I. p. 252.

86   E.g., Brown, *The Story of Maps*, pp. 86–7; Wilford, *The Mapmakers*, pp. 34–5.
     Beazley believed Solinus influenced the history of geography "mischievously"
     (*Dawn of Modern Geography*, vol. I. p. 247).

87   E. Diehl (*RE* X [Iulius 492] 827) expressed the belief that the composition was
     not governed by things important and worth knowing, but by the things Solinus
     found interesting.

88   Letter I.3.

89   Letter I.2.

90   E.g., I §78, X §1.

91   Letter I.2.

92   Letter I.3: inclitus terrarium situs et insignes tractus maris.

93   See, e.g., X §§6–11, 20–23.

94   Another suggested identification for "Adventus" has been Q. Antistius Adventus
     Postumius Aquilinus, consul in A.D. 168 (see Mommsen, *Collectanea*, p. VI).
     For Oclatinius, see Dio LXVIII.14. Oclatinius apparently served as a common
     soldier, and performed the duties of an executioner, spy and centurion before
     his meteoric rise to the roles of procurator, senator, consul and City Prefect. For
     detailed discussion of Oclatinius, see N.B. Rankov, "M. Oclatinius Adventus in
     Britain", *Britannia* 18 (1987), pp. 243–249. H. Usener added a layer of interest to
     the Oclatinius identification by discovering the remark *Iulius Solinus sub octiviano
     fuit* (which he took as a reference to Oclatinius) in an anonymous chronicle in the
     Codex Monacensis lat. 14429 fol. 223 (for references, see Brodersen, "Mapping
     Pliny's World" p. 64 n.12). Columba ("La Questione Soliniana", p. 181) instead
     suggested *Iulius Solinus* should be read as Iulius Hyginus, in reference to Augustus'
     freedman, precluding the need to amend *Octiviano*. He also adduced the improbable
     usage of the word *sub* with the name of a consul.

95   The closing lines of the letter beg the addressee to understand that he occupies the
     same place "as he to whom I dedicated the culmination of my labour". Schmidt is of
     the opinion that the second letter, rather than the first, was addressed to Adventus
     ("Solins Polyhistor", p. 33).

96   Many additional exemplars have since been unearthed (see Milham, "C. Iulius
     Solinus", p. 73 and K. Brodersen, "A revised handlist of manuscripts transmitting

Solinus' work" in *Solinus: New Studies*, ed. K. Brodersen [Heidelberg, 2014], pp. 201–208).

97   See R. H. Rouse, "Solinus", in *Texts and Transmission*, ed. L.D. Reynolds (Oxford, 1983), pp. 391–3.

98   Mommsen adduces the Class III "additions" on the British Isles and Lake Constance as evidence supporting this theory (see *Collectanea*, pp. XCII–III). Even more specifically, Mommsen suspected the culprit to be one of the monks in St. Columbanus' retinue which stayed at Bregenz.

99   Mommsen includes the second letter and the suspected additional passages as an appendix (Collectanea, pp. 217–221).

100 Walter, *Die Collectanea.*

101 Some manuscripts from the 12th century allow Letter I to be addressed to one "Constantius".

102 Schmidt ("Solins Polyhistor", pp. 25–6) thus summarily rejects Mommsen: "Mommsen's scholarly temperament, prone to impatiently and rapidly building up an argument, culminates in our particular case, as per the temperament of his age, in a foisting on us of his own assessment (and overassessment) of history" ("In Mommsens wissenschaftlichem Temperament, das zu Ungeduld und raschem, dann aber unerschütterlichem Urteil neigt, kulminiert auch in unserem konkreten Fall die Tendenz seiner Epoche, die eigene Ein (und Über)- schätzung der Geschichte unterzuschieben".)

103 In connection with Mommsen's refusal to take the evidence of the letters at face value, one is put in mind of the words of Frithjof Schuon: "Those who reproach our ancestors with having been stupidly credulous forget that… one can also be stupidly incredulous." (*Light on the Ancient Worlds* [*Regards sur les mondes anciens*, Paris, 1980], trans. Deborah Casey [Bloomington, 2006], p. 83). F. J. Fernández Nieto, in the introduction to his Spanish translation of Solinus, published in 2001, opted to follow Mommsen in keeping the title *Collectanea rerum memorabilium*, as he believed the older manuscript group represented the more authoritative version (*Solino, Colección de hechos memorables o El erudite* [Madrid, 2001], p. 28).

104 *quid enim proprium nostrum esse possit, cum nihil omiserit antiquitatis diligentia, quod intactum ad hoc usque aevi permaneret?*

105 II §9.

106 For the list, see Mommsen's *index auctorum a Solino Laudatorum* (*Collectanea*, p. 237); compare. Beazley, *Dawn of Modern Geography*, vol. I, p. 251, n.1.

107 I §§17, 75, 99, II §23, VII §§ 12, 20, 27, XI §§7, 30, XIX §3, XXVII §4, XXXIII §1.

108 XXIV §15, XXVII §15, XXXII §2, XXXIII §8, LII §19, LVI §§6, 14.

109 E.g., I §27, on the date of Rome's foundation, and II §9, on the foundation of

Praeneste.

110 This is not necessarily a point against Solinus having used Pliny as a source. It is accepted by some that ancient authors did not customarily acknowledge their principal sources (see Hermann Peter, *Die Quellen Plutarchs in den Biographieen der Römer* [Amsterdam, 1865/1965], p. 107; R. H. Barrow, *Plutarch and his Times* [Bloomington and London, 1967], pp. 153–154), although I have yet to come across a sustained scholarly argument that this was indeed a secure general rule.

111 *History of Roman Literature*, p. 292. In this idea he has been followed by Kenneth F. Kitchell and Irven Michael Resnick, in their translated and annotated version of Albertus Magnus' de Animalibus (Albertus Magnus *On Animals: A Medieval Summa Zoologica* [Baltimore and London, 1999], vol. I, p. 38).

112 Some modern commentators have declared two-thirds or even three-quarters of the *Polyhistor* to be Plinian in origin (see, e.g., Walter, *Die Collectanea*, p. 56, Robert Grant, *Early Christians and Animals* (London & New York, 1999), p. 115; Mark Griffith, "A possible use of Pliny's *Historia Naturalis* in the Old English *Rune Poem*", *Notes and Queries* 57 [2010], p. 1 n.8). Paul Dunbavin (*Picts and Ancient Britons: An Exploration of Pictish Origins* [Nottingham, 1998], p. 62) goes so far as to cite a figure of 90%. Even the former estimates are somewhat of an exaggeration; in his edition, Mommsen cross-references approximately 54% of Solinus' text to sections of Pliny (18,362 words of 33,811, including the sections Mommsen designates "*Plinius auctus*").

113 This is the subject of a book chapter by T. W. Hillard in *Solinus: New Studies* (Heidelberg, 2014), ed. K. Brodersen: "Prosopograhia shared by Pliny and Solinus: The question of Solinus' sources", pp. 43–74.

114 See also, by way of further examples, VII §20 on Cos/Ceos, XXVI §3 on the existence of African bears, and XXX §29 on the *pegasus*.

115 On the grounds that Bocchus' contributions cited in Pliny and Solinus principally concern Spain, and on the basis of two Bocchi epigraphically attested in Lusitania, Mommsen suggests a Spanish origin for the author and that Bocchus composed a work *de admirandis Hispaniae* (*Collectanea*, p. XIV).

116 II §12, §40.

117 Mommsen, Collectanea, p. XVII.

118 Schanz-Hosius, *Geschichte der römischen Literatur* III (Munich, 1927), pp. 224–244.

119 The name "Sicinius" Dentatus (§102), "Siccius" in Pliny (VII.101).

120 H. A. Sanders, "The Annals of Varro", *American Journal of Philology* 23 (1902), p. 42ff.

121 G. M. Columba, "La Questione Soliniana" pp. 179–328.

122 *Quaestionum Solinianarum Capita Tria* (Wischan, 1909).

123 *Die Collectanea*, pp. 22, 54 etc.

124 It must be noted that Hillard's paper (see n. 109) returns to a point closer to that of Columba—except that Hillard rejected the need for, or probability of, an intermediate source, consigning Pliny to the same ignominy as had customarily been meted out to Solinus. (That is to say, Hillard would assign the close verbal similarities to a common source and the practice of *both* Pliny and Solinus to offer verbatim transmissions of material found in that source.)

125 *Colección*, pp. 43–48.

126 For the theory that this was common practice amongst ancient authors, see n. 110 above.

127 This is the opinion of Brodersen ("Mapping Pliny's World", p. 71).

128 F. J. Fernandez Nieto, *Solino, Colección de hechos memorables o El erudite* (Madrid, 2001); K. Brodersen, *Solinus: Wunder die Welt*, Edition Antike (Darmstadt, 2015).

129 *Roman Science*, p. 141.

130 We have no certain knowledge of the identity of Solinus' dedicatee. In different manuscripts the name is variously written "Constantius" or "Herennius" (rather than "Adventus"). For further on this, see Introduction, pp 17, 25.

131 The last sentence of this letter clearly shows the second dedicatee (in contradiction to the salutation) is not the same person as the first. For the evolution and transmission history of Solinus' work, see Introduction, pp. 23-25.

132 The legendary Arcadian leader said to have brought Greek culture to Italy.

133 "Valentia" signifies bodily strength or vigour, from valens (valeo). Ῥώμη, accordingly, holds similar meanings. Like many ancient etymologies, this one was probably mistaken: the name "Rome" was likely of Etruscan origin.

134 arces = "citadels". Another fanciful etymology; arx most probably derives from the Greek ἀκρόπολις.

135 Heracleides Lembos, the 2nd century B.C. Alexandrian scholar.

136 The Greek historian Agathocles of Cyzicus.

137 The topic of Rome's "secret" name, appropriately enough, is shrouded in the deepest obscurity. There seems to have been not one, but two separate secret names. While Plutarch (Moralia, 278f) speaks of only one name, which he identifies with that of the guardian deity whose province it was to protect the city, Macrobius (3.9.4) speaks of two: the name for this tutelary deity, and the name for Rome

herself. The reticence surrounding the name of the tutelary deity at least, and probably also of the "real" secret name, stemmed from a fear of besieging enemies luring the god/dess away by evocations. Pliny tells us (Natural History, XXVIII.4), on the authority of Verrius Flaccus, that it had been the practice at sieges for Roman priests to call forth the besieged town's tutelary deities, and to offer them the same or superior rites as an incentive to swap sides. The name of Rome's own deity, he writes, had been carefully concealed to preclude Rome's enemies from acting in a similar manner. Plutarch offers the comparable example of the Tyrians, who kept chains on their sacred images to prevent their escape if they were called. As for the "real" secret name, even the most learned men, Macrobius states, do not know it. John the Lydian (On the Months, 4.73), contradicting Macrobius' "Latin name" assertion, says that the secret name was "Eros"—hence the pleasing speculation that "Rome" was Amor ("love") backwards (Eros was the Greek deity of erotic love).

138 In ancient literature, Cacus figures variously as a monstrous Italian cave-dweller, or a more civilized character deriving from Etruscan legend. Solinus' portrayal seems to be a conflation of the two; the mention of Hercules' lost cattle and punishment of Cacus acts as a frame for a contrasting, more rationalised version of events recorded by the 2nd century B.C. annalist Gnaeus Gellius.

139 An ancient patrician family.

140 The name "Myiagrus" is Greek, signifying "Fly-Catcher". According to Pliny, he was an Elean god who, when duly propitiated, killed vast multitudes of pestilence-bringing flies (NH X.75). Solinus is the only authority to place Myiagrus in a Roman context.

141 Balatus = "bleating".

142 Silenus was an historical writer, writing in the first half of the second century B.C. His work on early Roman history is mentioned by Dionysius of Halicarnassus (I.6).

143 Evidently the famous story of Romulus' birds (Romulus saw twelve vultures and his brother Remus only six; Romulus claimed this represented divine approval for his chosen city foundation site on the Palatine).

144 Marcus Terentius Varro, the famous and prolific 1st century B.C. Roman author. Solinus cites him 12 times, more than any other authority. Most of Solinus' section on Rome almost certainly derives from Varro, though probably via an intermediary source.

145 Where the concept of "Square Rome" (Roma Quadrata) came from, or what it originally meant, was unknown even to the ancient authorities. T. P. Wiseman suggests that Varro (via Solinus) connected it with the equal plots shared out amongst Romulus' citizens, i.e. he saw Roma Quadrata as the first standard (square) Roman plot (see T.P. Wiseman, "Rome on the Balance: Varro and Rome's Foundation Legend", in Varro Varius: the Polymath of the Roman World, ed. D. Butterfield, [Oxford, 2015], pp. 274–77).

146 The mysterious phrase "set out on the the balancing-point" (ad aequilibrium posita) is also difficult to interpret. Wiseman (pp. 278–84) sees the "balancing-point" as signifying the summit of the Palatine, as well as a reference to the moon being in Libra at the time (as per Tarruntius' horoscope, §18).

147 Tarruntius was the Roman astrologer for whom the beautiful lunar crater Taruntius (between the Mare Fecunditatis and the Mare Tranquilitatis) is named. This is Riccioli's (Almagestum Novum, 1651) nomenclature; he may have taken the spelling of the name from Solinus, as other ancient authorities refer to him as "Tarutius" (without the "n"). Tarruntius, or Tarutius, lived in the 1st century B.C, and was an intimate both of Cicero (On Divination, 2.98) and of Varro (see Plutarch, Romulus, 12). His area of expertise was astrology, and he evidently made a special study of Romulus, concerned in particular with the actual dates of his birth and of Rome's foundation. According to Plutarch, this study was instigated by Varro, who gave Tarruntius the task of deducing the day and hour of Romulus' birth from astrologically significant events known to occur during his lifetime. The chart derived by Tarruntius for Rome itself, not preserved by Plutarch, seems to be what Solinus is here referring to.

148 It is unclear what is meant by this sentence ("The explanation for this custom, it is believed, is derived from Ilia's progeny"). Possibly Solinus meant to indicate that the tradition of spilling no blood on the Parilia was instigated by Romulus (Ilia's son), owing to the guilt he felt for murdering his brother Remus. Romulus' deep remorse is mentioned elsewhere (see Ovid, Fasti, 4.835–855), though no other authority connects it to blood-free status of the Parilia. Plutarch (Romulus, 12) says the reason for the custom was a wish to keep Rome's birthday free from blood.

149 "Choice spoils", i.e., spolia opima. This term referred to an extremely honourable kind of war-trophy in the form of spoils stripped by a Roman commander from the body of an enemy leader whom he had slain in single combat. According to Plutarch (Marcellus, 8), up to his time, there had been only three examples, the first of which was Romulus.

150 The text in fact reads "Fagutaline Lake" (Fagutalem lacum), but we are forced by context to conclude lucum ("grove") to be the correct reading. Fagutal was an early name for the western part of the Mons Oppius.

151 "Cincius", i.e., the celebrated Roman annalist and antiquary, Lucius Cincius Alimentus. He was praetor in Sicily in 209 B.C. "Pictor" = Quintus Fabius Pictor, early Roman historian (he wrote in Greek). Pictor flourished during the 3rd century B.C.

152 Cornelius Nepos, the earliest extant Latin biographer, who lived in the 1st century B.C. "Lutatius" probably refers to the author of an historical work entitled Communes Historiae, mentioned by Probus (Commentary on Virgil's Eclogues and Georgics, III. 280) and Servius (Commentary on the Aeneid, IX.710).

153 Eratosthenes, the versatile and renowned 3rd-century Greek scholar, most famous for calculating the circumference of the earth, also studied chronology. His work on this subject was highly successful, in that his dates were widely accepted in antiquity, e.g., by the Apollodorus mentioned by Solinus (probably the 2nd century Athenian).

154 Marcus Tullius Cicero (famed 1st century B.C. writer) and his friend Titus Pomponius Atticus.

155 The third year of the 6th Olympiad, = 753 B.C., the most familiar foundation date for Rome in both ancient and modern times.

156 Although Solinus specifically states menses (months), he must have meant "seasons". The Egyptians had twelve months, in later popular usage named after their principal festivals (Thot, Paophim Athyr, Choiak, Tybi, Mecheir, Phanemoth, Pharmuthi, Pachon, Payni, Epeiph, Mesore) plus an intercalary month of five epagomenal days.

157 The Lavinian thirteen-month year, as well as the years of the Arcadians and Arcananians, is referred to by Augustine (City of God, 13.12), who writes that it is mentioned by several writers. One of these writers may well have been Solinus, as we know Augustine read him.

158 The importance of odd numbers was a well-known element of Pythagoreanism. According to Pythagorean teaching, odd, or "masculine" numbers were "limited", and even the "feminine" numbers were "unlimited". The reasons for this particular doctrine were complex (see R. Waterfield, The First Philosophers: The Presocratics and the Sophists [Oxford, 2009], p. 93 n.6).

159 These remarks about the nefarious behavior of the priests echo those of various other ancient commentators (e.g., Plutarch, Caesar, 59). The truth of the assertion is borne out by a letter of Cicero's written during his proconsulate in Cilicia, requesting that his year as governor not be increased by intercalation (Letters to Atticus, V.13).

160 Testimony on Caesar's re-modeling of the calendar is plentiful: see, e.g., Plutarch (Caesar, 59), Cassius Dio (XLIII.26), Ovid (Fasti, III.155), Suetonius (Caesar, 40), Pliny (NH XVIII.57), Censorinus (XX), Macrobius (I.14). The purport of the evidence is that Caesar had 90 days intercalated to bring the year back into accord with the seasons, and thus, Solinus' observations here are a puzzle. He asserts Caesar added 21 ¼ days and that one year alone thus had 344 days. Of course, 21 subtracted from 365 gives 344!

161 Solinus expresses the problem in terms of Roman inclusive reckoning. In effect, the intercalation of one day came every third year rather than every fourth.

162 In classical antiquity, multiple births aroused ambivalent reactions, ranging from acceptance to superstitious fear and rejection.

163 Gnaeus Pompeius Trogus, a near contemporary of Livy, frequently quoted by Pliny.

164 Democritus of Abdera, the Pre-Socratic philosopher.

165 The Dead Sea.

166 I.e., the electrical phenomenon known as St. Elmo's fire, or corposant. In the ancient world, these curious lights were ascribed to Helen and her brothers, the Dioscuri. From the earliest times the appearance of the double corposant was certainly associated with the Dioscuri, believed to be sailors' saviours. On the other hand, a single corposant, called "Helen", represented a bad omen. That menstrual blood could drive away the ill-fated fire of Helen is not attested elsewhere, though it is easy to see the connection between the two different types of dire "female" power.

167 King of Numidia, and ally of Rome during the second and third Punic Wars, Masinissa was a byword for aged vitality and bodily vigour.

168 Cato the Elder or the Censor (234–148 B.C.), famous for his stern, traditionalist morals. Like Masinissa, he was renowned for being well-preserved towards the end of his long life. The son Solinus mentioned, known to later historians as Cato Salonianus, lived to attain the praetorship, and fathered Marcus Porcius Cato, the friend of Sulla, whose son was Cato of Utica (Cato the Younger).

169 It was thought that the name represented a corruption of aegre partus, "born with difficulty".

170 Almost certainly gout. According to Pliny (NH XXVII.58) Agrippa suffered to such a degree from this affliction he resorted to risky treatments.

171 Tiberius and Gaius Gracchus (the "Gracchi") were revolutionaries who respectively met violent ends in 132 and 121 B.C.

172 I.e., "toothed" or "toothy".

173 A claim unquestioningly taken up from Aristotle (see History of Animals 509b), who has been famously ridiculed in modern times for failing to count his wives' teeth.

174 Agelastus: i.e., "laughterless". M. Licinius Crassus, the grandfather of the triumvir who was killed fighting in Parthia, was praetor in 127 B.C. Cicero (On Ends, 5.92, see also Tusculan Disputations, 3.15) quotes Lucilius the satirist as the source for this story; he reports Lucilius claimed Crassus actually did laugh, but only once. We should naturally like to know exactly what, on that memorable occasion, succeeded in coaxing a chuckle from the mirthless Crassus, but history does not explicitly record it.

175 The pancratium (pankration) was an athletic event involving wrestling and boxing, possibly akin to modern mixed martial arts.

176 "Samnites" were a class of gladiator armed in the style of warriors from Samnium (a region in Southern Italy).

177 Milo was a byword in the ancient world for great physical strength. An athlete from Croton, a Greek colony in southern Italy, he was six times an Olympic victor, six times victor at the Pythian games, and ten times victor at both the Isthmian and Nemean games (Pausanias, 6.14.5).

178 It seems probable that a portion has here dropped out of Solinus' text. This snippet may be aligned with Pliny NH. XXXVII.144. Pliny in this passage details that Milo was said to have carried this same alectoria (from the Greek ἀλέκτωρ, "cock") about with him, and that it rendered him invincible in his athletic contests.

179 The murmillo was another gladiator type. Armed in the fashion of the Gauls, they were apparently so called as they carried an image of a fish (mormyrus) on their helmets (see Festus, On the Meaning of Words, s.v. Retiario).

180   An obvious quip; "Pusio" signifies "little boy" and "Secundilla" is a diminutive form of "Secunda".

181   Adrienne Mayor (The First Fossil Hunters, [Princeton, 2001] p. 111), notes that Tegea lies in a prehistoric lake basin that contains the remains of mammoths and other Ice Age mammals; it is likely that the "Orestes" discovered there was of Pleistocene date.

182   Cornelius Bocchus, the author deemed by some (see Introduction, p. 28) to have been Solinus' source (direct or indirect) for chronological information. He possibly lived in Roman Hispania: Pliny also used Bocchus, and his citations all refer to the Iberian peninsula.

183   A geographer of the 1st century B.C.

184   A kind of sculpted disc or crescent made of metal, often gold.

185   Lucius Sergius Catalina (Cataline) was infamous for mounting a failed conspiracy to violently overthrow the Roman state in 63 B.C.

186   Solinus refers to an episode recounted by Livy (29.14), when Scipio Nasica was chosen by the Senate as the best and noblest man in the State, worthy to meet the cult image of the Idaean Mother goddess (Cybele) upon her arrival at Ostia from Pessinsus (in Asia Minor) in 205 B.C. The Romans imported this new cult at a low point during the struggle against Carthage in the Second Punic War, in response to dire prodigies and consultation of the Sibylline Books. At this time, according to Livy, Nasica was not yet old enough to be quaestor; Livy adds that history does not record those qualities of Nasica's which induced the senators to come to their decision. Claudia Quinta was also involved in the reception of the goddess.

187   According to tradition, the killer (singular) of the 7th century Parian poet Archilochus was accused by the Pythia at Delphi when he came to consult the god there. According to the Suda (s.v. Archilochus), the killer, by name Kalondas, later gained Apollo's forgiveness.

188   Public officers known as lictors accompanied Roman magistrates as attendants and bodyguards. They carried fasces, a bundle of rods containing an axe head in the middle, as a symbol of state authority.

189   Solinus is almost certainly referring to Q. Caecilius Metellus Pius, consul in 80 B.C. He received the cognomen pius on account of his efforts to recall his father (Q. Caecilius Metellus Numidicus) from banishment in 99. On this, see Valerius Maximus, V.2.7.; Valerius later (IX.1.5) deplores Pius' fall from the "old morals" of his youth when proconsul in Spain.

190   Claudia Quinta miraculously set free the cult image of Cybele when it ran aground, thus disproving rumours of her unchastity (for the story, see Livy, 29.14).

191   Technically, Sulla "owned" the title of happiness, as he took the cognomen Felix following his victory at the battle of the Colline Gate in 82 B.C (see, e.g., Plutarch, Sulla 34).

192 An allusion to Cato the Elder's lost Origines, an historical work in seven books. According to Cornelius Nepos, who authored a life of the stern Censor, the Origines contained accounts of noteworthy sights in Italy (Cato, 3.3), presumably to which Solinus is specifically referring.

193 Mommsen plausibly took this story (Collectanea Iulii Solini Collectanea rerum memorabilium [Berlin, 1895], p. XIII; "Polycle" is unattested elsewhere) to be the end result of confusion concerning a passage from Dionysius of Halicarnassus. At I.44 of the Roman Antiquities, Dionysius refers to a πολίχνη (polichné, "a small town"), i.e., Herculaneum, being established by Hercules.

194 Presumably the Zenodotus of Troezen quoted by Plutarch in his Life of Romulus (14).

195 According to Servius (Commentary on the Aeneid, VII.678; Caeculus figures in the Aeneid as one of Turnus' Italian allies), there were at Praeneste two brothers called the Divi (presumably Solinus' Digidii), whose sister was made pregnant by a spark from the hearth. Later the sister gave birth to a boy, whom she abandoned. The child was found by maidens (whether or not they also were sisters of the Divi, as Solinus has it, Servius does not specify) near a fire. The child, called Caeculus, because he had small eyes (an effect of exposure to the smoke) was thought to be the son of Vulcan; hence Solinus' adjective "fortuitous"

196 Cassius Hemina, an early Latin historian (2nd c. B.C.).

197 I.e., from the Greek ὄμβρος, a shower of rain. This Antonius is certainly M. Antonius Gnipho , the 1st century B.C. grammarian and rhetorician. He was said to have been a native of Gaul himself (see Suetonius, Grammarians 7).

198 Granius Licinianus, who composed a history of Rome perhaps based on Livy. He is thought to have lived in the 2nd century A.D.

199 Almost certain to be the Cosconius mentioned by Varro (On the Latin Language, IV.36, 89), who wrote about grammar and "actiones". Very little else is known of him.

200 The iugerum was a Roman unit of area, equal to about ¼ of a hectare, or 5/8 of an acre.

201 According to this tale (as told by Varro as quoted by Lactantius in his Divine Institutes, I.6, Pliny, NH III.88 and others), the Sibyl appeared in Rome and offered to sell nine books of prophecies to the king (Varro says the asking price was 300 pieces of gold). When, laughing at her foolishness, he refused to buy them, she destroyed three of the books, and asked the same price for the rest. The king, who thought her insane, again refused to buy the books, so she burned three more, and demanded the original price for her last three. At this point the king was awakened to the possibly portentous nature of these events, and capitulated.

202 The ancients did not conceive of the Italian peninsula as a boot-shape, as we do, but rather as a spur ending in two major projections (roughly corresponding to the modern Italian regions of Calabria and Puglia). It seems to have been a habit of Eratosthenes (and of other later ancient geographers) to visualise the shapes of geographical features by comparing them to common objects — e.g., Spain to an ox-hide, Sardinia to a footprint (see IV §1) and the Peloponnesus to a plane-leaf (see VII §15). Strabo (2.1.30), indeed, believed it incumbent on geographers to do so. For further, see Francis Celoria, "Delta as a geographical concept in Greek

literature" Isis 57 (1966), p. 388.

203 That is to say, Italy's "toe" and "heel".

204 Gades is modern Cádiz, in Spain. This passage may be better understood by way
     of reference to Pliny (NH III.5). Pliny explains more fully, speaking of Europe as
     hollowed out into four chief "gulfs". The first (he writes) begins at the southern
     extremity of Spain and ends at the "toe" of Italy. For the third and fourth great
     gulfs of Europe, see VII §1, X §22 and XII §1.

205 The conjunction of Sirius with the sun occurs during the hottest part of the
     Northern Hemisphere summer. The heat of Sirius, added to the heat of the sun,
     was believed to be responsible (see Pliny NH, II.107). This period was known as the
     dies caniculares or "dog days".

206 Lucius Coelius Antipater, contemporary of Gaius Gracchus . He is known to have
     written a history of the Second Punic War, and some Annales.

207 On Amunclae and the Greek Amyclae, see 7 §8.

208 The "deer-wolf" (lupus cervarius) of ancient literature is thought to have
     represented a type of lynx, or possibly a badger.

209 This story is almost certainly the result of an imaginative etymology of λυγγύριον,
     a Ligurian term for amber (mentioned by Strabo at 4.6.2). Possibly this originally
     meant "the Ligurian stone".

210 The Granius Licinianus cited at II §12.

211 Possibly Metrodorus of Scepsis (mentioned at I§109. The name gorgia may
     be connected with the artistic story about the gorgon Medusa told by Ovid
     (Metamorphoses, IV.735–52). As the tale goes, Perseus, having delivered
     Andromeda from the sea-monster, laid the head of Medusa the gorgon down on a
     bed of seaweed so he could wash his hands. The weeds were transformed into hard
     coral by the petrifying power of Medusa's eyes.

212 The river Rhône. Marius, according to Plutarch (Marius, 15), built his canal in 102
     B.C. (after he had been elected consul for the fourth time), ostensibly in order to
     assuage the difficulties experienced by supply ships sailing up the river from the sea
     to his camp.

213 I.e., from planus, "flat". The phrase "or from the wanderings of Ulysses" (vel Ulixi
     erroribus) is an addition from the third manuscript class which Mommsen deemed
     corrupt (see Collectanea, p. 218).

214 I.e., doves (columbae).

215 Timaeus was a 4th – 3rd-century B.C. historian. The name Sandaliotis, derived
     from the Greek σανδάλον (sandal) was given in view of the island's shape. The
     name Ichnusa was given for the same reason (ἴχνος = "footstep"). On shapes used
     to visualise geographical features, see also n. 73 (II §21).

216 Gaius Sallustius Crispus, notable historian of the first century B.C.

217 The unpleasant effect ascribed to this plant led to it being considered the basis for Homer and later writers describing an unwholesome smile as "sardonic".

218 Sardinia's archaeological record adds a tantalising layer of meaning to Solinus' comments, as the Sardinian Bronze Age Nuragic culture, responsible for the many thousands of singular structures known as Nuraghi, is thought to have practised some description of water cult. Some Nuragic complexes include fountains, and there are many "well-temples", constructions built around springs, which include stairs descending from paved areas to the water sources (see, in summary, Miriam S. Balmuth, "Archaeology in Sardinia" American Journal of Archaeology 96 (1992), p. 685).

219 That is, deriving from the Greek word for breakage or fracture, rhēgma (ῥηγμα), as the coasts of Italy and Sicily were thought to have broken asunder here due to an earthquake.

220 Solinus' etymology points to the Greek word for "fawn", nebros (νεβρός). The native Sicilian deer (now extinct; similar to Sardinian and Corsican deer) is doubtless what is referred to.

221 By "here the badinage of mimicry remained on the stage" Solinus presumably meant that Sicily retained a strong theatrical tradition. The truth of this is borne out by the large number of Greek and Greco-Roman theatres remaining in Sicily today, notably at Syracuse, Segesta and Taormina (Tauromenium).

222 Possibly Lais the daughter of Timandra, a famous courtesan native to Hyccara in Sicily, who, according to tradition, was sold as a prisoner of war during the 5th-century B.C. Athenian invasion and later lived in Corinth. The purported existence of another Corinthian courtesan of the same name makes it impossible to construct an even vaguely clear history of either woman. There are many anecdotes about both ladies, but Solinus' comment ("she preferred to choose her country rather than to confess") seems to be an allusion to one we no longer possess.

223 Arethusa was the name of a spring which rose on the island of Ortygia, in the harbour of Syracuse. Alpheus, a river in the Greek Peloponnese, was supposed to flow underneath the sea and empty itself at Arethusa. According to the myth told by Ovid and others, Arethusa was originally a Nereid who, fleeing from an admirer, the river god Alpheus, prayed to Artemis for help. Artemis turned her into the fountain on Ortygia. Nothing daunted, Alpheus diverted his river underground so their waters might mingle (see Metamorphoses, V.572–641).

224 Greeks and Romans almost always drank their wine watered down (not to do so was regarded as dangerous, and as a mark of barbarism: see e.g., Herodotus, VI.83–6).

225 "Salt of Agrigentum" may have been a term for a different substance (not salt), possibly lime.

226 The tibia or aulos was a wind instrument comprising double pipes with cylindrical bores, held out in front of its player. The word flute is often used in translations, but this is misleading, as the instrument bore no resemblance to the modern idea of a flute. Reeds were used for the mouthpieces (hence this section of Solinus' work). The Sicilian reeds mentioned by Solinus were probably arundo donax or the Giant

Reed, indigenous to the Mediterranean Basin, still used today as mouthpieces for modern woodwind instruments.

227 Solinus seems to be referring to the phenomenon known today as a "mud volcano".

228 i.e., the Aeolian Islands.

229 4th century Greek historian.

230 "Milk-stone".

231 According to the charming story told by Herodotus (I.23–4), Arion was a breathtakingly skilful poet and cithara-player who spent most of his time in Corinth. Herodotus' Arion was originally Lesbian (Methymna is a town in Lesbos). As the story goes, after winning sundry musical competitions in Sicily, Arion set sail for home, only to be set upon by the crew of his vessel, who coveted his prize money. They demanded he either commit suicide, and receive a proper burial on land, or be cast overboard at once. Seeing that their minds were made up, Arion begged to be allowed to sing one last time before he did himself in. After doing so, he leapt into the sea, and was carried to Taenaron by an appreciative auditor, a culturally inclined dolphin. Herodotus says that the statue was a little bronze of a man riding a dolphin. For further on dolphins, see XII§6.

232 The site of the famous Spartan defeat at the hands of the Theban general Epaminondas in 371 B.C. was actually a village in Boeotia called Leuctra. Solinus refers to the Laconian Leuctra, where no such battle took place, in error. This Leuctra was located on the western side of the Messenian Gulf (it is described by Pausanias [III.26.4–6] and mentioned by Pliny [NH IV.16]).

233 The destructive silence of Amyclae was proverbial in Latin literature, and was alluded to by Lucilius, Virgil and Cicero. However, these authors referred to another Amyclae (or Amunclae) which, according to tradition, once existed in Latium. Accounts of how silence came to destroy the city varied; one version involved serpents and silent Pythagoreans; in another the Amunclaeans, tired of false reports of the approach of enemies, promulgated a law forbidding the subject to be mentioned. But one fine day, when their enemies at last arrived, the terrified Amunclaeans did not dare to announce their approach, and were slain. It has been suggested that this latter story was in reality a translated fable about the Laconian Amyclae, a theory to which Solinus' reference gives credence (see Ettore Païs, "Amunclae a Serpentibus Deletae", American Historical Review 13 [1907], p. 2). Solinus mentions the other Amyclae at II §8.

234 The philosopher Arcesilaus in fact emanated from the Pitane in Aeolis, in Asia Minor.

235 The "memorable war" is probably a reference to the so-called Battle of the Champions.

236 The "fight of Hercules" Solinus refers to is doubtless the fourth Labour, the capture of the Erymanthian Boar. The Boar is represented by most writers as being resident in Arcadia, though with reference to Mount Erymanthus rather than the river of the same name. The Ladon was known as the scene of the nymph Syrinx's transformation into reeds in order to escape from Pan.

237 Sciron, it is said, was a bandit who robbed passers-by and then kicked them off a
     high rock; Theseus, exacting retribution, hurled Sciron himself into the sea. See,
     e.g., Plutarch, Theseus, 10.

238 Solinus erroneously includes the island of Cos among Athens' "suburbs", as it is
     close to the coast of Asia Minor, over the other side of the Aegean. Interestingly,
     however, he correctly attributes Varro's anecdote about fine silken garments to Cos,
     in contrast to Pliny (NH IV.62), who mentions the story in connection with the
     similar-sounding Ceos, when listing the islands close to the Attic coast.

239 "Storms of civil war" is a reference to Julius Caesar's victory over Pompey here in
     48 B.C. at the famous Battle of Pharsalus.

240 If, as in Solinus' opinion, the legend of the wedding of Thetis and Peleus (the
     parents of Achilles) had been "done to death" by other writers, it was because
     it engendered the fateful Judgement of Paris, the precursor of the Trojan War.
     Pelium (or Pelion) was therefore the backdrop to the opening scenes of probably
     the most celebrated episode in Greek cultural history. While the Cypria, the part of
     the Epic Cycle dealing with this portion of the story, is lost, sufficient later versions
     and references survive (e.g., in the works of the later poets Catullus, Ovid, Lucian
     and Hyginus) for Solinus' resolve to keep "huggermugger" (taceri—translation
     borrowed from Golding's inimitable vocabulary) to seem justified.

241 The blinding wound Philip received in the siege of Methone (Solinus' "Mothona")
     acquired a rich accompanying tradition, which has been discussed in detail by A.
     Swift Riginos ("The Wounding of Philip II of Macedon: Fact and Fabrication",
     Journal of Hellenic Studies 114 [1994] pp. 103ff). Solinus' version, while amusing,
     is almost certainly apocryphal, though it is just possible that the Aster story was
     inspired by real artefacts (or tales of them); Riginos (p. 109, n.20) refers to some
     arrows found at Olynthus bearing the inscription "TO PHILIP" cast in relief on
     the stems.

242 The legendary Philoctetes was the most celebrated archer of the Trojan War.

243 Solinus refers to the colossal feat of civil engineering accomplished under the
     Persian king Xerxes. Xerxes, in preparation for the passage of his fleet in the
     480 B.C. invasion of Greece, ordered a canal to be dug through the Mt. Athos
     peninsula. The reason for doing this (according to Herodotus VII.22; see also
     Thucydides, 4.109) was to prevent repetition of the disaster of 492, when
     Mardonius' expedition came to grief attempting to round Cape Athos (Herodotus,
     VI.44, 95, VII.22, 189).

244 The legendary Orestes killed his mother Clytemnestra, in revenge for her murder
     of his father Agamemnon.

245 "The Flood" is probably a reference to the myth of Deucalion (though other great
     floods featured in mythology – see XI §18). According to the story, Zeus became
     infuriated by the hubris of Lycaon (Lycaon had sacrificed a boy to Zeus, and his
     sons had served him with a stew of sheep's guts mixed with the innards of their
     brother Nyctimus) and engineered a great deluge, drowning all life save Deucalion
     and his wife Pyrrha, who escaped in a small boat. Most sources describe the waters
     as covering all but the highest mountain(s), and while the exact locations of these
     mountains were not specific, the mountains of Thessaly do seem to have had
     special connections with Flood stories. The presence of marine fossils there is not
     specifically advanced as evidence of Deucalion's flood by any other extant ancient

authority, though suppositions analogous to Solinus' had been drawn long ago from other inland deposits of such fossils. In the 6th century B.C. the philosopher Xenophanes proposed that there were cyclic encroachments of sea and land, giving empirical examples of fossil shells on mountains, fossil fish and seaweed in quarries (see Mayor, The First Fossil Hunters, p. 210f). Xanthos of Lydia, Herodotus and Eratosthenes reached similar conclusions from similar evidence. Later, Tertullian and other patristic authors used the same evidence for the universality of the Flood, which later became a standard argument in mediaeval writing (on this see M. J. S. Rudwick, The Meaning of Fossils [London, 1972], pp. 36–7).

246 That is, the Flood.

247 Not the Homeric warrior, but a brutish Thracian king, who figured in the story of Hercules' 8th Labour.

248 The Ister (or Hister) = the river Danube.

249 Presumably, as per Pliny NH IV.51, "Tenedus" here should be "Tenos". The distance between the former island (modern Bozcaada, near the entrance of the Hellespont) and Chios is too great to be a practicable designator, while Tenos (modern Tinos) lies directly south-west of Chios.

250 An author on Cretan matters about whom virtually nothing is known.

251 Presumably the Milesian Pre-Socratic philosopher.

252 Possibly the 2nd-century B.C. Crates of Mallus, who visited Rome in 159 B.C. and gave a series of lectures whilst recovering from breaking his leg in the Cloaca Maxima (Suetonius, Lives of the Grammarians, 2).

253 A convoluted reference to the "pyrrhic" dance, the Greek war-dance par excellence.

254 The Idaean Dactyls were a group of mythical beings, to whom the discovery of iron and the art of working it were ascribed. Their name ("Fingers") was variously explained by their number being five or ten, by their having served Rhea as fingers, or by their living at the foot of Mount Ida. The story of the Dactyls having invented music and the dactylic rhythm may be related to a later tradition crediting them with discovering various other things useful to humankind. The "rattling and clanging" doubtless refers to the dance of the Curetes (a group of warriors with whom the Dactyls were closely associated) to protect the child Zeus (see above).

255 By "our language" (nostro sermone), Greek rather than Latin is obviously meant. Originally a Minoan goddess, Britomartis was absorbed into classical Greek mythology via the culture of the Mycenaeans. By Hellenistic and Roman times, she had acquired a genealogy and attendant tales, which adapted her well and truly to the classical context. Owing to several points of similarity, these stories came to closely associate her with Artemis/Diana.

256 The peculiar inconsistencies of this section (§§15–16) suggest a manuscript error; Euboea must have been named in the text before Carystus, unless Solinus would have Carystus taken for an island. Hermann Walter is of this view (see Die Collectanea Rerum Memorabilium Des C. Iulius Solinus: Ihre Entstehung und die

Echtheit ihrer Zweitfassung, Hermes Einzelschriften 22 (Weisbaden, 1969), pp. 15–18), arguing that a displacement occurred, and that §§24–5 (on Euboea) should directly precede §§15–16 (or that §§15–16 should follow §§24–5).

257 Delos = "visible".

258 Paros is an island south of Delos. The "town Abdelum" (Abdelo oppido) was never in existence; the chief town bore the same name as the island itself. The genesis of this was almost certainly the phrase which appears in Pliny as Paros cum oppido, ab Delo XXXVIII ("Paros, with a town of the same name, 38 miles from Delos"; NH, IV.67). This particular error has been the butt of much derision on the parts of commentators (see e.g., Mommsen, Collectanea, pp. VIII–IX, H. J. Rose, A Handbook of Latin Literature [London, 1966], p. 438).

259 Maeotis was the ancient appellation for the Sea of Azov, the shallow north-eastern portion of the Black Sea.

260 This was accomplished in 481 B.C. for the Persian invasion of Greece.

261 An author of uncertain date, also cited by Pliny.

262 For the story of Arion, see VII §6.

263 Peuce = "Pine-tree"; Naracustoma = "Naracian mouth"; Calonstoma = "Fair mouth; Pseudostoma = "False mouth"; Borionstoma = "North mouth"; Spilostoma (Psilonstoma) = "Barren mouth". Today the Danube empties through three main channels.

264 According to Pliny (NH, XXXII.28) the salient feature of beavers' testicles was an odiferous secretion called castoreum ("beaver-oil"). As Solinus states, this substance was credited with a plethora of medicinal properties, from curing hiccups to arousing sufferers from coma. Castoreum retained its position in the European materia medica until well into the 20th century, being considered useful as an antispasmodic. It was also extensively used as an ingredient in perfumery. It is still used as a fixative, and is included in the recipes of such iconic scents as Shalimar by Guerlain, Emeraude by Coty, Magie Noire by Lancôme, and Givenchy III by Hubert de Givenchy (the modern versions contain it in synthetic form). It must be noted, however, that castorem is not produced from beavers' testicles, but from the two castor glands, situated near the anus of the animal of either sex; the error was doubtless due to the appearance of the castors, which, when removed from the body of a beaver, do recall a pair of testicles. The voluntary castration story seems to have been popular among the ancients, and plentiful allusions to it are to be found (e.g., Cicero, For Scauro, I.7, Juvenal, Satires, XII.34ff, Ammianus Marcellinus XVII.5.3).

265 The Dnieper River (rises in Russia and flows through Belarus and the Ukraine before emptying into the Black Sea).

266 Anthopophagi, i.e., "Human Eaters". Also mentioned at L §7 and XXX §7 (Aethiopians).

267 I.e., the eastern side of the Caspian Sea.

268 Albus signifies "white".

269 This is a reference to a Herodotean passage (Histories, I.73–4), wherein it is
     detailed that the Medes and Lydians cemented oaths by licking shallow cuts made
     on each other's arms. Herodotus also describes the five-year-long Lydian/Median
     conflict being concluded in this fashion. The Median king in question was not
     Astyages, but his father, Cyaraxes (Astyages went on to become the last Median
     ruler, being dethroned by Cyrus in 550 B.C.). The war, relates Herodotus, had come
     about because Alyattes had taken some Scythians who had wronged Cyaraxes under
     his protection (they had, in fact, murdered a high-born Median boy and served him
     up to Cyaraxes as a dish of game). Peace was concluded at the famous Battle of
     Halys, when both sides, in awe of a solar eclipse, decided to stop fighting.

270 Ges Clithron = the "Earth's Door Bolt". The Arimaspi, in the Greco-Roman
     tradition, were a legendary people inhabiting the nebulous extreme north of
     Scythia. The curious characteristics ascribed to them certainly stem from the
     Arimaspea, a lost poem by the archaic poet Aristeas, mentioned by Herodotus
     (IV.14, 27) and others.

271 Pterophoros = "featherbearing" or "wing-bearing".

272 The word smaragdi is sometimes translated as "emeralds", though it must be noted
     that in ancient times there was much confusion between the precious stone we
     know today as emerald, and a variety of other green stones. The smaragdi known
     as "Scythian", which were, as Solinus states, in high esteem in the ancient world,
     were probably emeralds from the Ural Mountains, from which emeralds are still
     obtained today.

273 A very literal translation. The meaning appears to be that the best smaragdi are
     those with a smooth and level upper surface.

274 "Cuprous smaragdi" (chalcosmaragdi) possibly refers to the mineral malachite,
     which often results from the weathering of copper ores.

275 It was common among the ancients to categorise stones as "male" and "female". See
     e.g., Pliny, NH, XXXVII passim.

276 An enduring figment of Greek literature, the Hyperboreans were a legendary race
     of people said to dwell in a fabulous land hyper Boreas, i.e., "beyond the North
     Wind". This place was a kind of Utopia— eternally joyful and endlessly distant.

277 The "hinges of the world" (cardines mundi), i.e., pole, a point around which the
     world revolves. Possibly related to the Gesclithron of the Arimaspi mentioned at
     XV §20.

278 The inappropriate use of the word "spots" (maculae) to describe the appearance of
     the tiger may be accounted for by the fact that in ancient times, these beasts were a
     relative rarity in the Mediterranean countries—in contrast, say, to lions and bears.

279 Pardialanches = "panther-choke".

280 Solinus is commonly credited with being the earliest known authority to use the

adjective mediterraneus of what is now known as the Mediterranean Sea.

281 Presumably Alexander, though Pliny (NH, VI.52), states on Varro's authority that this "passage" was discovered during exploration under the leadership of Pompey.

282 Solinus describes a westward route from the Oxus to the Caspian, up the Cyrus (Kura) with an overland journey to Phasis, and thence to the Black Sea. These and the other attestations of a navigable route between "India" (i.e., central Asia, modern Afghanistan/Turkmenistan) via the Oxus (Amu Darya) and the Caspian are highly interesting, mostly because the Oxus has not in modern times flowed into the Caspian, but into the Aral (today it is lost in the desert before it reaches the remnants of the Aral). Whether the Oxus (or a branch of it) did in ancient times empty into the Caspian is a moot point.

283 An obscure author of whom little is known, though it may be inferred he wrote on geographical matters.

284 The Danube. This terminology is in contrast to that used by Solinus at X §23, XIII §1 and XIX §1, where he refers to this river as the Ister (or Hister).

285 Solinus' assertion that amber "weeps" is probably a poetic/mythic allusion. According to a popular legend, the maidens known as the Heliades, having turned into poplars, wept tears of amber over their dead brother Phaëton.

286 I.e., the word sucinum ("amber") is similar to sucus ("sap").

287 The "Padanian woods" are also a reference to the story about Phaëton; he was meant to have crashed into the river Padus, and it was there his sisters were supposed to have wept their amber tears.

288 At XXIII §9, Spanish ceraunium is mentioned.

289 Caledonia, an appellation first used by Pliny (NH IV.102), was a name applied to the northern parts of Britain (i.e., modern Scotland). What is meant by Solinus' "Calidonian angle" (Caledonicum angulum) is uncertain. No such name appears in the works of any other extant author. While the words angulum and recessu indicate a bay, the distance given (800 Roman miles, roughly 1200 kilometres) indicates the very top of Scotland, rather than, say, the Moray Firth. Conceivably, however, angulus did refer to the firth, and the measurement was taken from its northern extremity.

290 The savagery of Hibernia's inhabitants is also mentioned by Pomponius Mela (III.53), who labels them as undisciplined and ignorant of all virtue; Strabo, though embarrassed by lack of reliable sources, reports that the Irish, even more savage than the Britons, were cannibals, devouring their deceased parents like the Scythians. They also, he writes, are reported to have sexual relations with their near kin (4.5.4). At this point, Arthur Golding annotates (in the margin) of his translation: "The manners of Irishmen of Old, not altogether altered to thys day".

291 The Isle of Thanet, now connected to the mainland by the deposition of silt from the River Stour. Solinus is the only Roman writer to mention it, correctly describing it as prime farmland.

292 §§{11}-{16} is the longest addition from the Class II/III manuscripts (See Introduction, p. 24.). Theodor Mommsen was thereby led to theorise that the hypothetical interpolator was native to the British Isles.

293 Though no location is mentioned, almost certainly the springs of Aquae Sulis (Bath). Minerva, in conjunction with a local goddess, Sulis, was worshipped there. It is unclear what is meant by "perpetual fires" which produce "stony globules". The fuel may have been Somerset coal.

294 There were three Spanish provinces during Solinus' time (Baetica, Tarraconensis, and Lusitania), but they were not instituted as a direct result of the Second Punic War. Subsequent to the Carthaginian defeat of 206 B.C., the Romans had gained dominion over only about half of the Spanish peninsula, and were continually under attack from the native Spaniards, a state of affairs which continued until 133/2, when Scipio Aemilianus established Roman dominion in central Spain, consolidating the successes of Dec. Iunius Brutus Callaicus in the west. From 197 the peninsula was divided into two provinciae, the flexibly defined regions of Hispania Citerior in the east, and Hispania Ulterior in the west. This division remained in force until the time of Augustus, when Hispania Ulterior became Baetica and Lusitania, and Citerior became Tarraconensis. On this topic, see John Richardson, Hispaniae: Spain and the Development of Roman Imperialism 218–82 B.C. (Cambridge, 1986) .

295 I.e., flax or esparto grass. In the ancient world, spartum fibre was a noted Spanish production. It was particularly gathered from a place known as the Campus Spartarius, an arid plain in the hinterland of Carthago Nova, which, according to Pliny (NH XIX.30), was less than 100 by 30 miles in size. One of the plant's principal uses was, as Solinus mentions, rope-making.

296 This item refers to the crimson dye derived by the ancients from the dried bodies of kermes beetles (distantly related to the cochineal insect). These beetles were thought by the ancients to be of a vegetable nature (hence the name coccum, "berry").

297 The original ancient concept of the Ocean (Oceanus) was very different to our own; rather than a body of water, Oceanus was thought of as a swift-flowing river encircling the earth. Presumably the sentence "the Ocean, which the Greeks thus name because of its swiftness" refers to this idea.

298 That is, from the legendary Myrtilus, who found a watery grave courtesy of the ungrateful Pelops, who had bribed him to engineer his master Oenomaus's defeat in a fateful chariot race, and Helle, the sister of Phrixus, who fell to her death from the back of the goat with the golden fleece, en route to Colchis.

299 Presumably from Ionius son of King Adrias (who gave his name to the Adriatic Sea). The Ionian Sea was also thought to have acquired its name from the voyage of Io, or from another Ionius, whose corpse (he was accidentally killed by Heracles) was said to have been thrown into the water there.

300 For the Bosphorus, "the transit of a cow" presumably refers to Io. Bosphorus, of course, signifies "oxen ford", as per Solinus' second, more literal interpretation.

301 Axine = "inhospitable"; Euxine "hospitable". The former appellation was applied by the Greeks, it was said, because of the wintry weather that prevailed, as well

as because of the customs of the fierce Scythian inhabitants (see Pliny NH VI.1; Strabo 7.3.6; Pomponius Mela I.109).

302 Propontis = "before sea", i.e., it is named for its "order", as it comes "before" the Euxine.

303 Antaeus was a legendary Libyan giant who murdered passers-by by compelling them to wrestle with him. According to Pindar (Isthmian Odes 4.3), he used their skulls to thatch a shrine to his father Poseidon. He was thought to be the son of Gaea, and, by touching the earth, to gain his strength from her. This is presumably what Solinus is referring to with his sentence "[Antaeus] knew very well how to interweave and disentangle knots on the ground, as though born from Mother Earth". The original source or inspiration for this passage may have been poetry: Antaeus and his relationship with the earth seem to have been a common subject for poetic allusion. See, e.g., Ovid, Metamorphoses IX.9.183.

304 This evocative passage, unsurprisingly, found its way into mediaeval literature (e.g. John Mandeville [Chapter XXXI]). It is also used, with effect, in the influential Victorian short story The Great God Pan by Arthur Machen (ch. V, 1890). The genesis of this curious description is certainly the Periplus of a Carthaginian named Hanno (Solinus refers to Hanno's account in §15), who led an exploratory journey down the west African coast. We still possess a document purporting to be a Greek translation of Hanno's report, though in which epoch he made his journey is difficult to accurately determine.

305 Juba II of Mauretania, a loyal client king of Rome, who reigned in the first century B.C., during the time of Augustus. He wrote on history, natural history, geography, grammar, painting and theatre.

306 The same general who put down the rebellion of Boudicca, and father of the biographer, Paulinus was propraetor in Mauretania in A.D. 42.

307 Arthur Golding translates the phrase "meets the solstitial region" (solstiali plagae obvia est) "where it butteth upon ye northwest"; Lewis and Short cite this passage to explain solstitialis plaga as meaning "south" (A Latin Dictionary [1879], p. 1723). This latter interpretation is probably the right one; after all, Tingitana did border upon the solstialis or "summer-like" desert regions to the south.

308 I.e., the war with the Epirote king Pyrrhus, from 280–275 B.C. The Romans first encountered Pyrrhus' 20- or- so-strong elephant contingent at the Battle of Heraclea in Lucania in 280. According to Plutarch's account of the battle, the Roman cavalry was put to flight by the elephants, and Pyrrhus subsequently claimed victory (Pyrrhus 17). Plutarch also includes an amusing story of how the king, having unsuccessfully tried to bribe the Roman envoy Fabricius, equally unsuccessfully tried to frighten him with a concealed elephant (Pyr. 20).

309 Icosium = modern Algiers. "Twenty" in Greek = eikasi: thus, "Icosium".

310 "Tripolis", i.e., "Three cities".

311 Perhaps this means something like "snakes on the defensive (e.g., a hissing cobra) are more reluctant to bite".

312 "Heliotrope" signifies "sun-turner".

313 This reference is to Gnaeus Servilius Caepio and Gaius Sempronius Blaesus' raid of the African coast in 253 B.C. Polybius (I.39) gives an account of the incident, which apparently occurred at Meninx, in Syrtis Major. According to Polybius' story, the Roman fleet actually did run aground, but was able to be refloated in the nick of time by dint of heavy equipment being thrown overboard.

314 When Marius was on the run from Sulla in 88 B.C., he is said to have hidden (vainly) in a marsh near the Italian city of Minturnae, whence he escaped, via Menis (i.e., Meninx, modern Djerba) to Africa.

315 Located in the middle of Syrtis Major, the altars of the Philaeni were supposed to have marked the boundary between Carthaginian and Cyrenean territory. According to Sallust's wild story (The Jugurthine War, LXXIX), the monument was originally set up in honour of two Carthaginian brothers called the Philaeni, who, in order to settle a border dispute with the Cyreneans in favour of their own city, gave themselves up alive to be buried in the sand. Marked on the Peutinger Table, the locality is assigned to a headland known today as Ras Lanuf.

316 Probably a reference to Athene. Certain traditions nominated Poseidon and Lake Tritonis as Athene's parents and her birthplace as Libya.

317 The wondrous and elusive substance more commonly known as silphium, for long the wealth and pride of Cyrene. It was widely used as a seasoning and a medicament and provided Cyrene with both wealth and fame (the Cyreneans even included stalks of silphium on their coinage), but the resource ran permanently dry by the 1st century A.D., probably due to overharvesting and overgrazing. The identity of the plant has been much debated, but it is often thought to have been a now-extinct kind of giant fennel, of the genus Ferula.

318 The "Oenses" = the people of Oea (later, along with Leptis Magna and Sabrata, one of the three towns of Tripolis; see XXVII§8). The war mentioned took place in A.D. 70; according to Tacitus (Histories, IV.50), the Oenses had summoned the Garamantes (Tacitus calls them "a wild race incessantly occupied with robbing their neighbours") to their aid in a feud with the people of Leptis. The Oenses eventually got more than they bargained for, as the Garamantes performed their part with such gusto as to leave the Leptitani cowering behind their walls in terror, and the Roman army, under Valerius Festus, was moved to intervene.

319 See XXVII§5, XXXII§5.

320 "Dog-heads"; previously identified by Solinus as a type of ape (XXVII §58).

321 Agriophagi = "Wild animal-Eaters".

322 Pamphagi = "Everything-Eaters".

323 Anthopophagi = "Human-Eaters".

324 Cynomolgi= "Dog-milkers".

325 Meröe was a region bordering the Nile, between modern-day southern Egypt and northern Sudan; it was often described by ancient geographers as an island (see XXXII§7), hence the phrase "Meröe, which the Nile makes with his first embrace".

326 Solinus here uses the word "Orient" (Oriens) in a novel sense, denoting a region. As with "Mediterranean", "the Orient" has since become a common term (Kai Brodersen notes this instance in his arguments for Solinus' innovative presentation of space; see "Mapping Pliny's World: The Achievement of Solinus", Bulletin of the Institute of Classical Studies 54 [2011], pp. 63–88). Solinus uses Oriens in the same way at XXX §16, I §121 and LIII §29.

327 Salmasius (Plinianae Exercitationes, vol. I. p. 274) believed this statement, that Aethiopia's groves were most verdant in winter (hieme), was a misreading or mistranscription of hebeno. That is to say, the groves should properly flourish not in winter, but with ebony trees.

328 "Sixtystone".

329 "Lower" in this case, as per the ancient parlance, describes Egypt's northerly regions.

330 Also mentioned as separating the Aethiopians and the people of Atlas (XXX §1), and Aethiopia from Africa (XXVII §5).

331 That is to say, in the language of the native people, "Astapus" signifies "water flowing out of the shadows".

332 This statement appears to be a vague reference to the Sothic year, the beginning of which was determined by the heliacal rise of the star Sirius (or Sothis).

333 Adipsos = "thirst-quenching".

334 By the world (mundum) "recommences its yearly motion", Solinus may have meant the rising of Sirius, the Dog Star, which occasion he above labels the "world's birthday" (§13).

335 This story is virtually identical to that told at VII §23 of two Boeotian rivers, which is also ascribed to Varro. It is possible confusion and/or duplication of the tale arose from the old literary association of sheep with Arabia: according to Herodotus (III.113) the country possessed two types of indigenous sheep, one with extraordinarily long tails (obviating the use of carts to carry them by their shepherds) and one with extraordinarily fat tails.

336 Scaenitae = "tent-dwellers".

337 This section is an addition contained in the Class III manuscripts. Almost precisely the same is said of the Aethiopians, at XXX §§30–31.

338 During Hellenistic and Roman times the Phoenix was certainly seen as a symbol of the Sothic Cycle (i.e., 1,461 Egyptian years). The Sothic Cycle was the Egyptian Great Year (Censorinus, De die natali 8.10, 21.11), but clearly something else was

envisioned here by Solinus and his sources. Solinus may have had in mind ideas expressed by authors such as Cicero (quoted by Tacitus in his Dialogue on Oratory 16.7), who calls a period of 12,994 (not 12,954) years, in which all the celestial bodies have completed their courses and once again coincide, a "great and true year" (magnus et verus annus).

339 For the bitumen produced by Lake Asphaltites, see I §56.

340 One assumes the destruction of Jerusalem here referred to is that of A.D. 70. Following the Siege of Jerusalem, the Roman army under Titus thoroughly sacked the city, destroying the Temple in the process. The authority Solinus was working from at this point must then have been composed later than 70, and possibly before 130, when Hadrian commenced a rebuilding program.

341 This statement of Solinus' is unparalleled in earlier sources. Most deem the Artaxerxes in question to be the Achaemenid Artaxerxes III Ochus, who reigned from 358 to 338 B.C.; this passage is often cited as evidence of Jewish involvement in the revolt which led to the destruction of Sidon. Others, however, link the reference with Ardeshir I, founder of the Sassanid dynasty, who reigned from A.D. 206–41, and who was also known as Artaxerxes (Theodor Reinach, "La deuxième ruine de Jéricho" in Semitic Studies in Memory of Rev. Dr. Alexander Kohut [Berlin, 1897] pp. 457ff, and John Pinkerton, in his Dissertation on the Origin and Progress of the Scythians or Goths [London, 1787], p. xx).

342 Mallet-shoots (malleolis) refer to new shoots cut from old wood, in shape resembling mallets.

343 The "apple of Sodom", also mentioned by Tacitus (Histories V.7.1) and Josephus (Jewish Wars, 4.484). These descriptions almost certainly refer to the fruit of the small tree Calotropis procera, found in Palestine, Arabia and Egypt. The poisonous fruits of the tree are actually hollow.

344 For the first Mount Cassius (Casius), see XXXIV §1.

345 Gnomonici, I.e. "sundial experts".

346 I.e., things easily float in its waters.

347 This remark of Solinus' has been reasonably interpreted as a reminiscence of the kingdom of the Hittites after Muwatalli II moved the capital from Hattusa (near Boğazkale, in northern Turkey) to Tarhuntassa, around 1285 B.C. The Land of Tarhuntassa almost certainly encapsulated at least some of Cilicia (on this see T. Bryce, "Lukka revisited" Journal of Near Eastern Studies 51 [1992], pp. 122–3). If this interpretation is correct, this passage is remarkable as being the sole Roman mention of the Hittites.

348 Solinus calls the mythical, fire-breathing Chimaera "three-formed" as it was said to have had the forepart of a lion, the body of a goat, and the tail of a serpent. According to Hesiod, it also had three heads (Theogony, 319ff).

349 This description (from the mouth of the Nile to the Don, which flows into the Sea of Azov [Lake Maeotis]) encompasses Asia in its entirety, as viewed by the

ancients (see Pliny NH V.47 for various citations). Solinus seems to be saying that he means to describe a part of Asia only. The area he delineates more or less corresponds with the Roman province of Asia during Imperial times.

350 For Dinocrates and Alexandria, see XXXII §41 above.

351 The so-called "Seven Sages of Greece" were seven 6th-century individuals renowned for their wisdom; the earliest quotation of this "list" is in Plato's Protagoras (342e–343b). Plato also includes Solon, Cleobulus, Myson and Chilon. There was some disagreement as to who should have been included (see Diogenes Laetius, I.41), but Bias of Priene, Thales of Miletus and Pittacus of Mytilene appear to have been fixtures.

352 Solinus is referring to the well-known tale of Marsyas, a satyr who lit upon the aulos (or tibia) Athene discarded after she had invented it. Emboldened by the beautiful strains he could produce, he foolishly challenged Apollo to a musical competition. The terms of the competition were that the victor could do as he pleased with the loser. After the appointed judges, the Muses, decided in Apollo's favour, the god flayed Marsyas alive and nailed his skin to a nearby tree as punishment for his hubris. The tears wept for him formed a stream later called the "Marsyas".

353 Niobe's children (as the story went) were murdered by Apollo and Artemis in revenge for her having boasted of her superiority to Leto. She was said to have metamorphosed, in her grief, into a rock on Mount Sipylus (see e.g., Ovid, Metamorphoses IV.310).

354 Pythonos Come = "Python Village", "Snakeville".

355 The Bithynian ritual was supposed to have been inspired by Hercules' search for Hylas. According to the story, when the Argo landed on the coast of the Propontis, Hylas was sent to fetch water. However, the nymphs of the spring he visited fell in love with him and drew him down into the water; he was never seen again. So long did Hercules search, vainly calling the name of his beloved, that he was eventually left behind by his other companions.

356 That is, the Dictator, Gaius Julius Caesar. The same story is to be found in Pliny (NH VIII.155) and Suetonius (Julius 61).

357 This story is along the same lines as the one told by Plutarch (Alexander, 20.13), wherein Alexander and his followers are astounded by the perfumes and accoutrements found in Darius' tent following the battle of Issus The obvious theme in Plutarch's story (and Solinus') is the contrast between native Macedonian (or Roman) simplicity and Eastern luxury.

358 Pliny (NH XIII.25) is even more contemptuous than Solinus, saying that scented men such as Plotius deserve to die, and that the proscription was thus absolved of guilt.

359 I.e., the Georgics of Virgil. The citron, or "Median apple" is described at II.126ff (J. B. Greenough's translation [Boston, 1900]):
      Media yields the bitter juices and slow-lingering taste
      Of the blest citron-fruit, than which no aid

Comes timelier, when fierce step-dames drug the cup
With simples mixed and spells of baneful power,
To drive the deadly poison from the limbs.

360　The Amu Darya.

361　"Behind" possibly signifies "to the east".

362　The Syr Darya.

363　Little is known of Demodamas, beyond the fact he wrote about Asian geography.

364　This presumably refers to the splaying of a camel's foot when standing on hard surfaces.

365　A writer of uncertain date. According to Pliny (NH, VI.55) he wrote a work entirely devoted to the history of the Attacori.

366　The author of an influential work on India, based on at least one Indian sojourn. He was sent by Seleucus I Nicator as ambassador to king Sandracottus, whose capital was Palibothra, probably around 300 B.C.

367　Nothing further is known about this author. "Philadelphus" refers to Ptolemy Philadelphus, who reigned 283–246 B.C.

368　Baeton was employed by Alexander to measure the distance of marches, and apparently wrote a book upon the subject (see Athenaeus, X.422b).

369　Meros is the Greek for "thigh".

370　Said to have been a physician from Cnidus (see Suda s.v.), Ctesias sojourned for some years at the court of the Persian king Artaxerxes II Memnon, composing the most comprehensive pre-Alexandrian description of India.

371　A writer on geography, also cited by Pliny. Nothing further is known of him.

372　Taprobane was the name given by the ancient Greeks to the island of Sri Lanka, later adopted by the Romans. The name may have originally derived from the Sanskrit Tamraparni. Solinus' statements relating to Taprobane being an unknown quantity in the west prior to the expedition of Alexander are also to be found in Pliny (NH, VI.81). That the island was "another world" (orbem alterum) was no doubt due to vague travellers' tales relating to its immense size. Antichthones = "counterlanders", i.e., those living on the opposite side of the earth. Despite the qualifying adverbs and verb tenses, Taprobane is in many ways represented by both Pliny and Solinus as an inverted version of their own Mediterranean world.

373　Unio = "one of a kind", "unique gem".

374　"Sea-dogs": likely sharks.

375 Ichthyophagi = "fish-eaters".

376 "Turtle-eaters".

377 The schoinos ("rope") was a Mediterranean unit of measurement. The parasang was an ancient Persian unit, the actual length of which is differently reported in the various authorities.

378 More commonly, Pasargadae.

379 See XXIII §13 (also XVIII §1). Solinus means to say that he will now describe the eastern side of the Ocean, as he has already treated the western.

380 From the Greek word ἀσκός, wine-skin.